Today no one denies either the importance or the complexity of international affairs. But it is not yet widely appreciated that in the universities they have provided the subject for an entirely new academic discipline—the professional study of international relations as a field of specialized expertise, distinct both from history and the study of ephemeral current affairs.

So far, much of the benefit of the academic study of international relations has been available only to specialists. *Studies in International Politics* are designed to bring the fruits of this new field of inquiry before a wider audience without lowering the intellectual standard.

Deterrence and Persuasion

Studies in International Politics

THE FOREIGN POLICIES OF THE POWERS

DETERRENCE AND PERSUASION

DETERRENCE AND PERSUASION

*French nuclear armament in the context
of national policy, 1945–1969*

WOLF MENDL

PRAEGER PUBLISHERS
New York · Washington

BOOKS THAT MATTER

Published in the United States of America in 1970
by Praeger Publishers, Inc.
111 Fourth Avenue, New York, N.Y. 10003

Library of Congress Catalog Card Number: 75–104770

Printed in Great Britain

FOR KEIKO

Contents

Preface

A book of this kind is never finished. Two months after the manuscript was handed to the publisher, President de Gaulle resigned and abruptly brought to an end a remarkable and unique phase in French policy. It is possible that within the next twelve months we may witness some dramatic changes in the French positions over defence and foreign relations. On the other hand, it is equally reasonable to assume that some of the basic decisions taken under de Gaulle will not be reversed, just as he built on some of the basic policies of the Fourth Republic.

In spite of the hazards of writing contemporary history, one might make a modest claim for the use of this study. In the first instance it tries to examine the impact of events on the more permanent features of national policy. Secondly, it tries to show the complexity of national policy-making and the interplay of many factors which must always qualify simplifications about why a nation opts for a nuclear weapons programme. Lastly, it may help to throw some light on the pressures which lie behind the proliferation of nuclear weapons in the world. Non-Proliferation Treaty or no Non-Proliferation Treaty, the problem of the spread of nuclear weapons will continue to exist for as long as such weapons exist and those states which possess them cannot agree upon a convincing programme which will lead to their control under an international authority.

This book would not have been written without three years of study and research made possible by the generosity of the Joseph Rowntree Charitable Trust. It may appear under the name of one author. In reality it has been a co-operative venture in which very many people have taken part in different ways. Most thinking is group thinking and it would be impossible to list the names of all those who have helped me in one way or another to see problems from a new angle or more clearly.

PREFACE

My advisers have included scholars and specialists on both sides of the Channel. I am particularly indebted to M. Jacques Vernant, Secrétaire Général of the Centre d'Etudes de Politique Etrangère and to his colleague, Dr. Walter Schütze; to Professor Raoul Girardet of the Fondation Nationale des Sciences Politiques; to M. Jean Planchais of *Le Monde*; to M. Paul Collet, Secretary of the Commissions des Affaires Etrangères and de la Défense Nationale of the National Assembly; all of whom not only gave me freely of their time but rendered all manner of assistance and opened many doors. Many others discussed aspects of this study with me and shared their knowledge and insights generously.

I derived much profit from talking with Professor Max Beloff and Mr. William Pickles about the governmental institutions of France. Sir Basil Liddell Hart very kindly allowed me to read his personal correspondence with some of the leading military figures of post-war France. Mrs. Margaret Gowing helped me to find my way through the tangled wartime relations in the atomic field. Dr. Martin Gibson kindly checked Chapter 4, which deals with scientific and technical matters, so as to save me from the worst blunders. Mrs. Dorothy Pickles and Mr. David Thomson offered invaluable advice and criticism as examiners of the doctoral thesis which formed the basis of this book.

The editors and the publishers of the series of which this book forms a part have not only rendered every assistance but have gone out of their way in their generosity and understanding. The staff of the press library of the Royal Institute of International Affairs, where most of the spade work was done, met the author's many requests with unfailing courtesy and remarkable efficiency. Miss Walker and Miss Wilmot gave much technical assistance in the preparation of the manuscript. I am most indebted to Mrs. Jane Goater for her splendid work in preparing the manuscript for the publishers and to Norman and Margaret Marrow for indexing the Book. My mother provided me with a haven where I could spend many undisturbed hours in great comfort. My wife bore the inevitable trials which attend such work with great fortitude. In spite of difficulties with which she had to contend, she has always encouraged and supported me and has contributed her skills as a proof-reader to the enterprise.

My friend Sydney Bailey gave some badly needed counsel in the preparation of my study for publication. I owe, above all, an incalculable debt to Mr. Michael Howard for his unfailing encouragement and for being my guide, philosopher and friend during the long gestatory period leading to publication.

To all these and many others I express my thanks and appreciation. They have done their best and any blemishes in the book are entirely due to my own shortcomings.

WOLF MENDL

Watford
Spring 1969

1 · Introduction

Some people argue that French defence policy under de Gaulle was but a transient phenomenon which will not outlast him and that, if it contains material of more general interest, a study of British defence policy since 1945 would be as fruitful an exercise and for English-speaking students a far easier and more comprehensible task.

This approach is due to an understandable irritation with the French position in international affairs and to a misreading of the situation in France. French defence policy has its roots in the past. Although it may have assumed a somewhat idiosyncratic aspect under de Gaulle, it will be impossible to wish away its core, constituted by the French nuclear force (Force Nucléaire Stratégique Française). The financial, economic and military stakes in this enterprise constitute an enormous vested interest. Even if a political group came to power with the intention of changing current military policy, the problem of how to set about it and to dismantle, dispose of and replace the sophisticated and elaborate military machine may well be too much for the political inertia which affects most governments. Moreover, de Gaulle's military policy corresponded to the deep-seated image and aspirations which many Frenchmen share about the place of their country in the world. Such sentiments encouraged them to support the general lines of Gaullist external policy even though they may have been among the President's bitterest political opponents.

To think that the wider implications of French defence policy can be equally well discovered by studying British policy is to ignore the fundamental differences between Britain and France. The France of the 1970s may of course face the same problem of deciding what to do with the national nuclear force that faced Britain in the 1960s, but the answer will be determined by the

13

very different national policy objectives of France as well as by the different genesis of the French nuclear effort.

Our study had its origin in a simple, perhaps naïve, question. Why did France embark upon a course which led it to become the fourth military nuclear power? In retrospect it seems almost inevitable that the first three nuclear powers should have followed this course. Once the United States had developed the atomic bomb the Soviet Union was sure to accept the challenge as the only other state aspiring to a role of world leadership. Although it is often overlooked that Britain was the first country to start the process of proliferation among lesser powers, her role in the atomic effort during the war and her part as one of the 'big three' of the alliance, coupled with the fact that she had emerged from the war with her empire largely intact, made it most likely that she would want to continue her national nuclear effort.

France was the first power to launch a nuclear programme outside the context of the Second World War, although one could argue that governmental interest in atomic research went back to the first year of the war. French scientists had participated in the Anglo-Canadian-American wartime effort to develop atomic energy for military uses but France had only a very tenuous official connection with the programme. After the war the French government laid the foundations of an atomic energy programme in the midst of a shattered economy. The celebrated Parodi statement of June 1946 led to the assumption that France would choose the Canadian way of concentrating on the peaceful uses of atomic energy. However, from the early 1950s onwards it became clear that the programme was being steered towards military objectives and it is likely that some of those most intimately associated with it had intended this from the beginning. Progress towards a French nuclear armament proceeded inexorably throughout the 1950s, in spite of misgivings on the part of some ministers and in spite of doubts as to what use a small national atomic force would be in a world where the two super-powers were acquiring a highly diverse and sophisticated armament in this field. Even after the development of the hydrogen bomb in

14

the middle of that decade, when French public opinion for the first time became alarmed at the prospect of thermonuclear war as a result of the arms race, France prepared to become a thermonuclear power by setting up a factory for the production of U235. Throughout this period, while Jules Moch played a prominent part in efforts to halt the nuclear arms race and himself opposed French atomic armament, the French programme was moving towards the first test explosion in 1960.

Until 1960 the French only gave passing attention to the purely strategic arguments for nuclear weapons although they have played an important part in the debate since. Strategic thinking about nuclear weapons has two aspects: it can be a theoretical structure built around the existence of nuclear and thermonuclear weapons; it is also an attempt to place nuclear armament into the context of defence and foreign policy objectives.

There is no doubt that the second aspect applies particularly to the development of French nuclear policy. As far as the problems of national defence are concerned, nuclear weapons were first discussed in the light of their effect on military operations, then as a factor in the Cold War with its emphasis on indirect strategy, and in recent years as a guarantee of vital national interests in the face of the strategic equilibrium between the super-powers. In foreign policy they were discussed in terms of a status symbol for great powers and of the diplomatic leverage they conferred on France. The need for a French nuclear armament was largely justified in the context of concrete situations of which the diplomatic events surrounding the end of the war in Indochina and the experience at Suez in 1956 are outstanding examples. Both these incidents provided a basis for the theory that in conditions of nuclear stalemate between the super-powers a nation cannot rely upon its ally for protection when the issue is not of vital interest to that ally.

Although the theoretical arguments in support of French strategic doctrine were voiced on various occasions before the 1960s, the full elaboration of a thesis, in the best tradition of French theory and logic, with its doctrines of proportionate

15

deterrence and of multipolarity, did not come until the Force Nucléaire Stratégique was the centrepiece of the French defence system. Even so, one suspects that there is a far more pragmatic basis to French policy than its theoreticians would have us believe.

Notable contributions to a discussion of the French doctrine of nuclear strategy begin with the work of General Pierre Gallois[1] and continue with that of General Beaufre[2] as well as an increasing number of books which attempt to deal with the merits of a national nuclear force from various angles.[3]

In this book we have therefore tried to analyse the basic external objectives of France since 1945, the relationship between these objectives and French defence policy and the role of a national nuclear armament in it. The later chapters will examine the domestic factors involved in the evolution of French nuclear policy and the public debate surrounding it. This may reveal not only how the French have looked upon nuclear weapons in the past but how they may think about them in the future. In the concluding chapter we discuss the influence of the independent nuclear force on the position of France in international politics.

References

1. General P.-M. Gallois, *Stratégie de l'Âge Nucléaire* (Calmann-Lévy, Paris, 1960); *Paradoxes de la Paix* (Presses du Temps Présent, Paris, 1967).
2. General Beaufre, *Introduction à la Stratégie* (Librairie Armand Colin, Paris, 1963) and *Dissuasion et Stratégie* (Librairie Armand Colin, Paris, 1964).
3. For example, Raymond Aron, *Paix et Guerre entre les Nations* (Calmann-Lévy, Paris, 1962) and *Le Grand Débat, initiation à la stratégie atomique* (Calmann-Lévy, Paris, 1963); Maurice Bertrand, *Pour Une Doctrine Militaire Française* (Editions Gallimard, Paris, 1965); Marc de Lacoste Lareymondie, *Mirages et Réalités, l'arme nucléaire Française* (Editions de la Serpe, Paris, 1964); Jules Moch, *Non à la Force de Frappe* (Robert Laffont,

Paris, 1963); Club Jean Moulin, *La Force de Frappe et le Citoyen* (Editions du Seuil, Paris, 1963); Alexandre Sanguinetti, *La France et l'Arme Atomique* (René Julliard, Paris, 1964); Club de Grenelle, *Siècle de Damocles: La Force Nucléaire Stratégique* (Les Editions Pierre Couderc, Paris, 1964).

2 · French nuclear policy in the context of French foreign policy

Since defence policy is a function of foreign policy it is necessary to examine the basic lines and problems of French external policy. Although the pressures for embarking upon a national nuclear armament came from within the administration, particularly from circles in the Commissariat à l'Energie Atomique* and from some military groups, the responsiveness of a few influential politicians and their ability to persuade their more reluctant colleagues to follow this direction were influenced by factors in international politics which favoured the development of such a policy.

As far as the military uses of atomic energy were concerned, the problem had two facets. The first involved the basic objectives which French governments set themselves: objectives which arose from the image of their country's place in the world. The second concerned the more specific relationships of France to other great powers which could be classified as allies or potential enemies. As the war receded and the world was beset by the Cold War, the problem of French relations with the principal opponent, the Soviet Union, was transmuted into the problem of relations with the allies of France. Thus, French nuclear weapons were thought of not so much as a 'force de dissuasion' than a 'force de persuasion'. French nuclear armament had little to do with a military posture against a potential enemy, in spite of a good deal of theoretical argument on the subject. However, it had a great deal to do with the French position *vis-à-vis* the principal allies.

* Hereafter referred to as C.E.A. or the Commissariat.

18

(i) Basic objectives

In the immediate aftermath of war, the overriding purpose of French governments, before and after the establishment of the Fourth Republic, was to ensure the country's economic recovery and to reassert its independence and position in the world. They wanted France to return to the concert of great powers from which she had been excluded at Yalta and Potsdam. The war had left a legacy of physical destruction and exhaustion; it had masked a civil war which was carried over into the political feuds of the Fourth and Fifth Republics; it had caused France to lose status as a world power and had marked a serious decline in her prestige. The effect of all this and the disorganization of national life under the occupation culminated in a profound demoralization of the people.

The problem of recovery and the restoration of national prestige was tackled by far-reaching economic measures. They included the nationalization of basic industries, the setting up of machinery for national economic planning and the creation of a potential for the future, exemplified in the founding of the C.E.A. There might have been differences over methods of approach, but the basic motives were shared by all – even the communists.

The need to reconstruct the country naturally affected the debate over military policy and was a principal reason why the defence budgets never met the needs of the defence planners. It also affected French relations with the United States. Until the mid-fifties France, like her European partners in the Atlantic Alliance, readily accepted the protection of the American shield against Russia although there were no signs of real fear of a Russian attack, except during the year after the outbreak of the Korean war in June 1950. Behind this shield the French and other European peoples could recover socially and economically from the wounds of war. It is important to note that within France the majority, who favoured membership of NATO, and the minority, who were opposed to it and favoured a neutralist course, were agreed that French efforts should be concentrated on economic

19

reconstruction and not on armaments. The result of this attitude was to lead to a conflict between NATO's 'declared strategy' and 'actual capability'.[1] The former was a commitment to the defence of each member state, the latter involved a reliance on the American threat of nuclear retaliation. In the early years the reliance on the American guarantee and the priority of European economic recovery were accepted on both sides of the Atlantic. The outbreak of the Korean war and the much slower impact of the first Soviet atomic explosion in August 1949 quickly brought about a divergence between the American and European viewpoints. The United States, increasingly anxious as the Cold War was intensified, exerted pressure on her allies to integrate defence planning, to make greater military efforts and to accept German rearmament. The Europeans were apprehensive that this line of policy would slow down, if not halt, economic recovery. Countries with large communist parties, like France and Italy, argued that this would be the best way to undermine the security of the West.

We might, therefore, summarize the problem of Franco-American relations by saying that in the period between the end of the war and the mid-fifties France was under strong American pressure to rearm and did so unwillingly. After the mid-fifties, French armament policy took a turn towards nuclear weapons, which, though it was not at first openly discouraged, was in due course to meet with strong American disapproval. These tensions with her principal ally reflected the different preoccupations of the two countries. Bearing in mind French determination to restore the nation to its position as a major power, we must examine the objectives France set herself on the road back to international status.

It is important to remember in this connection that although the reassertion of French sovereignty over territories which had passed under enemy or allied control during the war was obviously a major aspect of France's effort to regain some of her former greatness, her main attention was focused on the European scene. During the Algerian war, French strategists justified the priority

given to it on the grounds of preserving Europe's natural hinterland and the bridge to her important outlets in Africa. France
never ceased to be Europe-centred, even when her domestic
politics were overshadowed by the conflict in North Africa.

Ever since the seventeenth century France has sought to achieve
primacy in Europe. This search for domination was frustrated by
two states: Britain and Germany. British opposition to French
policy arose from a totally different concept of the desirable
pattern of international relations on the Continent. Britain's basic
objective since the sixteenth century was to prevent the domination of Europe by any one power, whether it be Spain, France,
Germany or Russia. Germany, on the other hand, challenged the
French for the leadership of Europe since the mid-nineteenth
century.

After 1945 these rivalries were dwarfed by Russian-American
rivalry in which Europe was only one, although the most important, prize. There was no question of France challenging Russia
on the Continent. Accordingly, French sights were lowered to
encompass the western half of Europe. Within this restricted area
France had to make sure that Germany would play a subordinate
role in the international political and military field; that Britain
would not pursue her traditional game of balancing the European
states against each other; that the United States would assume the
role of guarantor against Russian domination without, however,
dominating the west European scene.

Broadly speaking, these objectives were reflected in French
nuclear policy. We can see their impact on the arguments
advanced in support of a national nuclear armament during the
years leading to 1960 and on the prescribed function of
the French nuclear force in support of French diplomacy after
1960.

(ii) The problem of German revival

For France the historic anxiety about Germany did not come to
an end with the decisive victory of 1945 and Germany's uncondi-
tional surrender. Remote as it seemed, the spectre of a revived and

vengeful Germany haunted all Frenchmen who had lived through the years after the First World War.

French policy towards Germany since 1945 may be divided into several distinct historic phases. The first lasted until about 1948. During these years French diplomacy concentrated upon creating assurances against the re-emergence of a strong German state. They took two forms: an attempt to dismember the country and to create a group of client states in the Rhine basin, thereby reviving the dreams of some Frenchmen after the First World War. By 1948 the failure of this policy was marked by the Declaration issued on the 7th June after the London conference of the three western powers. The three main points of this statement were the international supervision of the Ruhr which was, however, recognized as part of Germany; the decision to proceed with the forming of a German government; and the fusion of the three western zones of occupation, which had been agreed upon on the 16th April 1948 and was hereby confirmed. The second element in the assurance policy had been the attempt to strengthen Franco-Russian co-operation and thus hold Germany in pincers. The purpose of such an alliance, in the eyes of some French statesmen, was not only to contain Germany but to forestall any attempts at establishing an 'Anglo-Saxon hegemony'.[2] For these reasons, the French delegation to Moscow in December 1944 had no difficulty in accepting the Oder-Neisse line as the delimitation of Germany's eastern frontier. The Prague coup, the deepening crisis over Berlin and general Soviet pressures on the peripheries of the communist world forced the French to abandon this line of approach, especially since the French Communist Party had passed into opposition in May 1947 and was a serious threat in an unstable domestic situation.

The second historical phase is marked by the French search for Anglo-American guarantees against both Germany and Russia. The latter was never openly referred to as the enemy but there can be no doubt that, apart from the communists and some socialists, Frenchmen felt the need for protection against Russia. This sentiment was particularly true of the army which was not only

fighting the communist-dominated Vietminh in Indochina but
has had a markedly anti-communist ideology since the First
World War.[3]

Nonetheless, a careful study of contemporary writings and
speeches makes it clear that the Anglo-American presence in
Europe was just as much a measure of safety against Germany. In
themselves, the Brussels Treaty of 1948, which mentioned Germany as the potential aggressor, though it was also directed against
Russia, and the North Atlantic Treaty Organization of 1949
satisfied French demands in this respect since they assured the
continued presence of British and American forces on the Continent. The three dilemmas facing the French leaders at this time
have been well summarized as to whether priority should be
given to anti-German or anti-Soviet defence; whether they should
work for a united European army or French military autonomy;
whether to follow a policy of 'Atlantism' or 'Neutralism'.[4]

Almost immediately after the launching of the project for an
Atlantic alliance the question of German rearmament loomed
large. It became acute after the outbreak of the Korean war. A
statement by Hervé Alphand, ambassador to the United States, at
a press conference which he gave jointly with M. Gazier, Minister
of Information, underlined French concern in this matter: 'As far
as we are concerned, we had no intention to promote, propose or
accept the rearmament of Germany.'[5]

Under pressure from a menacing international situation and
from an impatient United States, the French evolved the ill-fated
Pleven Plan which tried simultaneously to satisfy the American
demand for a German contribution to western defence and to
allay French fears of German rearmament. For the subsequent
four years, which mark the third phase, the debate over the
European Defence Community (E.D.C.) dominated French political life. The intent of the Plan was clear. Under no circumstances
should a German government be allowed to control German
troops.[6]

In the same debate warnings against the dangers of German rearmament came from both the right and the left. For Frenchmen,

therefore, the issue turned on the single problem of the best way to keep Germany under control so that there was no danger of her re-emerging as the dominant power on the Continent and of trying to exploit her position by playing off East against West. The different solutions offered to achieve the commonly agreed objective provided the fuel for polemics which cut across party lines.

The integrationist solution had as its leading champion the Alsatian Robert Schuman, even though the plans for the European Coal and Steel Community and the European Defence Community owed most to the inspiration of Jean Monnet.* It is significant that a politician from Alsace and a party, the M.R.P., which was particularly strong in that region, should have championed the European cause in France. It is no accident that Alsace Lorraine, the coveted prize for which three wars had been fought within seventy years, should have become the crucible of the European idea. Even so, for Schuman and for the M.R.P. the movement for European unity carried with it an implication of security for France against Germany. General Béthouard, for instance, voiced the fear that Germany might succumb to the Soviet peace offensive and make a deal with Russia. The only way to avoid the danger was to follow a policy which would multiply Germany's ties with the West and which would prevent the re-establishment of a German army.[7]

The socialist party also endorsed such a policy for the same reasons. At its forty-third congress in May 1951 it passed a resolution which insisted that European unity was essential and thus supported 'La création rapide d'une armée européenne unifiée, capable d'appuyer une politique européenne autonome', provided that Germany remained disarmed.[8]

In the debate on the defence budget in 1955 Paul Reynaud

* There was at this period a whole series of 'plans' which included a Pflimlin (another Alsatian) Plan for European agriculture, proposed in March 1951, and a Bonnefous Plan for the co-ordination of European transport, launched in August 1950. The project for the Council of Europe, which the French hoped would lead to a supra-national development, might well be included in this list.

neatly summed up the position of those who had supported the plan. He was as attached as anyone to national independence, but what was independence without an assured defence? E.D.C. would have provided American aid for all the allies. Since its defeat, that aid would go to the new German army with its general staff and war college.[9] Not all took the view that E.D.C. was an insurance against German militarism. Some, like M. Edgar Faure, thought that the German danger was exaggerated and that Franco-German rivalry had ceased to be the centre of attention on the world stage.[10]

Various arguments were advanced against French ratification of E.D.C. The emphasis given to each one depended on the outlook of the particular critic. The opponents were to be found within the whole range of the political spectrum, from extreme left to extreme right, as well as within the armed forces and the administration.

The politicians made great play of the plan's threat to national sovereignty and appealed to patriotic instincts in support of their opposition. The foremost and most vitriolic of the critics was Michel Debré, the Gaullist member of the Conseil de la République. He concentrated his attack on the danger of a German military revival within the context of the revised treaty.[11] He argued, in a manner which seems strange in the light of his master's policies under the Fifth Republic, that the reason for this lay in the fact that the original plan had included all the free states of Europe and that it had since been reduced to a union of five or six without Britain.

In all aspects, the opposition of the military chiefs was based on similar reasons to those advanced by the politicians. With the exception of a handful of generals, notably de Larminat and Crépin, the military hierarchy was opposed to the project and its principal figure, Marshal Juin, came into open conflict with the government over the issue, a conflict which culminated in his dismissal.[12]

On the other hand, many of the younger officers stationed in France and more of those in Germany supported the proposed treaty. Some of the ablest air force officers, including General Stehlin and Colonel Gallois, later to become the foremost apologist for a national nuclear force, were on the same side in the debate.[13]

Much of the military opposition was not inspired by fear of German rearmament, but by the fear that the French army would lose its identity under the terms of the European Defence Community. Many officers had resigned themselves to the inevitability of German rearmament and they were more concerned about the continued existence of the French army. The conflict in Indochina and the prospect of military operations in North Africa, as a result of the deteriorating situation in the three countries of the Maghreb, no doubt played an important part in military thinking. E.D.C. threatened to absorb French military strength so that the French presence overseas would be weakened. The very arguments employed by the British to excuse their participation – responsibilities to the Commonwealth and world-wide commitments – were eagerly repeated by the French, even by those who supported the basic objectives of the treaty. Yet many officers serving in Indochina were partisans of E.D.C. because it offered a way to western unity against the communist menace. They saw their operations as part of the global struggle against communism and not as a campaign to preserve French domination in that part of the world.

Notwithstanding these reservations, it would be an error to neglect the important place which German rearmament occupied in the minds of E.D.C.'s opponents. The three main points on which Marshal Juin attacked the project were the absence of the United Kingdom, the danger that other members of the Community might acquire a share in French overseas commitments, and that it would lead to a German preponderance in Europe while France was occupied elsewhere.[14] It is no exaggeration that the last was probably the most important of the three reasons. Juin's views were echoed in parliament by General de Monsabert (R.P.F.), who suggested that concerted Anglo-French action was the only way in which to avoid the danger of German military domination.[15]

26

At the back of this concern lay the basic fear that Germany would not only dominate the Continent in a conventional military sense, but that she might become another nuclear power. As early as 1948 the three Western High Commissioners had begun negotiations in Berlin on the restrictions to be imposed on the Federal Republic of Germany in the nuclear field. Experts of the C.E.A. advised that the annual production of plutonium in Germany should not exceed five hundred grammes. However, at the outset of the negotiations over E.D.C. Chancellor Adenauer had won allied agreement that there should be no discrimination against Germany.[16]

By 1953 and 1954 France had embarked upon a programme of industrial production of atomic energy whose military potential was obvious to most. Here lay the hope that France might establish her pre-eminent position on the Continent and minimize the effect of German rearmament. The concession to Adenauer over E.D.C. threatened this possibility. Its stipulations had, under the terms of article 107, paragraph 1, forbidden any production of war material, including the making of prototypes and the pursuit of technical research, except on authorization of the Community's commissariat. Furthermore, the definition of an atomic weapon in annex II, paragraph 1 of the article, limited the amount of nuclear fuel which could be freely produced by a member state to five hundred grammes, with the effect that practically all work of the Commissariat à l'Energie Atomique – whether pacific or military – would have been subject to the authority of the European Community. Obviously, all those who wished to develop an independent nuclear programme were as opposed to the treaty as were those who wanted to maintain the national identity of the French army. In 1953, for example, the Commissariat's administrator-general, Pierre Guillaumat, had warned the government about 'certains inconvénients' of the proposed treaty.[17]

One military publicist argued for the manufacture of French atomic weapons on the grounds that the terms of E.D.C. would make Germany a potential nuclear power. Starting with the authorized production of five hundred grammes of plutonium, there could be little doubt that the patriotism of German scientists, led by Heisenberg, would lead to collaboration in an enterprise which would restore at least part of Germany's military might.[18]

In the opinion of others the treaty prepared for the likelihood of a European bomb, created by a joint Franco-German research and production centre. Thus, the work of the C.E.A. would no longer be under purely French control. On the 24th August 1954 the partners of France in the negotiations at Brussels rejected proposals to preserve the independence of the French nuclear industry. A week later the National Assembly had buried the treaty.

If the nuclear question lay hidden in the debate over E.D.C., especially during the last two years before its final rejection, it was more prominent in the subsequent negotiations which led to the rearming of Germany within the context of Western European Union and NATO.

The crucial developments which culminated in this decision occurred under the premiership of Mendès-France. In the light of his subsequent opposition to the Gaullist policy of nuclear armament, Mendès-France's action in bringing the question of the manufacture of nuclear weapons to the cabinet's attention seems strange at first sight. Various explanations have been offered to account for it. There is no doubt that international events greatly influenced his attitude. 1954 was the year in which the French suffered their most humiliating defeat since 1940. The failure to secure American intervention in Indochina may well have influenced the service chiefs to start thinking that France should dispose of her own nuclear weapons to meet emergencies such as the one caused by the battle of Dien Bien Phu.[19] Around this time the idea of using tactical nuclear weapons gained ground among NATO strategists. There was not only the need to balance Soviet superiority in conventional armament, once the fantastically high target for NATO's forces set by the council meeting in Lisbon, in February 1952, had been shown to be a chimera, but there was need to make the allied superiority in nuclear weaponry more credible, now that the Russians were developing their own potential. The failure of the European Defence Community and the inevitability of German rearmament had a close bearing on Mendès' decision to bring the issue before the cabinet.

His own attitude towards E.D.C. had been ambiguous and, at best, tepid. After its defeat on the 30th August 1954, he immediately set to work to break his country's threatened isolation. From his and others' efforts emerged the Paris Agreements and the extension of Western European Union to include Germany and Italy. One of the most interesting facets of the new agreement was the establishment of an armaments pool and the control of the maximum armaments which the member states were allowed to have on the Continent. It is true that the new treaty suppressed the ceiling of five hundred grammes for nuclear fuel and that the controls only came into effect when 'la fabrication des armes atomiques, biologiques et chimiques aura dépassé le stade expérimental et sera entrée dans la phase de production effective'.[20] The French could, therefore, pursue their experimental work unhindered, but the article implies that once France had passed that stage, she would be willing to have her atomic force subject to European control and would presumably operate it in the European interest. As we know, the armaments pool and the related controls came to nothing, but that belongs to the post-Mendès era.

Thus, when the question of a French nuclear programme for military purposes was first raised at cabinet level on 26th December 1954, at the same time as the National Assembly debated the Paris Agreements, Mendès-France was concerned not so much to make France an independent nuclear power, so that she could throw her diplomatic weight about, but to make sure that France would not be dominated by a rearmed Germany within the Western Alliance. A witness of this historic meeting records the premier's concluding remarks after a discussion which lasted three hours. Mendès-France said that he had become very conscious of the gap in the international field between the atomic powers and the rest, 'ainsi que de l'avantage que la France avait en cette matière sur l'Allemagne, du fait de la renonciation de celle-ci à la fabrication de l'arme.' Therefore he had decided to launch a secret programme of studies and preparations for a prototype of a nuclear weapon as well as for an atomic submarine.[21] The 'Europeans' never forgave him his equivocation over E.D.C., but his nuclear policy was by no means identical to that of the Gaullists.

One may note in passing that it was perhaps not unfitting that the problem should for the first time have been posed at the cabinet level on the initiative of Mendès-France. In spite of differences in policy and temperament, he was in some respect closest to de Gaulle among all the leaders of the Fourth Republic and of all its prime ministers he enjoyed the General's warmest support. Like the President of the Fifth Republic, his view ranged far beyond the immediate horizon and he loved France more than the French. He shared with de Gaulle an impatience with party squabbles and political manœuvres. Ever since the end of the war, only these two men have succeeded in focusing upon their persons the aspirations and hopes of forward-looking Frenchmen.

The attitude of Mendès-France to nuclear rearmament emerges clearly from his comments on the first French nuclear explosion in February 1960. He definitely rejected the international military system based upon discriminatory and aristocratic principles, such as were implied in the idea of a nuclear club of three.[22] He doubted whether unilateral renunciation would have any effect on other countries about to embark on a weapons programme and asked whether there could be any guarantee that one of the three nuclear powers might not want to share its secrets with a special friend. Russia had given submarines and tanks to Egypt in 1956, why should she not offer nuclear weapons to her in a similar crisis of the future?

Notwithstanding, Mendès-France saw the immense danger of the spread of nuclear weapons and believed that the three-power monopoly gave some temporary guarantee against a world war. Such weapons should, therefore, not be forbidden to France alone, but the control of nuclear arms must be universal. France should take the initiative by offering to renounce the bomb 'contre une réglementation collective', which was essentially the implied

The critics feared that Germany was trying to tie French hands over the military production of atomic energy through the terms of the treaty. M. Mutter alleged that M. Spaak had been induced to raise the whole issue of banning the military uses of atomic energy in order to gain the support of the German socialists for EURATOM, thus introducing a condition of which there had been no question at the Messina conference in 1955 when the treaty was first discussed.* M. Michel Maurice-Bokanowski warned that EURATOM was a pretext to further political union in which French rights would be submerged by those of Germany. Germany was sure to be dominant in such a situation.

It has been argued that the failure to gain a standing equal to that of the United Kingdom with the United States drove France towards EURATOM and the attempt to form a consortium with West Germany and her Common Market partners. Thereby Germany would have had access to the atomic secrets of her partners and would have been well on the way to becoming a military nuclear power.[30] In the light of the government's attitude, the pressure to which it was submitted to safeguard a strictly national programme for the military exploitation of atomic energy and the elaborate precautions written into the final text of the treaty, it is unlikely that this possibility was seriously envisaged on the French side.[31]

The theme of keeping ahead of Germany runs like a thread through subsequent debates on foreign and defence policies. It did not necessarily provide the prime consideration at any one

* M. Mutter's purpose was to press the government for an explanation of its change of position from the 'pacifistic' declaration in M. Mollet's investiture speech in January 1956 to its 'open mind' about a national nuclear armament programme in July. The official reply was that at Messina the problem had not been touched upon as the talks had represented a preliminary reconnaissance of the whole question of atomic co-operation. Since then, substantial progress in the negotiations had made it necessary to consider the problem of the military utilization of atomic energy. Furthermore, M. Mollet's initial stand had been intended to encourage progress in disarmament negotiations and he had only made the undertaking for his government and not its successors.

time, but it was always there, lurking persistently in the background. During the debate in the Conseil de la République in June 1956 on the proposal to establish a military division within the C.E.A., M. Michel Yver, spokesman of the foreign affairs commission, argued that without nuclear weapons France would not be able to maintain her superiority over Germany and thus keep in check her extraordinary 'dynamisme'.[32]

In 1960, when the debate on nuclear weapons had finally passed from the stage of hypotheses and projections to become an issue of everyday politics, the protracted discussions in the National Assembly on the government's 'loi-programme' for the creation of a national atomic striking force included many warnings of its likely effect on Germany. One of the most influential parliamentarians, M. Paul Reynaud, outlined the dangers concretely. In his view, assuming that the Algerian war was over by 1965, the government's plans would lead to the following situation by 1970: France would have six divisions and Germany twelve. Germany, having fulfilled her obligations to NATO and having the largest army in Western Europe, would be well placed to ask for a revision of the Treaty of Paris which would enable her to have a national nuclear striking force. All this pointed to the need for creating a nuclear force within an integrated Europe.[33] For M. Jacques Douzane, who had the same fears about the effect of the government's policy on Germany, the 'force de frappe' would not be a deterrent force but a persuasive force conjuring up a terrible perspective.[34]

M. Mollet aptly summed up the issue. Speaking later in the debate, he recalled the motives of those who had pushed through the EURATOM agreement and the place of Germany in their calculations. Addressing ministers, he exclaimed that there was no doubt in his mind that the government's opposition to integration condemned the whole of its German policy to failure. Besides, it was paradoxical to observe the very men who had opposed E.D.C. and were hostile to the principle of German rearmament, now taking decisions which made the remilitarization of an independent Germany inevitable. How could they oppose German demands for a national nuclear striking force in the light of the equality of rights and the principle of non-discrimination in a Europe of fatherlands? Referring to a brochure of the German High Command calling for the supply of tactical atomic weapons to the Bundeswehr, Mollet reverted to his warnings of 1956 about a Bonn-Washington axis and the spectre of what he described as a 'nouveau pacte Ribbentrop-Molotov'.[35]

Other orators pursued a similar theme. M. Debray explained that the opposition was not so much to nuclear weapons as to the way in which they were fitted into the context of French foreign policy and to their effect on the West, particularly Germany.

The roles were reversed. In the debates over E.D.C. and EURATOM, M. Debré and his friends attacked the integrationists for preparing the way for a German dominated Europe. In the debate over the 'force de frappe' the 'Europeans' attacked M. Debré's government for preparing the way for an uncontrolled German rearmament.

Throughout the period since the end of the war, one might well ask, 'Whom were the French watching on the Rhine – the Russians, or . . . the Germans?' One of the functions of the French nuclear programme was, therefore, to add military and, more important, diplomatic weight to the position of France vis-à-vis the potentially greatest power on the Continent, outside Russia. This was certainly Charles Ailleret's motive when he started on his long crusade for the creation of a national nuclear armament.[36]

Many of the policies pursued by President de Gaulle since his assumption of power: the withholding of French divisions from NATO, while those of Germany are integrated into the allied system; the creation of a French atomic armoury, while Germany is forbidden to have one; the proposal for an Anglo-American-French directorate of the Western Alliance,* confirming France's

* Contained in a secret letter to President Eisenhower and Prime Minister Macmillan in September 1958, in which he not only suggested the establishment of a directorate of three within the Western Alliance, but also the extension of its interests to cover the whole world and not merely the North Atlantic and West European region.

35

pretensions to be the leading Continental power in NATO; all pointed to French determination in keeping Germany under control.

However, Gaullist policy towards Germany was not hostile. On the contrary, it was firmly based on the concept of partnership in which France should play the leading role thanks largely to the existence of the French nuclear force. Such an attitude may appear to be patronizing and might have been resented by the Germans. It was founded on the fact of Germany's defeat at the end of the Second World War and on the consequences arising from that event. Among them are the status of Berlin as a city still under four-power occupation; the series of agreements which tie the Federal Republic of Germany to the Western Alliance, particularly the renunciation of any right to the manufacture or ownership of a national nuclear force; the existence of a separate East Germany, which the French do not regard as a state. These three factors limit German sovereignty and make it impossible to settle the future of Germany without the approval of the four allied powers of the Second World War. On the other hand, the French were realistic enough to know that a European settlement could not be effective unless it was reached in co-operation with the Germans. For various reasons Russia and the United States preferred a continuation of the *status quo* on the Continent. The Europeans were no longer willing to accept a situation which consecrated the political, military and economic hegemony of those two powers. Hence pressure for a European settlement was emerging from beneath the strategic deadlock.

The French argued that because of their history and present obligations the Germans could not take the initiative in promoting the changes which were necessary to make an eventual settlement possible. The French, however, were in the position to do so because they were Europeans and because they were friends of the two great powers. In order to take advantage of this, it was necessary first to weaken the control of the United States over Western Europe and then to begin the dialogue over a European system with the Russians. The Federal Republic of Germany was

36

a necessary partner in the pursuit of such a policy but was dependent on French initiatives. The French approach to Germany, therefore, rested on the dual concept of partnership and leadership.

The Franco-German Treaty of the 22nd January 1963 was the cornerstone of the relationship between the two countries. While establishing a fairly precise procedure for consultation at various levels, including that of the ministers of defence and their chiefs of staff, the subjects of these consultations were left vague. In the field of defence there was the intention to align strategic and tactical doctrines so as to arrive at common conceptions.

The treaty has so far withstood the vicissitudes of the Franco-German relationship but its functioning has been marked by periodic German complaints of French high-handedness and unilateral action, in exactly the same way that the French complain about the United States within the framework of the Atlantic Alliance. Moreover, the Germans have continued to accept the principle enunciated by Fritz Erler in the debate on Chancellor Erhard's investiture in 1963: No Europe without France and no European security without the United States.

The partnership was also emphasized in President de Gaulle's speech at the Military Academy in Hamburg in 1962, in which he extolled the role of Gauls and Germans in European history and tactlessly reminded his audience of the pre-eminent part played by the military in their countries' past.[37] On a more concrete level, military collaboration has extended to joint training against which the French Communist Party failed to arouse any significant opposition. Joint missile research goes back to the days immediately after the end of the war when France, like other allied powers, sought to benefit from the advanced German rocketry. A number of Germans worked in the French missile research programme and one of them, Hubert Schardin, became Director of Ballistics at the D.E.F.A. (Direction des Etudes et Fabrications des Armements) research establishment at St. Louis. On the 31st March 1958 this establishment became bi-national with two directors, one from each country. In fact, Germany and the

United States have become the principal foreign contributors to French ballistic missile technology.[38]

In recent years, the partnership found expression in the moves to open the dialogue with the East European states in which France took the initiative and apparently hoped to play the role of guide on the path to German reunification.

The French government never allowed the Germans quite to forget their subordinate relationship to France. The scheme for an Anglo-American-French directorate within the Atlantic Alliance was designed to distinguish the powers with global interests and responsibilities from the remaining alliance partners whose interests and influence were confined to the Atlantic and European regions. The failure of this move led to the step by step withdrawal from the North Atlantic Treaty Organization over which the German partner was not consulted, not even after the signature of the treaty of 1963. Indeed, the Germans had cause to complain of a lack of warning, let alone consultation, prior to various French moves, such as the recognition of the People's Republic of China. French high-handedness was not confined to diplomatic manœuvres. The kidnapping of the O.A.S. (l'Organisation de l'Armée Secrète) leader, Argoud, in Munich in February 1963 provoked the most serious discord between the two states.

In his press conference of the 4th February 1965, President de Gaulle hinted at the limitations of national territory and of national armament that Germany must accept if she wishes to achieve reunification. In his view the German problem could only be solved in the context of a European security system, the construction of which would have to be the work of all the neighbours of Germany. Even after de Gaulle one may assume that France would accept the Oder-Neisse Line as Germany's eastern frontier and agree to the denuclearization of the state in return for a Soviet acceptance of German reunification. Until the time when such a settlement enters the realm of practical politics, the French will continue to insist on their special rights *vis-à-vis* Germany, particularly in the occupation of Berlin.

The agreement over the role of the French forces in Germany, reached between Generals Lemnitzer and Ailleret after France's withdrawal from the North Atlantic Treaty Organization, further underlines this privileged position. It is left to France to decide whether to join in repelling an attack. There is no guarantee of French participation in a defensive battle, so that French troops are stationed in the rear in accordance with their reserve mission.[39] Yet the troops remain on German soil at the express wish of the German Chancellor. The convention of the 23rd October 1954 provides the juridical basis of their continued presence and a letter from the French Foreign Minister, dated the 21st December 1966, outlined the modifications of administrative arrangements made previously under NATO. They mainly concern the notification of troop movements and other military dispositions; questions of protocol, such as the display of national flags, and the use of both languages. The French garrison in Berlin is excluded from these arrangements.[40]

President de Gaulle recognized the great importance and power of Germany, but certain factors in the European situation, notably the division of Germany and the course of Russian policy, forced Germany to operate within a restricted field of manœuvre. Thus France had the opportunity to exercise her leadership. The national nuclear force played its role in this respect not so much as a means of protection against the Soviet Union but as a means of adding weight to French diplomacy and as a means of keeping German pretensions under control.

The French government was unimpressed by fears that French policy encouraged the Germans to want their own nuclear force and that the heavy emphasis on nuclear weapons weakened French conventional capabilities in relation to those of Germany. According to the Gaullist view, Germany's obligation under the 1954 agreements and her position *vis-à-vis* the Russians excluded the acquisition of nuclear weapons.[41]

(iii) The British example

While one may argue whether French nuclear policy was setting an example for the Germans to follow, there can be little doubt that Britain set an example for France.

There are strong similarities between the origins of the British and French nuclear energy programmes. The atomic research of both countries became important but subordinate parts of the allied war effort, although British inferiority was obscured by various wartime agreements between the allies. Both states aimed at independence in this field after the war. The motives for a military orientation in Britain and France were related to prestige and influence rather than to defence against a specific enemy. Both saw its relevance to their world-wide interests.

Here the resemblance ends. The British operated within the framework of a policy directed towards the American alliance. The British interest was to tie the Americans to Europe. The British nuclear force was to serve as a trigger for the American defence of Europe. For a time the French had a similar objective but it was more limited and soon the nuclear force became a symbol of the French escape from dependence on the American alliance. The British moved in the opposite direction.

The decision to develop an independent nuclear programme in the period after 1946 was due partly to the belief, justified to a certain extent, that a British effort would eventually lead the Americans to provide scientific and material assistance. Subsequently, the British weapons systems were built increasingly around American technology after the virtual abandonment of an independent missile development base with the cancellation of Blue Streak in 1960. The long hesitations about a full commitment to the European Community and the consistent support for NATO integration were further signs of the basic orientation in British policy.

France, too, hoped to benefit from American co-operation, but only as a means to restore her independence and freedom of manœuvre, particularly within Europe. French statesmen since 1945 have been very conscious of the difference in their geopolitical and strategic outlook when compared with that of the Anglo-Saxon maritime powers.

40

Nevertheless, the influence of the British example in nuclear armament may be seen in the light of various functions: it stimulated a country of similar economic potential and power to follow suit; it provided a challenge for the leadership of Europe; it was a guide to relations with the nuclear giants, particularly the dominant partner in the Western Alliance.

French wartime experiences in the atomic field had caused some bitter feelings towards the United States.* Similar sentiments were not entertained towards the British, apart from general remarks about 'Anglo-Saxons' who took all the credit for the achievements without allowing for the French contribution.[42] This indulgence towards the British was due to their more generous attitude towards the French scientists working on the allied projects and to the fact that the British were in an obviously weak position *vis-à-vis* the Americans. In spite of a mishandling of the triangular relationship by the British authorities, the French saw the Americans as the principal instigators of allied policies in this field.

The British atomic energy programme passed through two distinct phases after the war. Following the American cut-off as a result of the McMahon Act of 1946, the British set about developing their own military potential in atomic energy so that they might eventually obtain American scientific and material assistance in weapons development as the result of their independent progress. The amendments to the McMahon Act of 1954 and 1958 justified this view. The second phase involved the development of a strategy to justify Britain's nuclear and thermonuclear power. This could be said to have begun with the first British atomic explosion in October 1952 when the idea gained ground that the United Kingdom might escape the burden of maintaining large conventional forces by developing her nuclear capability. The evolution of British defence thinking was contained in a series of White Papers from 1955 to 1957, which eventually led to the abolition of conscription in 1960. The basic argument in support of an independent nuclear deterrent lay in the belief that

* See below, pp. 125–129.

the next war would be nuclear and, though Britain was defence-less against a thermonuclear attack and depended upon the effectiveness of the American deterrent in the ultimate resort, her own nuclear force was a necessary reinforcement of the Alliance. As the Americans had lost their nuclear monopoly, a British deterrent would ensure some independence of the United States and would enable Britain to influence allied strategy.

Since one could not defend the validity of the British deterrent on purely military and technical grounds, the government was forced to support it on political grounds. These were best sum-marized in a television interview in 1958 when Mr. Macmillan justified the British nuclear force in these terms:

> The independent contribution gives us a better position in the world, it gives us a better position with respect to the United States. It puts us where we ought to be, in the position of a great power. The fact that we have it makes the United States pay a greater regard to our point of view, and that is of great importance.[43]

It was argued that Britain could play a particularly effective role in East-West relations and disarmament negotiations, only because of her nuclear prowess.

One might add a third phase which began with the cancellation of Blue Streak and brought the country face to face with the problem of keeping up in the development of ever more costly and complicated weapons systems, which raised the question for how long Britain would be able to stay in the nuclear race.

The French watched British developments closely. Each major step in Britain can be matched by corresponding developments in France. The decision of the United Kingdom to launch a programme of its own after the war was paralleled by the be-ginnings of the French programme, though their points of departure were wide apart. The first British atomic test coincided with the first stirrings of interest in a weapons programme in French military circles. The debate on British nuclear strategy and the search for a military justification of the atomic programme in the middle fifties found its echo in the writings of the small military pressure group, which appeared in the *Revue de Défense Nationale*.

Captain Pierre J. G. Maurin argued that only those powers which had nuclear weapons were entirely independent and that the British example disproved the thesis that only the greatest powers can be atomic powers. Although the middle powers could not hope to rival the capacity of the United States, they could still have a certain weight.[44] Colonel Ailleret suggested that because Great Britain had the will and intelligence to make the necessary effort, she had established herself as a civil and military atomic power.[45] Colonel Debau concluded from the British example that a country with resources similar to those of France could carry the economic burden of atomic research and production.[46]

The first British thermonuclear explosion in May 1957, coupled with British aloofness towards EURATOM, provided more grist for the mill of the advocates of a national deterrent. The United Kingdom had taken her place among the atomic powers at considerable cost and had acquired the dignity of an 'inter-locuteur valable' and of an accepted intermediary, while France was proposing to abandon her atomic privileges to EURATOM.[47]

The British example was again invoked in support of the initial proposal for the construction of a plant to separate isotopes, under the terms of the second Five Year Plan in 1957. The 'rapporteur' of the Finance Commission, M. Max Brusset, bolstered his arguments in favour of the Plan with comparisons of the atomic programmes of the United Kingdom and France.[48]

When it came to debating the government's 'loi-programme' for atomic armament three years later, the argument about the British example became double-edged. M. Michel Debré asked why France should not do the same as Britain and made his own the arguments about reinforcing the Atlantic Alliance used by ministers at the Conservative Party Conference.[49] Referring to the plans for an intermediate stage in the creation of 'la force de dissuasion', which would depend on aircraft as vehicles of delivery,

43

he added that this was merely following the British pattern.

But M. Guy Mollet had no difficulty in showing the obverse side of the coin. The British had always been reticent about European integration. Now that the Communities were established and were proving themselves, Britain tried to get closer to them. In the field of defence, on the other hand, the British had pursued an Atlantic integrationist policy with the result that, after the failure of the Blue Streak project, they had negotiated a treaty with the United States which enabled them to share in the developing American strategic power. Both examples pointed to the fact the the British experience was an argument for integration and not isolation.[50]

M. Mollet used the British example to juxtapose his policy of nuclear integration, which had led him to sacrifice his pacifist stand over atomic weapons in order to save EURATOM, against the government's policy of nuclear autarky. This appears to have been a reversal of his position three years earlier.* His ally, M. Maurice Faure, went further and used the British example to demonstrate the uselessness of a small national atomic force. In his opinion, British influence in Asia and Africa did not rest on nuclear weapons but on successful decolonization. The members of the Commonwealth either relied for their security on the American deterrent or took refuge in neutralism. Britain had turned her back on Europe and yet had not acquired any real advantages in return.[51]

The arguments of both men point to the assumption that not only must France integrate her efforts with those of her European neighbours in order to keep up with modern economic and military developments, but that she could only hope to retain a position of world influence within the context of such an integration. In a sense, therefore, French reactions to British progress in the nuclear field were governed as much, or more, by the need to keep up with the neighbours across the Channel as by the example of how to become an atomic power.

Thus, the Gaullists (Républicains Sociaux) insisted at the time

* See below, Chapter 2, p. 95.

of the debate over EURATOM that because of her position in the world and the state of her research, France had the same claim as Britain to be the only nation of Western Europe which should dispose of the nuclear weapon.[52] During the debate in the National Assembly it was symptomatic of this concern that M. Francis Perrin had to point out that although France was not so far behind the United Kingdom in plans for the industrial production of atomic energy, she would be about three times as far in arrears in its military development.

Finally, there was the contrast in the treatment meted out by the United States to Britain and France. Various attempts at Franco-American co-operation had failed. The failures were all the more bitter when it was recalled that in 1955 North American Aviation entered into a licence agreement with Rolls-Royce Ltd. without any opposition or interference from the United States government. Thereby all the engineering details of the only large rocket engine in an advanced state of development in the United States were made available to the British firm. In addition, a system of inertial guidance using gyroscopes could be produced under licence in the United Kingdom.[53]

Nevertheless, shrewd observers were not slow to expose the so-called preferential treatment derived by Britain from her special relationship with the United States. M. Faure asked in the debate over the censure motion on the government's atomic policy in 1960, whether the United States had in fact systematically supported the United Kingdom over international issues. He reminded the House of the Suez crisis and the American attitude in support of the Common Market against the British position. Nor did the British carry much weight in the determination of American strategy in the Pacific.[54]

Yet, the idea that all France had to do was to reach a certain stage of development to benefit from American co-operation persisted into the 1960s, in spite of the growing difficulties which faced the British independent deterrent. Emulation and aspirations to a similar relationship with the United States marked one aspect of French atomic policy *vis-à-vis* Britain. Another aspect is

45

provided by various abortive attempts to ensure a Franco-British collaboration in this sphere.

These efforts date back to the period immediately after the war. At a meeting of the Atomic Energy Committee, presided over by Félix Gouin in March 1946, Frédéric Joliot-Curie had argued that France should help Britain in her atomic effort because no aid could be expected from the United States. As a result of wartime collaboration the French position in relation to Britain and Canada was strong and through continued collaboration one might help the British to free themselves from the American embrace. Subsequent discussions between Joliot-Curie, Raoul Dautry, Lew Kowarski, John Wilmot, the British Minister of Supply, and Sir John Anderson, came to nothing because the British were hoping to renew their relations with the United States and were particularly sensitive to Joliot-Curie's political affiliations. It has been suggested that the French failure to make much impression on the British in these early years was also due to Joliot-Curie's failure to appreciate the importance of the French contribution to the allied war effort, which led him to assume a weak negotiating position.[55]

In later years there was some collaboration with the British in the creation of C.E.R.N. (Centre Européen de la Recherche Nucléaire) in 1953. The two countries shared the cost of the venture on a fifty-fifty basis. A renewed attempt at bilateral co-operation came to nothing in February 1955. The French were to give preference to British nuclear exports in return for information and materials to help in building a plant for the separation of U235. However, the United States formally opposed the deal on the grounds of the Anglo-American agreement over atomic secrets.

In recent years the situation of the two countries has reversed dramatically. Some people in the United Kingdom now look enviously at French achievements in the nuclear weapons field, particularly in the development of missile technology. In Gaullist eyes the British policy of priority for the American connection disqualified Britain from entry into the European Community. It was the declared policy of the government to achieve the greatest degree of self-sufficiency in the procurement of strategic weapons, including nuclear explosives and the means of their delivery, while accepting co-operation with other countries in 'les secteurs moins essentiels'.[56] If necessary, such co-operation could be dispensed with.

France may have followed the British example and tried to secure British co-operation in the 1940s and 1950s but the basic objective behind her nuclear policy was different. In so far as the British sought an independent role, it was conceived as a continuation of Britain's function as one of the 'Big Three' of the wartime alliance with global responsibilities. This meant by implication that no one power must be allowed to dominate the European Continent.

The French search for independence was only partly dictated by the desire to play a role in the world at large. It was principally inspired by the search for leadership in Europe–at least in the western half of it. The impulse was there under the Fourth Republic but it emerged as a more clearly defined policy under de Gaulle and was sharpened by his personal resentments, particularly against Mr. Macmillan who had wounded his pride during the war.[57] The aim was to achieve a freedom of manœuvre in which the French would serve as a balancer between the Germans and the Slavs. In fulfilment of it France had to exercise influence over Germany, had not to be too dependent on the maritime powers for her security and had to be able to exploit the African hinterland as an additional source of strength for the French position in Europe. In support of such a national policy the French nuclear force played an important part as a means of deterrence and as an ultimate guarantee of defence.

If President de Gaulle did not need much convincing that every time Britain had to choose between France–or Europe–and the United States she would choose the latter, the Nassau Agreement of December 1962 proved it for all to see. His conversations with Macmillan at Rambouillet which preceded it epitomize the psychological difficulties of the Anglo-French dialogue. De Gaulle was probably quite sincere in offering some form of nuclear

47

partnership to offset the effects of the cancellation of Skybolt, for it was in line with earlier attempts at technical co-operation with the British. His habit of 'thinking aloud' on such occasions left the offer vague and ambiguous. It is most likely that the General expected the British to make the first public move in the direction of an Anglo-French collaboration as, in his view, the onus lay on Britain to prove her credentials as a 'European' state. British suspicions of French machiavellianism and unwillingness to let go of the American connection when it came to the test account for Macmillan's neglect of the French gesture.

The same problem appeared in a different context over the so-called 'Soames Affair' of February 1969. By this time the British had gone a long way to make themselves respectable Europeans but the General, still unconvinced, set another test by 'thinking aloud' about the possibilities of a future transfiguration of the European section of the Atlantic Alliance. The British government again suspected French trickery and reacted in a way which caused deep offence in Paris. So the two partners were caught in mutual suspicions whose roots lay in their historic relationship and their traditionally different outlook on Europe. However, the French President had become aware of the restrictions on his more grandiose ambitions imposed by French economic weakness. For some months before his resignation in April 1969 there had been a mellowing of attitudes towards the 'Anglo-Saxon' powers and some indication that Britain might again be regarded as a reinforcement in the face of German strength.

(iv) **Relations with the United States over atomic weapons**
The ingredients of French relations with the United States consisted of two elements. One is the coincidence or conflict of French and American interests in Europe and, to a lesser extent, elsewhere. The other is composed of the personal feelings of President de Gaulle and of most Frenchmen who lived through the humiliations of the 1940s and 1950s. The first element is the more important because it is the more lasting.

48

[Leaving aside the historic and sentimental ties between France and the United States we note that in the early post-war period, France, like the other European members of the Western Alliance, was to a large extent economically, politically and militarily dependent on the United States.] She had to rely on America to provide a guarantee against Russian threats and the danger of a potential German revival.] Once she became involved in the Indochinese war she relied to an ever-increasing degree on American financial and material support to provide the means with which to continue the struggle. By the time the war came to an end, American involvement was so great that it led to serious difficulties in the relations between the two countries over the newly independent states of the Republic of Vietnam, Cambodia and Laos.*

[The basic problem facing French governments after 1945 was how to reconcile this necessary dependence with a policy of restoring national independence and French influence in international relations.] As long as the emphasis was on economic and social reconstruction, there were not many critics, apart from the communists and those who favoured a neutralist foreign policy, of the need to accept military protection from the United States.

In relationships over atomic questions one accepted American leadership and superiority but insisted on the right of France to have a stake in nuclear policy as one of the three principal allies. France claimed equality with Britain, even though the facts hardly warranted the assumption that Britain enjoyed a favoured status in this field between 1946 and 1954. However, the motives which governed British efforts during this period were also present in French minds.

* The United States had assumed the responsibility of arming the forces of those states as well as providing substantial economic aid to the region as a whole. This naturally led to American attempts to direct policy in the area, which was regarded by the French as an interference in their preserve. For an interesting account of Franco-American relationships during the first year after the armistice of July 1954, see General Paul Ely, *Mémoires: Vol. I: L'Indochine dans la Tourmente* (Paris, Librairie Plon, 1964), pp. 269–74.

Although the French programme started with greater handicaps than that of the British, the participation of French scientists in the allied wartime effort gave their country, in French eyes, the same right and even obligation to establish itself as an atomic power. Nevertheless, we can trace a fairly consistent line of thought which held that French advances in this field should be considered not so much as steps towards French atomic independence than as means whereby the United States could be persuaded to take the French programme seriously and be induced to help it.

From the earliest days immediately after the war, the American policy of secrecy came under heavy criticism on two grounds: first, that it was useless as it would only be a matter of time before other countries knew how to make atomic bombs; secondly, that it might eventually lead to a scientific arms race. At the same time there were occasional warnings that one day France would be able to make her own bombs if she wanted to.[58] Joliot-Curie, the High Commissioner for Atomic Energy, went even further and suggested at the end of 1948 that the problem of making a French bomb might have to be faced when the necessary information was at hand and that it would involve a 'great responsibility'.[59] This statement marked the entry into operation of the first French experimental uranium pile and could have been interpreted as an attempt to exert pressure or to exercise a kind of political black-mail. More significant still, Joliot-Curie took the opportunity to say that the secrets of the French process would be used to bargain with other nuclear powers for industrial purposes.[60]

French chauvinism about atomic energy was justified in the light of foreign reaction to the event. The Anglo-American press was disturbed by the implied loss of monopoly in this field and by the likelihood that the French would freely publish the results of their research. On the Continent there was some rejoicing about 'Un' Altra Vittoria della Scienza Europea'.[61] Anglo-Saxon concern was not, however, confined to the emergence of another atomic power in the world but included alarm at the extent of communist infiltration into the French programme whose scienti-fic leader, Frédéric Joliot-Curie, was himself a member of the party; an alarm which was shared by the non-communist French press.

The debate about the dismissal of Joliot-Curie in 1950 provides another clear indication that the French atomic programme was seen in the context of inter-allied relationships in which the underlying assumption was that of co-operation. The communists and their sympathizers insisted that the government was under American pressure and that the United States wanted to force France into producing atom bombs. Naturally, they linked their protests to their peace campaign. They found ammunition for their arguments in the attitude of the American and British press which repeatedly expressed concern over the presence of communists in the Commissariat. Much play was also made of a report by Drew Pearson that the American ambassador had urged the French government to replace Joliot-Curie.[62]

Elsewhere in the political spectrum the government earned support of varying fervour. Even the left-wing *Combat* recognized the need for Bidault's action, though not without asking why there was so much disquiet over Joliot-Curie's speeches if, as seemed obvious, the available resources did not allow France to turn her research into the manufacture of weapons.[63]

After the French programme had entered upon the industrial stage, attitudes towards the United States changed in the light of French technical progress. However, the basic approach was unaffected since it was still thought that American help was desirable and that there should be no discrimination between the American treatment of the United Kingdom and of France.

The problem of equality of treatment within the Alliance had exercised influential Frenchmen since 1949. On the 4th August 1949, *The New York Times* reported a speech by the chief of staff of the army, General Revers, to the Anglo-American Press Association in Paris. The General had said that in NATO's strategic plans France should have the place assigned to her by geography and 'that none should have a monopoly of one weapon'. Nonetheless, a report of discussions in NATO's Standing Group in November of that year suggested that France would not join Britain in asking for a share in atomic secrets or for a stockpile of atomic weapons on French soil.*

The French continued to claim a share in the discussions about atomic energy among the Alliance partners. They were told that atomic energy would not be on the agenda of the three-power conference to be held in Bermuda in December 1953. Accordingly, no senior French atomic expert accompanied M. Laniel to the venue. However, Lord Cherwell and Lewis Strauss were present, so that discussions about international co-operation in the atomic energy field and the relaxation of the policy of secrecy were conducted without French participation. To avoid a repetition of this experience the French sent an atomic expert with their delegation to the four-power conference of foreign ministers in Berlin in January 1954. This time the subject was not discussed.[64]

As France increased her capability to make atomic weapons, the demand for equality in the right to decide NATO policies became more pronounced. M. Gaillard, who had done more than anyone to put the French atomic programme on an industrial basis, was content to leave the disposal of offensive atomic weapons in American hands but used the threat of a possible French bomb as an additional argument in favour of a more liberal Anglo-American policy. He drew an invidious comparison between the information the enemy had acquired about the American atomic programme and that vouchsafed to the allies, adding that it was unacceptable that there was not the closest collaboration within the heart of the Atlantic Alliance over atomic matters, particularly defence against the effects of the bomb.[65]

Co-operation there should be, but without control by the supplier over the recipient. This point was emphasized during the debate on EURATOM. M. P.-H. Teitgen, for instance, argued

* According to this account, there had been differences between France and the United States in assessing the danger of nuclear war. The Americans argued that since the U.S.S.R. was at that time inadequately equipped to attack America directly, she would first attack Western Europe. In the French view, the Russians would not make a nuclear attack on countries which did not possess such weapons and France was, therefore, better protected by not having them. (*The Scotsman*, 26 November 1949.)

that if France bought fissile materials from America she would have to account for their use to the United States with the result that the Americans could send their inspectors into French installations.[66] But if they were bought by EURATOM they would be solely under EURATOM's control.

During the debate in the Conseil de la République on a private motion to set up a military division within the C.E.A., the most frequently expressed concern was to prevent an Anglo-Saxon monopoly from dominating the Western Alliance. EURATOM, with its exclusive interest in the peaceful uses of atomic energy, was well suited, according to M. de Maupeou, as an instrument of Anglo-American control over the allies because under the original provisions of the treaty France would be effectively prevented from making nuclear weapons for a number of years. He added that NATO should not be regarded as a permanent alliance and he saw many reasons (the Norwegian refusal to have NATO bases in peacetime, the British evacuation of Suez, the American withdrawal from Iceland, French difficulties in North Africa, British difficulties in Cyprus) why NATO was becoming the sick man of the West. M. Michel Yver, speaking for the foreign affairs committee, reminded his fellow senators that France, through her key position, had forced the Americans to adopt a forward strategy as opposed to a peripheral strategy, which might have been preferable to them. Unless France acquired an atomic capability she would play a secondary role in the directorate of the Atlantic Alliance.

M. de Maupeou, who spoke for the national defence committee, saw furthest of all and followed some of the arguments which are very much the ones currently used by some French apologists for a national nuclear force. Referring to the signs of a Russian-American agreement to establish a world-wide monopoly over the military uses of atomic energy, he said that in the presence of such a monopolistic policy the national defence committee had come to the conclusion that one should pursue a policy of 'vulgarisation des armements nucléaires'. Such a development, instead of increasing the risk of war, would provide a relative but

53

not negligible assurance of the independence and security of those states which could afford to have atomic weapons. He went on to suggest that the ultimate solution of it all did not lie in futile disarmament talks, but in an effective system of collective security with an international organ controlling weapons of mass destruction.[67]

The issue was, therefore, seen not only in terms of American discrimination within the Alliance but in the light of a possible Russian-American agreement which remained an obsession of French policy. Thus, M. Claparède, Secrétaire d'Etat à la Présidence du Conseil, told the Council of the Republic that the French delegate at the United Nations had secured the removal from all western proposals of any arrangements which discriminated against France.[68]

In the last years of the Fourth Republic the horizon had been extended to include the possible effect of an East-West détente on the French claim to great-power status, but the principal objective remained the assertion of French rights within the Alliance. The Fourth Republic's last effective Minister of National Defence, M. Chaban-Delmas, told a press conference, with reference to the production of nuclear weapons, that friendship demanded that there should be no discrimination.[69]

President de Gaulle's proposal for the establishment of a directorate within NATO was, therefore, only a logical extension of the concern for a French say in allied strategy. At this time French relations with NATO in general and the United States in particular were complicated by the Algerian war. The ambivalent attitude of the allies had greatly offended French susceptibilities. M. Debré's investiture speech in January 1959 linked French demands for a greater say within the Alliance to the demand for allied solidarity in the Algerian conflict.[70]

The general policy of the government over the control of nuclear weapons enjoyed widespread support in the country.*

* A public opinion poll in July 1959 had put the following question: 'Le gouvernement français refuse aux Etats-Unis la possibilité d'entre-poser des armes atomiques américaines en France tant que les alliés de l'OTAN n'accep-

We must, however, bear in mind that although there was general agreement over the question of equality within the Alliance, particularly in the status of Britain and France, the basic objectives of President de Gaulle, as far as they were understood, were not necessarily shared by those who supported him over this issue.

France had been set on the course of providing herself with an atomic armoury since the middle fifties, which did not exclude international co-operation to achieve this end. Gaullists and non-Gaullists alike envisaged substantial American help for the programme and certain aspects of American policy had given them reason to believe that they would not be disappointed. If this help had been forthcoming, one may well speculate about its effect on French policy. An important ingredient in Franco-American relations over nuclear policy was, therefore, provided by the unsuccessful French search for American support in creating an atomic force.

In retrospect, the French might well argue that amendments to the McMahon Act had raised their hopes only to be deceived. The terms of the Act* were first modified in 1954 as a response to the new NATO doctrine of using tactical nuclear weapons against conventional attacks. However, these changes only opened the

---

teront pas que la France puisse intervenir au cas où on déciderait de les utiliser. Approuvez-vous ou désapprouvez-vous la position du gouvernement français?' The replies were broken up as follows:

Approuvent	69%
Désapprouvent	4%
?	27%

(*I.F.O.P., Institut Français d'Opinion Publique, -S3210, 'L'actualité vue par le public', No. 4, July 1959, Rapport 1243.*)

* Under the terms of the original Act there was a complete ban on the exchange of information 'with respect to the use of atomic energy for industrial purposes'; the relevant passages are to be found under 'Control of Information', Section 10 (a) 1 and 2, (b) 1 (*Atomic Energy Act of 1946*, Public Law 585–79th Congress, Chapter 724–2nd Session, S. 1717, pp. 12–13).

door slightly to co-operation in the military sphere, a co-operation which remained rigidly circumscribed.*

A second series of amendments was carried through in 1958. In some respects these were more far-reaching in that the government was able to provide special nuclear material to allied powers and to share certain non-nuclear weapons components and delivery systems. Above all, the United States could render more direct assistance in the production of weapons to nations which had made 'substantial progress in the development of atomic weapons'.

The date of the first amendment coincided with the orientation of the French programme to military ends and it had an important influence on French thinking, particularly with the British example in mind. Officials continued to express the hope that American aid would be forthcoming, even after the decision to produce a French bomb had become public knowledge.

In an interview with the correspondent of *U.S. News and World Report*, the last but one Prime Minister of the Fourth Republic, M. Gaillard, clearly expressed the twin French concerns for equality of status within the Western Alliance and for the benefit of American co-operation.[71] A short while later, his Minister of National Defence, M. Chaban-Delmas, was much more specific at a press conference:

> In a spirit of co-operation we have asked the United States to consider:
> (1) That as far as the use of I.R.B.M.s is concerned it would be proper to share in the decision. This is the now well-known two-key system;
> (2) That we should be in a position to produce this type of

* For example, no nuclear weapons could be given to allies for training purposes unless they remained in the custody of American nationals; nuclear warheads remained under American control; certain information about the external characteristics of nuclear warheads could be shared with allies to facilitate training and operations with nuclear weapons, provided it did not facilitate the manufacture of warheads, which, in the words of John Foster Dulles, involved a 'difficult task of definition'. (Osgood, pp. 216–17.)

missile, which calls for technical assistance from the United States, whether it be in the form of production under licence or of blueprints transmitted by the Government in Washington;

(3) That there is no doubt that American financial aid would be necessary.

Our policy is one of intervention and risk: when we are capable of manufacturing this or that material, it is supplied to us more readily.

The manufacture of missiles would enter into the framework of European co-operation in the field of armaments, which has already been initiated at Bonn. We intend to be able to make modern weapons in order to maintain an equitable balance within NATO and to preserve it from what could become one day a ferment of disintegration.[72]

The warning of the last sentence was unmistakable and, as we now know, prophetic. In his speech at the Ecole Militaire in November 1959, President de Gaulle expressed his government's intention to create a 'force de frappe', whether self-made or bought.[73] Nevertheless, the possibility of American assistance was continually evoked in the years right up to and immediately after the first French atomic explosion.

It is necessary to set the repeated faith in American intentions against the background of what actually happened to Franco-American co-operation in the field of nuclear weapons.

The story of these relations divides into two parts. The first covers the period before the accession to power of General de Gaulle. The second starts with the amendment to the Atomic Energy Act of July 1958 which coincided with the early years of the Fifth Republic when French nuclear preparations were pushed more openly and when the declarations of intent of previous years were put to the test.

In the early fifties the French demand for enriched uranium and the United States demand for natural uranium dominated the problem of co-operation. Direct negotiations between the two countries were rarely successful. American policy also cast its shadow over parallel negotiations with other countries. We have already noted how discussions with the British failed on this score. Similar trouble occurred in negotiations with Canada between 1956 and 1957. The French refused to pay the same price for Canadian natural uranium as the United States because no restriction was placed on its use by the Americans whereas the French were only allowed to exploit it for peaceful purposes.[74]

There was no particular alarm in the United States about the development of a French atomic armaments programme. But there was apprehension at the prospect of the dissemination of nuclear weapons. The move to establish the International Atomic Energy Agency and various proposals for joint allied control of nuclear weapons were the concrete expressions of this anxiety.* American policy was crystallized at the NATO summit meeting in December 1957 when President Eisenhower offered to help NATO in developing an I.R.B.M. system in order to meet European doubts about the reliability of the American deterrent. The proposal included the dispersal of I.R.B.M.s in Europe and the use of the double veto, or 'two-key system', for their control. He refused to help individual members to develop national nuclear armouries.[75] Two months later an important French military and civilian mission went to Washington, headed by Buchalet and Ailleret, to collect information about the problems of an atomic test from the competent authorities in the United States. This was a technical reconnaissance but its success left the impression that there was no American hostility to French work in this area, although Colonel Ailleret was irritated by his hosts' condescension and their repeated warnings about the costs and difficulties, coupled with hints that the French would be best advised to put their trust in NATO. In spite of General de Gaulle's later claims for the achievements of the French programme, French technicians had benefited greatly from American papers published for the International Conferences on Atomic

* A proposal to transfer the custody of nuclear stockpiles to NATO was killed by Congressional opposition in July 1957.

Energy held in Geneva in 1955 and 1958, as well as from information gathered during various trips to America, such as the one mentioned above.[76]

Once the French military programme had taken shape, Franco-American relations in this field suffered a series of sharp set-backs which were made all the more painful to the French because of American vacillations. These reflected two levels of conflict within the American governmental system: the conflict between the executive, ever mindful of the delicacy of inter-allied relations, and Congress, resolutely hostile to sharing American atomic power; and the conflict between various departments of the American administration. Added to these disharmonies was the clash of interest between the great private corporations, anxious to do business, and the government's policy.

The first failure followed Mr. Dulles' visit to Paris in July 1958 when, bearing in mind the amended McMahon Act, he promised American help in the building of a submarine reactor. The French followed it up with a mission to Washington, in February 1959, but the offer had to be withdrawn after objections from the powerful Joint Congressional Committee on Atomic Energy. France had to content herself with 440 kilogrammes of enriched uranium but without any data for the construction of a propulsion reactor. The plan was revived in May 1960 but had to be abandoned again in the face of Congressional opposition.[77] American reservations were attributed at the time to fears of a leakage of information via the French programme to the Soviet Union. The basic motive, and the one which dominated the whole of American policy, was put in the following words by the Special Assistant to the Secretary of State for Atomic Energy and Disarmament:

The bar to our co-operation with France ... has not been security in the French defence establishment, but has been our own national policy of not assisting fourth countries to become nuclear powers.[78]

The second affair also took place in 1959. Two French concerns,

La Société pour l'Etude et la Réalisation d'Engins Ballistiques (SEREB) and La Société Nationale d'Etudes et de Construction de Moteurs d'Aviation (SNECMA), entered into detailed conversations with the American firm Aerojet General Corporation with the view to negotiating licence agreements for the production of solid fuel ballistic missiles. According to a statement made in the autumn of 1959 by M. Blancard, the French Secretary of State for Air, the atomic warhead was to have been developed by France and the delivery system by the United States. The I.R.B.M. was to have been ready by 1965, with a range of between 1,500 and 2,500 miles. In September an agreement between the State and Defence Departments prohibited all co-operation between the firms involved. The official reason given was that the object was to encourage the development of a joint European project to develop an I.R.B.M. The real reason was American anxiety over the French programme, now heightened by the presence of General de Gaulle at the helm.

The French and American companies hoped that President Kennedy might take the opportunity to lift the ban on his visit to Paris in May 1961. They were disappointed. Whereas President Eisenhower seemed willing for NATO to have its own I.R.B.M., it was soon clear that his successor was resolutely opposed to any kind of nuclear proliferation, whether by way of NATO or of its individual members. The failure to secure American co-operation in this venture had the effect of delaying the production of an operational French I.R.B.M. by a period of three to five years.[79]

French hopes continued to linger that nuclear weapons might be bought or their production made easier through American co-operation. In April 1962, Secretary of Defence McNamara and General Maxwell Taylor, Chairman of the Joint Chiefs of Staff, had conversations on this subject with the French Minister of the Armed Forces, Pierre Messmer. On their return to Washington they recommended a sharing of atomic secrets with France.[80] However, because of the growing divergence between American and French policies, this proposal was not taken seriously. Tensions and irritations continued to dog Franco-

American relations. In 1964 the Americans banned the sale of giant computers to France on account of their potential use for military as well as civilian purposes. The ban was eventually lifted but the incident only confirmed French suspicions of American discrimination against their country and encouraged the push towards national self-sufficiency in the computer industry.[81]

French reactions were not merely passive and regretful. They were expressed in various measures. The announcement in March 1959 that the French Mediterranean fleet would be withdrawn from NATO command in time of war followed hard on the failure of negotiations for the supply of a submarine reactor. In the spring of 1959 France refused to have I.R.B.M.s on national soil as long as the warheads remained under American control. In the following year she refused to allow the United States to stockpile tactical nuclear weapons on French soil, thus forcing the removal of American fighter-bombers to bases in Britain and Germany, so that they could be re-equipped with nuclear weapons.

Disappointment over the failure to obtain American co-operation was undoubtedly one of the reasons for French retaliatory measures. Nevertheless, these actions stemmed also from General de Gaulle's concept of international relations. For the President, nuclear power was necessary for the achievement of military autonomy which, in turn, was the prerequisite of political independence. Hence, in international relations military power must have a national character:

The defence of France must be in French hands. This is a necessity with which we have not always been familiar in the course of the past years. I know it. It is essential that it becomes so again. If it should happen that a country like France has to make war, its effort must be its own effort ... Naturally, French defence will be co-ordinated with that of other countries if need be. That is in the nature of things. But it is indispensable that it be a French defence and that France defends herself by herself, for herself and in her own manner.[82]

These words not only contain the General's belief in 'national' defence but also his concept of an alliance, clearly thought of in the image of the loose *ad hoc* coalitions of the eighteenth and nineteenth centuries.

After the end of the war in Algeria President de Gaulle was able to give free rein to his concept of military independence as the foundation on which to build his European policy. Although this policy passed through various vicissitudes and has occasionally been obscured by digressions elsewhere in the world, the pattern became steadily clearer. American domination of the Western Alliance must be removed by a determined attack on the integrated structure of NATO. By withdrawing from the Organization in 1966 France had hoped to begin this process. By remaining in the Alliance she expressed a readiness to accept the ultimate American guarantee which is the corollary to the super-power rivalry in the world. French policy followed the view expressed by Pierre Messmer, Minister of the Armies, in 1962: 'In the last analysis, and because of the inequality in numbers between the Soviet and Allied forces in Europe, Europe's defence is based on the existence of the American strategic nuclear forces.'[83]

Having relegated the United States to the role of benevolent but distant guarantor, France would then be free to assume her place as the keystone of a European security system. Germany would be kept under control with the help of Russia. Soviet domination of the Continent would be contained with the help of Germany and other European states. The United Kingdom had no part in this game so long as there was the slightest suspicion of a special link with the United States.

The emerging nuclear weapons programme under the Fourth Republic served as a support of various options in external policy. It was interpreted simultaneously as a reinforcement of European solidarity, as a means with which to achieve a special status within the Atlantic Alliance, as a guarantee against an eventual German military revival and as the base for an independent national policy. After its formal launching in 1960, the French nuclear force became the instrument of the Gaullist policy of national independence and grandeur. It was seen as freeing France from strategic dependence on the United States, as giving France the right to take a leading part in the settlement of Europe, and as restoring to her some of the military pre-eminence on the Continent, outside Russia, which she had lost after 1870.

References

1. For an analysis of the objectives of NATO in its early years, see Robert E. Osgood, *NATO – The Entangling Alliance* (The University of Chicago Press, Chicago, 1962), pp. 30–51.

2. Charles de Gaulle, *Mémoires de Guerre: Vol. III: Le Salut, 1944–1946* (Paris, Librairie Plon, 1959), p. 54.

3. Paul-Marie de la Gorce, *La République et son Armée* (Arthème Fayard, Paris, 1963), has a useful chapter dealing with the evolution of anti-communism within the army (Chapter X, pp. 259–80).

4. Alfred Grosser, *La Quatrième République et sa Politique Extérieure* (Paris, Armand Colin, 1961), p. 229. For a general discussion of the problems facing French foreign policy in the immediate post-war years, see Dorothy Pickles, *French Politics: The First Years of the Fourth Republic* (London, The Royal Institute of International Affairs, 1953), pp. 186–219.

5. *Le Monde*, 8th August 1950.

6. Robert Schuman, speech in the National Assembly, *Le Monde*, 13th December 1950.

7. *Le Figaro*, 26th June 1953.

8. *Le Populaire*, 16th May 1951.

9. *Le Monde*, 26th July 1955.

10. Edgar Faure, *Politique Extérieure et Défense Nationale*, report to the Congress of the Parti Républicain Radical et Radical-Socialiste, October 1952 (Etablissements Moullot, Marseille, 1953), p. 21.

11. Debate on defence budget in Conseil de la République, *Le Monde*, 3rd February 1953.

12. For accounts of the circumstances of his dismissal, see Maréchal Juin, *Mémoires: Vol. II: Libération de la France, Avènement de la Quatrième République 1944–1947, Maroc 1947–1951, Alliance Atlantique, 1951–1958* (Paris, Arthème Fayard, 1960), pp. 260–4; *Le Monde*, 30th March, 1st, 2nd, 6th and 7th April, 7th May 1954; *Le Figaro*, 3rd–4th April 1954.
13. Jean Planchais, *Une Histoire Politique de l'Armée: Vol. II: 1940–1967: De Gaulle à De Gaulle* (Editions du Seuil, Paris, 1967), pp. 243–4.
14. Juin, *Mémoires: Vol. II*, pp. 260–4.
15. Debate on the defence budget for 1953. *Le Monde*, 27th January 1953.
16. Bertrand Goldschmidt, *Les Rivalités Atomiques: 1939–1966* (Arthème Fayard, Paris, 1967), pp. 200–3.
17. Bertrand Goldschmidt, *L'Aventure Atomique* (Paris, Arthème Fayard, 1962), p. 115.
18. Captain Pierre J. G. Maurin, 'Perspectives Atomiques: II' (*Revue de Défense Nationale*, July 1954, pp. 70–1).
19. *La France et la Puissance Atomique* (Situation de la France, No. 2, 'Tendances', March 1960), p. 12.
20. Protocol III, section 2, article iii, quoted in *La France et la Puissance Atomique*, p. 12.
21. Goldschmidt, *Les Rivalités Atomiques*, pp. 206–7.
22. *Les Cahiers de la République*, Janvier-Février 1960, an unsigned editorial (p. 4), which, on the basis of a reference to it in the next issue, must be assumed to express his views, even if it had not been written by him. The subsequent analysis of his views is taken from this editorial and the one in the issue of Mars-Avril 1960.
23. Protocol No. III on the Control of Armaments, Part I, Annexes 1–3 (*Documents agreed on by the Conference of Ministers held in Paris, October 20–23, 1954*, Cmd. 9304, Miscellaneous No. 32 (1954), Her Majesty's Stationery Office, London), pp. 39–43.
24. Colonel E.-J. Debau, 'Les Armes Atomiques et la Défense Nationale' (*Revue de Défense Nationale*, July 1955, p. 5).

25. Jean Fabiani, *Combat*, 6th July 1956. See also the even more bitter anti-German tone of an article by Bernard Lavergne, Professor of Law at the University of Paris, entitled 'L'Euratom ou la nouvelle C.E.D. à abattre' (*L'Année Politique et Economique*, Paris, No. 131, June–July 1956, pp. 289–93). The author referred to Jean Monnet and other technocrats as '. . . les futurs Fuhrers de la Petite Europe cléricale' (p. 290).

26. *Combat*, 3rd July 1956.

27. Yves Moreau, *L'Humanité*, 5th July 1956.

28. J.O., *Débats Parlementaires, No. 80, A.N., 11 July 1956*, session of 10th July, pp. 3338–9.

29. *Ibid., No. 81, A.N., 21 July 1956*, session of 11th July, pp. 3382–3.

30. Osgood, pp. 218–19.

31. For a detailed exposition of how French rights to the military exploitation of atomic energy were protected, see July, *Dispositions Relative à la Communauté Européenne de l'Energie Atomique* (Rapport fait au nom de la Commission des Affaires Etrangères sur le Projet de Loi (No. 4676) autorisant le Président de la République à ratifier):

    1. le Traité instituant la Communauté Economique Européenne et ses annexes;

    2. le Traité instituant la Communauté Européenne de l'Energie Atomique;

    3. la Convention relative à certains institutions communes aux communautés européennes, signé à Rome le 25 Mars 1957. (No. 5266, Assemblée Nationale, Troisième Législature, Session Ordinaire de 1956–7, Annexe au procès-verbal de la séance du 26 juin 1957, pp. 239–62.)

32. J.O., *Débats Parlementaires, No. 39, C.R., 22nd June 1956*, session of 21st June 1956, p. 1244.

33. J.O., *Débats Parlementaires, 1960–61, No. 67 A.N., 19th October 1960*, session of 18th October, p. 2564, col. 1.

34. *Ibid., No.68, A.N., 10th October 1960*, session of 19th October, p. 2640, col. 2.

35. *Ibid.*, *No. 71, A.N., 25th October 1960*, session of 24th October, p. 2721, col. 2.
36. Edgar S. Furniss, *De Gaulle and the French Army* (The Twentieth Century Fund, New York, 1964), p. 299; General Charles Ailleret, *L'Aventure Atomique Française: Souvenirs et Réflexions* (Paris, Editions Bernard Grasset, 1968), p. 114.
37. Alfred Grosser, *La Politique Extérieure de la Vème République* (Editions du Seuil, Paris, 1965), p. 90.
38. Judith H. Young, *The French Strategic Missile Programme* (Adelphi Paper 38, The Institute for Strategic Studies, London, July 1957), pp. 1–2, 7–8. J. Pergent, 'Le Laboratoire Militaire Franco-Allemand de Recherches de Saint-Louis' (*Revue Militaire Générale*, October 1959), pp. 392–407.
39. M.C., 'Chronique d'Actualité' (*Revue Militaire Générale*, February 1967), pp. 281–2.
40. Letter of M. Couve de Murville to the German Government, 21st December 1966. Edmond Jouve, *Le Général de Gaulle et la Construction de l'Europe: 1940–66* (Bibliothèque Constitutionnelle et de Science Politique, Librairie Générale de Droit et de Jurisprudence, R. Pichou et R. Durand-Auziar, Paris, 1967), Vol. II, pp. 550–1, 470–1.
41. 'Les Allemands ... ne doivent pas se faire des armes atomiques.' (President de Gaulle in an interview with Michel Droit, 15th December 1965.) 'L'Armement nucléaire de l'Allemagne constituerait aux yeux de l'U.R.S.S. un acte grave dont on ne peut pas mesurer les conséquences.' (M. Pompidou in the debate on the second Five Year Plan for defence, 12th December 1964.) Jouve, Vol. I, pp. 130, 640, note 73.
42. Interview with Irène Joliot-Curie, *The New York Herald Tribune*, 14th April 1946.
43. *The Times*, 24th February 1958, quoted by Osgood, p. 243.
44. Pierre J. G. Maurin, 'Perspectives Atomiques: I' (*Revue de Défense Nationale*, June 1954), pp. 706–9; 'Perspectives Atomiques: II' (*Revue de Défense Nationale*, July 1954), pp. 70–1.
45. Colonel Ailleret, 'Applications "Pacifiques" et "Militaires"

de l'Energie Atomique' (*Revue de Défense Nationale*, November 1954), p. 422.

46. Colonel E.-J. Debau, 'Les Armes Atomiques et la Défense Nationale' (*Revue de Défense Nationale*, July 1955), p. 4.

47. Jean Fabiani, *Combat*, 9th–10th June 1956.

48. *J.O.*, *Débats Parlementaires*, No. 66, A.N., *1957*, session of 2nd July 1957, p. 3313, col. 2.

49. *Ibid.*, No. 68, A.N., *1960–61*, *14th October 1960*, session of 13th October, p. 2516, col. 2.

50. *Ibid.*, No. 71, A.N., session of 24th October, p. 2722, col. 1.

51. *Ibid.*, No. 71, A.N., session of 24th October, p. 2726, col. 1.

52. Jean Griot, *Le Figaro*, 4th July 1956.

53. Leonard Beaton and John Maddox, *The Spread of Nuclear Weapons* (London, Chatto & Windus for the Institute for Strategic Studies, 1962), pp. 53–5.

54. *J.O.*, *Débats Parlementaires*, No. 71, A.N., *1960–61*, session of 24th October 1960, p. 2726, col. 1.

55. Goldschmidt, *Les Rivalités Atomiques*, pp. 180–1.

56. General M. Fourquet, at that time Délégué Ministériel pour l'Armement, 'La Politique d'Armement à long terme' (*Revue de Défense Nationale*, May 1957), p. 746.

57. Jouve, Vol. I, p. 181.

58. Lew Kowarski in an interview in *Combat*, 5th December 1946.

59. Press Conference of 16th December 1948. *New York Herald Tribune*, *New York Times*, 17th December 1948.

60. *L'Humanité*, 17th December 1948.

61. *Il Messagero*, 18th December 1948.

62. *L'Humanité*, 7th February 1950.

63. *Combat*, 29th–30th April 1950.

64. Goldschmidt, *Les Rivalités Atomiques*, pp. 162–4.

65. Félix Gaillard, *La France et l'Energie Atomique dans la Paix et dans la Guerre* (Moullot, Marseille, 1954), p. 13.

66. *J.O.*, *Débats Parlementaires*, No. 78, A.N., *6th July 1956*, session of 5th July, p. 3260, col. 1.

67. *J.O.*, *Débats Parlementaires*, No. 39, C.R., *22 June 1956*, session of 21st June, pp. 1238–40.

68. *Le Monde*, 28th November 1957.
69. *Combat*, 23rd–24th November 1957.
70. *J.O., Débats Parlementaires, No. 4, A.N., 16th January 1959*, session of 15th January, p. 29, col. 1.
71. Interview with Robert Kleiman, *U.S. News and World Report*, 30th December 1957.
72. *Le Monde*, 9th–10th February 1958.
73. Discours prononcé par le Général de Gaulle le 3 Novembre 1959, lors de sa visite au Centre des Hautes Etudes Militaires et aux trois écoles de guerre, B.I.M.A., 13th November 1959, mimeographed copy, p. 3.
74. Goldschmidt, *Les Rivalités Atomiques*, pp. 230–1.
75. *Aviation Week and Space Technology*, Vol. 75, No. 8, 21st August 1961, p. 32.
76. Ailleret, *L'Aventure Atomique Française*, pp. 290–8; Lacoste Lareymondie, p. 31, pp. 34–5.
77. For accounts of this affair, see Osgood, pp. 226–7; Beaton and Maddox, p. 54; Goldschmidt, *Les Rivalités Atomiques*, pp. 242–3; Daniel Dollfus, *La Force de Frappe* (René Julliard, Paris, 1960), pp. 65–6.
78. Joint Committee on Atomic Energy; Hearings; Agreements for Co-operation for Mutual Defence Purposes; 86 Congress, i sess., p. 46, 17th June 1959. (Quoted by Osgood, p. 403, note 26.)
79. *Aviation Week and Space Technology*, Vol. 71, No. 18, 2nd November 1959, p. 37; Vol. 71, No. 23, 7th December 1959, p. 29; Vol. 75, No. 8, 21st August 1961, p. 32.
80. Lacoste Lareymondie, p. 53.
81. Goldschmidt, *Les Rivalités Atomiques*, p. 263; *Le Monde*, 20th May 1966; *Le Figaro*, 18th July 1966; *The Sunday Telegraph*, 21st October 1966.
82. General de Gaulle, speech at Centre des Hautes Etudes Militaires, 3rd November 1959, p. 1.
83. Interview with Frederick C. Painton, *U.S. News and World Report*, 24th September 1962.

3 · French nuclear policy as a function of defence policy

Up to 1939 the basic objective of French defence policy was clear: to provide the maximum security against attack from the east. Germany had to be contained and prevented from avenging her defeat in the First World War. This objective dominated foreign and military policy. It was the basis of French support for the League of Nations and for the 'Cordon Sanitaire' in Eastern Europe; of the conscription debate and of the Maginot Line.[1] If French attitudes shifted from militancy in the early 1920s via conciliation in the late twenties to purely defensive thinking in the 1930s, the fear of Germany lay at the root of all. The great controversy between the supporters of mass armies and of a highly professional army, which owed its origins to the Revolution and reached its height in the period between 1871 and 1914, reflected different political philosophies but a common military objective. Other aspects of defence policy, such as naval competition with the maritime powers and colonial expansion, were subordinate to this central concern.

After 1945 the issue was clouded by the effect of the war. The experience of the conflict had left two distinct and contradictory impressions on the French. They were all too well aware that they depended on others for defence against a powerful enemy and yet they had learnt to mistrust the intentions and capabilities of allies.

The events of the war years had clearly demonstrated that France was no longer mistress of her destiny. She had been defeated and she had been liberated by foreign powers. The reason for General de Gaulle's personal popularity undoubtedly lay in his ability to give humiliated Frenchmen the conviction that France, after all, had played a major part in her liberation.

Henceforth the country would be dependent on her allies against any major external threat. A close analysis of the state of affairs between the world wars would no doubt reveal that this condition was not a new one in 1945. Indeed, French alliance policy in the 1920s and 1930s expressed an awareness of dependence on others for national security, yet outwardly, at least, France was still a great power.

For many Frenchmen the Second World War also confirmed the unreliability of such dependence. The Alliance system before 1914 and the organization of collective security before 1939 had both failed to spare France great suffering and defeat. Thus it became the aim of French leaders, de Gaulle most of all, to lay the foundations of a truly independent system of national security so that France would no longer have to accept the strategy of her allies by forming the first line of defence in the West but would be able to take an equal share in determining allied strategy. The drive for this independence had started under the Fourth Republic but it was masked by the immediate aftermath of the war and by the subsequent colonial wars.

After he had finished with Algeria, President de Gaulle devoted all his energies to providing France with a self-sufficient national defence based upon a nuclear striking force. It was the theme of his address to the Centre for Higher Defence Studies and the three war colleges in November 1959. It was given a new emphasis by his chief of staff of the armed forces in a celebrated article eight years later[2] when France had come a very long way from the chaos of 1945.

The trauma of defeat, the humiliation of alien occupation and the exhilaration of resistance and liberation also had an important influence on civil-military relations in France. The events of 1940 and the Pétain régime had discredited the professional army and particularly the officer class which had for many years before the war become an isolated and embittered society, turned in on itself and profoundly distrustful of 'Les Politiques'. In the eyes of civilians and even of its traditional supporters, the bourgeoisie, the professional army had lost status, was regarded as a poor prospect

70

for a career and was viewed with suspicion as a possible source of some new form of Bonapartism or Boulangism.

Although a number of officers had taken an active part in the resistance and had organized it in various corners of the country, the resistance movement was basically anti-militarist and represented the revenge of the soldier over the officer, and of the civilian over the soldier.[3] These sentiments lent a highly emotional colouring to the revived controversy over the kind of army France should have: a popular army based on conscription or a professional army.

Lastly, the Second World War was responsible for two new factors which were to leave a profound mark on French defence policy, although they were not fully understood by the military, let alone the public, until the first post-war decade had passed. These factors were the changes in strategic thinking brought about by nuclear weapons and the impact of the revolutionary struggles in Indochina and Algeria.

(i) The place of nuclear weapons in French military thought since 1945

The attitude of the armed services to the new weapon which had emerged at the end of the war passed through several phases, each related to the condition of France and to her relative strength in the world as well as to the changes in international relations.

In the first seven years after the war the main emphasis was on protection against the effect of atomic weapons on the field of battle and on the civilian population. In addition, the structure and tactics of the army had to be adapted to the use of such weapons.

Military and naval commentators studied the enormous changes in military methods brought about by the Second World War and linked them with the possible future use of nuclear weapons and thus tried to discover their effect on the organization of the armed forces. Strategic concepts were changed. In the words of General de Lattre de Tassigny:

Our conception of a north-eastern frontier is out of date. The notion of strategic defence should give way to a conception of our security within the vast framework of the French Union.[4]

From this followed an emphasis on light divisions and battle-groups, easily dispersed and capable of operating at great speed over wide areas. These ideas in turn encouraged new training methods, such as were used in de Lattre's 'camps légers'.* Another approach was to analyse the damage caused by an atomic explosion and to draw conclusions about defence in depth and the dispersal of industry. Nor was it difficult to foresee the evolution of tactical nuclear weapons. Admiral Barjot even envisaged 'minuscules pistolets atomiques'.[5]

The navy and air force were equally affected. The emphasis shifted to aircraft carriers and submarines. The former were thought of as having primarily defensive functions and the latter, armed with atomic rockets, would increase their offensive value. In air warfare the North Pole assumed strategic importance through the improved range of heavy bombers. Some observers foresaw the development of atomic missiles. All agreed that the new weaponry would require the dispersal and hiding of factories and bases.

The impact of nuclear weapons was not confined to talk and speculation during these early years, but right from the beginning the armed services provided for the atomic training of some of their officers. The army annually selected a small number with good scientific background to study nuclear physics. Atomic engineers were also trained under the auspices of the Technical and Industrial Directions of the three services and the Direction des Poudres. In this way two embryonic services emerged: Le Groupement Atomique de la Section Technique de l'Armée and La Section Atomique de la Direction des Etudes et Fabrications d'Armement (D.E.F.A.). The major interest then was in preparing

* The 'camp légers' were controversial and there was no lack of those who questioned their effectiveness. The ebullient personality of de Lattre undoubtedly aroused enthusiasm in the young soldiers and his approach was refreshing in the traditionally garrison-bound metropolitan army. For a critical assessment of these training camps, see Paul-Marie de la Gorce, *La République et son Armée*, pp. 446–9.

to meet a possible atomic attack, rather than in the manufacture or use of such weapons. However, some of the officers trained in atomic science and technique were to play an important part in the elaboration of the first atomic bomb and its testing.

From the middle fifties onwards a small group of technicians, of whom the most noteworthy was Colonel Ailleret, published articles arguing in favour of a French atomic armament. Although these men did not have a major responsibility for the decisions which were taken with regard to the atomic energy programme, their advocacy helped to create a climate of opinion in military and political circles which encouraged the creation of a national nuclear force.

A number of quite specific reasons were advanced in support of a French effort to manufacture atomic weapons. Bearing in mind its appeal to the French politicians, the advocates specially stressed the cheapness of nuclear weapons in comparison with conventional explosives. They did this by setting side by side the damage caused by nuclear bombs and the equivalent amount of T.N.T. Thus they estimated that the damage caused by one twenty-kiloton tactical nuclear weapon was equal to that caused by the simultaneous firing of one hundred thousand salvos from six thousand 105 mm. howitzers. Next came the comparative costs of manufacturing conventional and nuclear explosives, so that it could be demonstrated how much cheaper and more effective it would be in the long term to produce nuclear weapons.[6]

For those who were more concerned with military operations and less with economics and finance, there was the argument that atomic weapons would restore the balance in face of the opponent's numerical superiority. The new weapons also implied new organization and new tactics. They called for the development of light units which were as self-sufficient as possible without excessive reliance on the rear; for an increased dependence on natural obstacles which would provide points of anchorage for a thinly held line of 'couverture' to prevent infiltration; for a scattering of forces over a large area as heavy concentrations would be subject to atomic bombardment.[7] Marshal Juin elaborated such ideas very

73

precisely in a letter to the Minister of National Defence in which he called for drastic changes in the structure and tactics of the ground forces.[8]

These ideas had a practical expression in the development of light motorized divisions and in the production of special vehicles like the A.M.X. thirteen-ton tank and the E.B.R. armoured reconnaissance vehicle. It is noteworthy that Colonel Argoud, later to become one of the principal apostles of 'la Guerre Révolutionnaire', not only led the movement to reform concepts of armoured warfare, struggling ceaselessly against the conservatism of most of his superiors, but also foresaw the needs imposed by atomic war.

There was a twofold significance in the campaign for nuclear arms. The first was the extent of its influence. It provided material eagerly seized upon by the press and some politicians, so that public demands for French nuclear weapons were based upon the data and conclusions provided by the military technicians. The other significant aspect was the confident assertion that these views were shared by some of the highest military authorities, thus revealing a definite movement of opinion within the armed services favourable to the military development of atomic energy.

Seen in its wider context, this movement of thought coincided with important changes in the orientation of French defence policy and with international developments to which we shall refer later.

With the wisdom of hindsight we can see that the arguments put forward in support of the manufacture of French nuclear weapons were based on insufficient knowledge and understanding of the problems involved. Thus, their alleged cheapness in comparison with the equivalent amount of conventional explosive ignored the rising costs of increasing the number of shells and bombs at one's disposal and of providing a suitable means of delivery. These costs were aggravated by the need to keep up with continued technological advances in this field, quite apart from the enormous expenditure involved in providing highly enriched uranium for tactical weapons. But the chief weakness in the position of Colonel Ailleret and his friends was their narrow military and technical conception of these weapons which recognized their revolutionary impact on tactics without taking account of their impact on strategy.

The evolution of thought in relation to nuclear weapons was reflected in the debates on the defence estimates. Apart from a few special issues, such as the dismissal of Joliot-Curie, the first and second Five Year Plans for the development of atomic energy, EURATOM, or debates initiated by groups of parliamentarians, as in June 1956 and January 1957, the military aspects of the atomic energy programme were usually brought up in connection with the military budget. Until the middle fifties the emphasis remained on the adaptation of the French forces to atomic warfare, rather than on the need for French nuclear weapons.

The long debate on the defence budget of 1954 marked a turning-point. M. Pleven not only gave the first official indication that military research in the atomic field was already under way but expressed his opinion that French defence policy was in a period of transition. So far, military studies carried out by the C.E.A. and the three services had produced some interesting results in protective measures against nuclear weapons. Within the next year, however, the advanced state of studies and preparations should lead to a full evaluation of the problem and its cost.[9]

M. Pleven's remarks were made in reply to pressures for an official policy of nuclear armament which came from various political quarters. Its advocates included staunch Gaullists like General Koenig; men of the right like Pierre André and M. Loustanau-Lacau; moderate socialists like Max Lejeune; members of the M.R.P. like M. Augarde.

A variety of arguments were advanced in support of defence expenditure on atomic energy. A principal concern was that France might otherwise be left behind in modern developments. Thus, General Koenig, speaking as president of the Commission de la Défense Nationale, suggested that 'On n'a pas apporté à la recherche atomique tout l'intérêt souhaitable.' M. André insisted that an army without atomic weapons was no real instrument

75

of defence.[10] The basic anxiety, however, arose from the fear of the consequences of American strategy and the danger of being dependent upon it. We shall return to this subject later as it lay at the heart of French defence problems in Europe. Henceforth the question of nuclear armament was raised regularly during the budget debates. In 1955 M. Pierre André, speaking as rapporteur of the Commission de la Défense Nationale, calculated that France could have an H-bomb within four or five years at the cost of twenty thousand million francs per annum.[11]

The emergence in official circles of a more clearly defined French doctrine of nuclear warfare may be traced to the budget debate of 1954 and the statements of government spokesmen during that year.

Having analysed the changing pattern of warfare and having indicated that France was working on the military application of atomic energy, M. Pleven had gone on to formulate the basic strategic concepts which should govern French defence policy. In the event of aggression, the enemy would aim at the allied means of atomic retaliation. The only protection against this lay in the threat of reprisal by an air force disposing of a larger number of weapons than were available to the aggressor. In the light of his analysis, M. Pleven concluded that France would need an active defence in the form of interceptory planes and missiles, and a passive defence in the form of the dispersal and hiding of targets. With these needs in mind he felt that the current naval and air construction policies could be safely pushed ahead, but that the effect of tactical nuclear weapons would have to be carefully studied before one embarked upon major new arms expenditure.[12]

M. Pleven's line of approach to defence requirements was later carried further by the revelations of M. Diomède Catroux, Secretary of State for Air in the Mendès-France government. Speaking to a dinner audience at the Aéro-Club, he took the long view and indicated that 'la défense de notre pays doit être repensée, je le crois fermement, autour de notre aviation'. He referred to studies of atom-powered aircraft engines (which were to come to nothing), an emphasis on vertical take-off planes and, most important, the acquisition of the means of reprisal which called for the development of long-range bombers and land-based missiles.[13]

The remarks of MM. Pleven and Catroux provide the first official allusions to the need for matching French nuclear explosives with suitable means of delivery. Nevertheless, until 1960 the debate about the delivery system, which lies at the heart of nuclear strategy, does not spread beyond a small circle of experts and technical-minded politicians. If the Algerian war had not broken out and rapidly absorbed the energies and attention of the military establishment, this might not have been so. But then, without the Algerian crisis General de Gaulle might not have come to power and though the nuclear debate would surely have taken place in any event, its course might have been very different.

Discussion did, of course, take place during the years up to 1959 and included some special pleading by the air force and the navy who were not so deeply involved in North Africa as the army. However, it was General de Gaulle who opened the formal debate with his celebrated speech at the Ecole Militaire in November 1959. This might be regarded as the official launching of the government's programme of atomic armament which was not, however, published and debated until the following year.

In essence, the President's remarks are not very different from those of M. Pleven in 1954. Since France was on the threshold of nuclear power he could be more incisive. France must have her own defence and cannot rely for it on others. Consequently she must provide herself with a 'force de frappe' within the next few years, which can be deployed at any moment and anywhere. Since France could eventually be destroyed from any part of the world, the French force must be constructed so as to be able to strike at any point on earth.[14] The crucial difference was in the intention behind the policy of national nuclear armament. For many leaders of the Fourth Republic the context remained a close co-operation with one's allies, for de Gaulle this co-operation was incidental and not axiomatic.

The debate was henceforth conducted on two levels: the rather esoteric military-strategic level on which the most distinguished French participants were Generals Gallois and Beaufre; and the politico-diplomatic level on which the President and his critics confronted each other.

The Force Nucléaire Stratégique Française (F.N.S.) is an instrument designed principally to serve Gaullist external policy. It is a means of deterrence. It should deter a potential enemy from acts of pressure or aggression against France and it should deter other states from interfering with the course of French policy. In the eyes of the French President a national nuclear force, like a sound national economy or a spirit of national unity, added to the weight of French influence according to the degree in which it enabled France to operate independently in world affairs.

However, de Gaulle is a military man and therefore justified the nuclear arm in military and strategic terms. Although the more extreme flights of fancy exhibited by some French military theorists did not meet with official approval, de Gaulle's own utterances and those of his ministers and generals enable us to follow the evolution of French strategic thought since 1958. In the course of time French nuclear theory shifted its emphasis to adapt to changes in weapons technology and the international situation. Economic restraints have also had an important influence in shaping strategic doctrine during the last year of de Gaulle's rule.

French doctrine rested on the proposition that nuclear powers dispose of two types of armament which may be described as classical and atomic. However, the status of powers depends on whether or not they possess nuclear weapons. Such weapons impose a strategy of deterrence in which their use is psychological and political and not military. If they were to be used in a conflict there would be no escape from mutual destruction. Hence, while the great powers may engage in armed conflict of the classical type, their nuclear capabilities cause these confrontations to take place over secondary and peripheral issues. Only when the very existence of the state is in danger will there be a real threat of nuclear war.

Since the United States and the Soviet Union are in a state of
nuclear balance it follows that neither will use its full might
except in defence of its heartland. Thus France cannot rely upon
American nuclear protection against the political and military
pressures of another nuclear power. She must, therefore, dispose
of a nuclear capability with which to defend her vital interests
and to make an aggressor calculate that the damage he would
suffer from a French retaliation would be disproportionate to the
value of his objective.

The central argument has received a different gloss at different
periods in the development of French atomic power. Around
1957 the reliability of the American deterrent became doubtful
not because of events in Europe but because of American conduct
over the Suez crisis. The realization that France could not depend
under all circumstances on the United States for protection and
that the United States might on occasion make common cause
with the Soviet Union, was used as an argument for the creation
of a national nuclear force. In the late 1950s there was as yet no
very strongly expressed fear that the United States and Russia
would settle European questions at the expense of the Europeans.
The existence of a small independent nuclear force was seen as an
instrument with which to bring American strategic power into
play. The French thus adopted the trigger theory which partly
lay behind the decision to create a British nuclear force in the late
1940s.

One way of dealing with the assumed unreliability of the
American nuclear guarantee was to think in terms of developing
a European nuclear force, presumably through a combination of
the French and British enterprises in this field. The French
government opposed the idea on the grounds that it was militarily
impracticable and politically inexpedient. In July 1960, the
Minister of the Armed Forces, Pierre Messmer, had denounced
the scheme as a ' "tarte à la crème" dont on se régale à la fin des
discours !'[15]

Almost at the same time the idea of a multilateral force (M.L.F.)
was floated. It was discussed at a conference at Lake Como, held

79

on the 6th September 1960. The Atlantic Council meeting at the end of that year marked the beginning of official American agitation in support of the proposal. In December 1962, the British Prime Minister, Harold Macmillan, secured the same rights for France as for Britain under the terms of the Nassau Agreement. If France participated in the M.L.F. her submarines would remain under French command, they would have Polaris missiles with French warheads, and they could be withdrawn in the event of supreme national danger.

For various reasons, not least of which was de Gaulle's personal rancour over the course of events at the end of 1962, the French government would have none of it and argued that the M.L.F. merely camouflaged the American monopoly of nuclear strategy in Western Europe. The M.L.F. would not increase the credibility of the American nuclear guarantee because it would merely subjugate European nuclear forces to American strategic direction. The only consequence would have been to throw into doubt the credibility of national nuclear forces.

The American proposals attempted to meet what was assumed to be European and particularly German pressure for a share in the formulation and conduct of western nuclear strategy. Whether such a demand had really existed or had been artificially stimulated, it made sufficient impression on the French to persuade them to hint at an alternative solution. They suggested that their national force might serve as the kernel of a future European defence system. The Secretary of State at the French Foreign Ministry, M. Michel Habib-Deloncle, told the Consultative Assembly of the Council of Europe on the 23rd September 1963 that once Europe had strengthened its political structure one could agree on how the French nuclear enterprise might be used by the community of European nations for their common defence. M. Pompidou argued a year later before the National Assembly that the fact that France was in Europe assured the Europeans that the French nuclear striking force would automatically operate in their interest as European defence could not be separated from that of France. The spokesman for the opposition, M. Maurice Faure, retorted that the French 'force de frappe' was not a European force but a force in Europe.[16]

According to some French theorists, the Cuban missile crisis of 1962 forced the United States and the Soviet Union into an unwilling and limited co-operation. Henceforth they would collaborate in attempts to control international conflicts and would seek to prevent the spread of nuclear weapons to other countries. In brief, the United States and Russia had a common interest to preserve their status as the world's super-powers so that they could continue the game of global rivalry as before.

A French nuclear force was therefore necessary not only to defend the vital interests of France but to frustrate this Russian-American hegemony and to provide France with freedom of action in world politics. In other words, the F.N.S. offered national security and manoeuvrability. However, when it came to confrontation with one of the super-powers, France could not act on her own but must have the support of an alliance with the other super-power. This special relationship might be necessary although it could not be expected to cover all French interests.[17]

The ever-expanding panoply and growing sophistication of nuclear weapons systems, as well as the developing French capabilities in this field, introduced a new note into the argument. The great number of tactical nuclear weapons available to both sides raised the spectre of a limited nuclear war in Europe which would devastate the Continent but spare Russia and the United States. To the French it appeared that the Americans were not only prepared to fight a nuclear war on the Continent but were also planning to abandon Europe in the interests of American global strategy. In support of the first thesis, the French have pointed to the American doctrine of flexible response. In support of the second thesis they have seen evidence of a return to the peripheral strategy of a maritime power, as illustrated by operation 'big lift' in which an armoured division was moved from America to Europe within sixty-four hours after fifteen days' warning, and by the development of a logistic base on the other side of the Pyrenees. As far as France was concerned, once the preliminary encounter in Germany had been lost, she would become a corridor for a 'bataille des restes' based on Spain.[18]

The scale of American nuclear armament and the context of American global strategy indicated that the greatest danger of nuclear war in Europe came from the American side, for the Americans would be least able to sustain a conventional war and most tempted to resort to tactical nuclear weapons first in order to halt the enemy's advance. The French nuclear force therefore became an instrument for lessening French dependence on defence by the United States–a policy based on the assumption that the global strategic balance, weighted as it appeared to be in America's favour, would suffice to protect Europe against inordinate Russian pressure.

French nuclear strategy was predicated on the instantaneous and total use of the national nuclear armoury once a serious aggression has been identified. This adaptation of a doctrine of massive retaliation–purer in its implications than the one asso-ciated with John Foster Dulles–was first slightly modified by the plans for producing French tactical nuclear weapons. It was agreed that such weapons would permit a delay between the identification of aggression and the use of strategic weapons directed against the opponent's cities. The deployment of con-ventional forces backed by the threatened or actual use of tactical nuclear weapons might force the invader to pause in face of this earnest of French intentions. However, such a delay could only be for a few hours before France let fly with all she had. Indeed, there seemed no other way in which to deal with the dreaded effects of a limited nuclear war in Europe. President de Gaulle put it in his customary dramatic style:

> Partout, à droite ou à gauche, on pourrait se battre avec des armes tactiques nucléaires sans que la France bouge. Mais si le territoire français est attaqué la riposte se fera avec des armes nucléaires stratégiques. Nous y sommes décidés.[19]

In the years 1964 and 1965 a strategic debate between the army and the air force burst into the open. Ostensibly concerned with the role of tactical nuclear weapons, it was really a quarrel over the control of the French strategic forces and is strongly reminiscent of inter-service rivalries in the United States during the Eisenhower administration. The air force had staked a claim to control the strategic and tactical use of nuclear weapons, thus consigning the army to the functions of ringing the alarm and protecting the nuclear weapon carriers. The army countered with arguments in favour of tactical nuclear artillery under its control and against the use of tactical nuclear air bombardment. Since then the army has been promised its battlefield weapons and the navy has acquired a share of the strategic forces.[20]

General Ailleret's article on 'Défense "Dirigée" ou Défense "Tous Azimuts" ', published in the *Revue de Défense Nationale* of December 1967, aroused a good deal of speculation inside and outside France about a new departure in French strategic doctrine. In fact, it contained passages almost identical to some in de Gaulle's speech of November 1959. However, when the President spoke it was an expression of intent. Eight years later the policy applied to an established and developing nuclear capability.

According to General Ailleret, France has always had a 'favourite enemy'. That role has fallen successively on Britain, Germany and Russia. Now that the threat from Russia had almost disappeared there was no specific enemy. Nonetheless, as a consequence of progress in weapons technology, a threat in the future could come from any direction in the world. In spite of her pacific intentions, France might be attacked by nations which were at war with other states. The attack might be launched because one of the parties wanted to control French territory and resources or because it wanted to deny them to its opponent. Hence the choice for France was between falling under the control of one of the super-powers—or of an alliance system dominated by it—and developing her own national deterrent. Since the second course was infinitely preferable, France must have a nuclear striking force which was not only azimuthal but which could eventually be deployed in space once it became technically feasible to do so.[21] The argument ended with a significant caveat. If the national

83

deterrent failed to prevent entanglement in a conflict, nothing need hinder France from becoming a member of an alliance formed to deal with a specific threat, although the F.N.S. would still give France freedom to act on her own account in the last resort. Here again we find a return to the concept of an *ad hoc* coalition on the pattern of the eighteenth and nineteenth centuries and a rejection of the idea of integration which was first tried towards the end of the First World War. General Ailleret translated into the military strategic terms of the late 1960s the formulation of basic defence policy made by President de Gaulle in 1959.

Through his untimely death in 1968 General Ailleret was spared the humiliation of a significant shift in French strategic doctrine little more than a year later. In an address delivered at the Institut des Hautes Etudes de Défense Nationale in March 1969,[22] his successor as chief of staff of the armed forces, General M. Fourquet, specifically rejected the doctrine of massive retaliation, described as 'tout ou rien', as well as the American strategy of meeting aggression in force at all levels. He advocated instead a strategy of graduated response in which tactical nuclear weapons would play their part independently of the strategic nuclear force and thus raise the threshold beyond which the latter would come into play.

Equally significant was the implicit abandonment of the concept of 'tous Azimuts' by the emphasis on meeting an attack from the east in co-ordination with allied forces. General Fourquet repeated the argument against integration and for the ultimate autonomy of national defence but he considered independent action as only a remote possibility.

The reference to the threat from the east; the linking of military action to that of one's allies; the insistence on graduated deterrence were all startling indications of the changes which had come about in the year before General de Gaulle's resignation. The changes were caused by the economic pressures which threatened to postpone development of a French I.C.B.M. system to the Greek Calends. They reflected anxiety over Russian activities in Czecho-slovakia and in the Mediterranean. Above all, they mark the declining authority of President de Gaulle. Although he was in office for eleven years, the handicap of the Algerian conflict and the crumbling of his power base in the last year of his rule reduced the period when the General was really master of his policy to the six years between 1962 and 1968.

Ever since the end of the Second World War the various stages in the development of a national atomic energy programme and the immediate preoccupations of those concerned with national security have influenced discussion about the significance of atomic weapons to national defence. French strategic theory and planning to a large extent reflect the problem of national security as it is seen at a given time. Much of the writing about the function of nuclear weapons begins characteristically with statements of principle followed by a lucid and largely theoretical analysis. This Cartesian method disguises the fact that such intellectual exercises are concerned with practical problems, so that a study of the objectives and difficulties of national security policy in France requires among other skills the ability to read between the lines of a journal like the *Revue de Défense Nationale*.

It is therefore necessary for us to turn to the problems of French defence policy since 1945 in order to discover how they were perceived and met.

(ii) **The problems of French defence policy after the war**
The predominant influence in the formulation of French nuclear policy was exercised by civilians. In spite of the keen interest of a small group of military specialists and their influence over the military hierarchy, those concerned with the shaping and execution of national defence policies were not too closely associated with developments in the nuclear field until the advent of the Fifth Republic. The reasons for this may be found partly in M. Guillaumat's jealous guardianship over the C.E.A.* and partly in the constitutional and institutional environment which favoured civilian control. A more fundamental cause lay in the confusion which beset French defence policy under the Fourth Republic.

* See below, pp. 142-3.

Defence policy and planning were conditioned by two factors. The first of these related to domestic politics. Since the scope and extent of measures of national defence were wholly dependent on the means at the government's disposal, the use of military estimates as a political football did not help long-term planning.

A typical example was provided in July 1948 when the Schuman Cabinet was brought down on a socialist motion to reduce the defence estimates by one half per cent in order to express the socialists' displeasure over their coalition partners' attitude to the schools question and over recent dismissals from the civil service. Matters had been further complicated on this occasion by party preparations for the forthcoming elections to the Council of the Republic and the Departmental councils.

The difficulties on the floor of parliament were, however, only a reflection of the tensions within the government consisting, as it did, of a collection of party nominees. This was particularly true of the relations between the Ministers of Finance and of National Defence. M. Ramadier, Minister of Finance in the Mollet government, regarded the army as a spendthrift whose least expenses must be closely checked.[23] He held interminable sessions examining the accounts, with the result that the armed services were tempted to inflate their estimates in full knowledge that they were likely to be cut.*

Behind this lay not only political manœuvre but the conflict between the need for a balanced budget and for a national strategy. The socialists, in particular, insisted on the principle that there could be no national defence without a healthy and strong economy. Political instability and inability to work out acceptable compromises frequently forced governments to resort to provisional budgets covering one, two or three months (douzièmes provisoires) merely to keep the machinery going. Fifty-four provisional budgets had been voted within the space of ten years.

* An excellent example of how this worked in practice is provided by the haggling in 1957 between the Minister of Finance (Ramadier) and the Minister of National Defence (Bourgès-Maunoury) over the budget for 1958. One might schematize the conflict as follows:

As France was never wholly free of financial difficulties under the Fourth Republic, the issue could be summarized as a choice between taxes to meet a programme of rearmament, which was implied in a coherent defence policy, or a reduction of the tax burden and a patchy and incoherent military policy. In spite of protestations supporting full French participation in collective security, the needs of a favourable image in the eyes of the electorate always predominated in the end.

In early years, the financing of the atomic energy programme from military sources was possible because of internal administrative arrangements which kept it outside the range of public debate, so that in this respect there was remarkably smooth progress and the opportunity for long-term planning. Military expenditures, on the other hand, were under constant public–and from some quarters hostile–scrutiny in which non-military considerations often played a decisive part.

The difficulties involved in the budgetary process and the uncertainty of the political scene provided a good excuse for the defence planners to explain their failure to work out a coherent strategic doctrine. While this was undoubtedly true, it ignored

Ramadier		*Bourgès-Maunoury*
Original Proposals		
150 milliard frs. economies (Demobilization of 100,000 men)		140 milliard frs. for supplementary expenses in Algeria.
Intermediate Positions		
100 milliard frs. economies (including Algerian war)		Waives claim for 140 milliard frs. for supplementary expenses.
Final Positions		
Expenses cut from milliard frs. to milliard frs.	1,361 1,295 ——	i. Conscription reduced from 30 to 24 months;
Economy of milliard frs.	66 ——	ii. Effectives in Algeria to be made up by transfers from Morocco, Tunisia, Germany and France;
		iii. Arms orders reduced.

Financial Times, 13 April 1957; *Combat*, 18 April 1957; *Le Monde*, 3 and 4 May 1957.

the second factor which influenced French defence policy: the problem of priorities.

The end of the Second World War saw a return to some of the traditional preoccupations of defence policy, notably the question whether it was best served by a mass army of citizen soldiers or a highly trained professional force.

In terms of strategy, the debate was dominated by the new ideas of warfare which had emerged out of the war and which included speculation about the use and effect of atomic weapons. Thus, M. Paul Coste-Floret, Minister for War, insisted that France must have a mass army to meet the characteristics of a future war, which included the defence of the country as a whole and not just its frontiers, the need for great mobility and the need for each region to be responsible for its own defence. For the purposes of military training it would be necessary to re-establish compulsory service for one year.[24] One of M. Coste-Floret's critics asserted that the new strategy required a highly trained and equipped professional army and a conscript force to provide the 'résistance intérieure', which could be used for reconstruction work in peacetime.[25]

The communists, the largest single political force in the early post-war years, were particularly hostile to the 'armée de métier' for political reasons. They called for the establishment of a citizen army, locally organized and controlled, based on the factory, the workshop, the village, youth organizations, etc. Because the war of the future would include atomic bombardment as a prelude to airborne landings, the notion of 'front' and 'rear' would disappear.[26] Hence the population must be ready for guerrilla war. The intent behind this advocacy was obvious enough and quickly recognized.

The lines of battle over this issue followed the pre-war pattern of political alignments: the left clinging to Jaurès' theory of the citizen army while the right was impressed by arguments for a highly professional army which were, perhaps, most succinctly expressed in de Gaulle's *Vers l'Armée de Métier*.[27] De Gaulle's concept of an 'armée de métier' did not, however, exclude the republican concept of the nation in arms. He saw the professional corps as the spearhead of the nation in arms. Before the war the spearhead consisted of the armoured forces and in recent years it is provided by the F.N.S. combined with the armoured divisions. His idea of the nation in arms found expression in plans for a 'Défense Opérationnelle du Territoire'.

Altered circumstances naturally required new arguments to support the theses, but the basic ideas remained essentially the same. Since the three main resistance parties, the communists, socialists and popular republicans, dominated the post-war scene and could all be placed on the left of the political spectrum, it is not surprising that the concept of a citizen army predominated in the debate about defence policy. It was not long before socialists and catholics had to draw a clear distinction between their views and the more radical ideas of the communists.

The socialists, in particular, abandoned their pacifistic anti-militarism. Nevertheless, as late as 1953 they still held to their traditional views about the nation in arms. The danger of a communist fifth column in a mass army would be countered by its integration into a European army which would, in turn, be part of the NATO defence structure.[28]

The traditional debate over the nature of the French army continued for the first decade after the war, though both sides accepted the need to see it in a new context. The possible effect of atomic warfare provided arguments for a citizen army as well as for a professional corps.

The debate died down after the outbreak of the Algerian war when conscription was essential to maintain French forces in North Africa. After 1962 the government clearly moved in the direction of a highly professional army based on selective service.

Another, though more indirect, consequence arising out of the experience of the Second World War was the preoccupation with local defence to deal with an invasion and occupation. These ideas took various forms since the war until they came to rest with the plan for a Force de Défense Opérationnelle du Territoire, D.O.T.*

* The idea of territorial defence found its first expression in the organization of

The organization of internal defence, involving the division of France into military regions, each with its own forces and with close co-operation between the military and civilian authorities, had several purposes: to counter airborne landings; to deal with land forces which had pierced the frontier defences and had penetrated deeply into the country; to provide foci of resistance in the event of a break-down of communications with the government and the central command–a contingency envisaged in a conflict involving the use of atomic weapons; to combat a fifth column–presumably the Communist Party; to be centres of potential resistance against an enemy occupation. It would seem natural that these ideas and plans should have arisen out of the experience of the occupation, but, in fact, they were dominated by the experience of the armed forces in Indochina and Algeria.

Until 1962 the lessons of revolutionary warfare were undoubtedly very much in the minds of those who were responsible for organizing the 'Défense en Surface' of France. Their speeches and writings were full of references to 'la Guerre Révolutionnaire' and make no mention of the lessons of the resistance during the Second World War. Similarly, it is interesting to note that for the French officers in Indochina 'la Guerre Révolutionnaire' came as a revelation for which the German occupation and the resistance movement had obviously not prepared them, even though many of them had taken a prominent part in the 'Résistance'. One explanation of this lack of connection may lie in the fact that the professional soldiers who had taken part in the resistance had been preoccupied with building up conventional military units and a command structure without realizing the value of 'la guerre dans la foule' under an enemy occupation. It was the Communist Party which fought a revolutionary war from 1941 to 1944, directed not

---

'La Garde Nationale' for the purpose of 'défense en surface' (Decree of 30 September 1950). This system was replaced by the organization of the 'Défense Intérieure' (Decree of 28 December 1956), which was largely a change in nomenclature. The D.O.T. was instituted under Ordinance No. 59–147 of 7 January 1959, 'portant l'organisation générale de la défense' (*J.O., Lois et Décrets, 91st Year, No. 8*, 10 January 1959, Titre IV, Arts. 21–4).

only against the Germans but also against the traditional order, and thus came close to taking over parts of the country at the time of liberation.

The relationship between 'la Geurre Révolutionnaire' and 'la Défense en Surface' must not, however, be pushed too far. The army had evolved a theory and practice of counter-revolutionary activity which would have been effective against serious subversion, but the principal object of D.O.T. was to protect the country from outside attack and to develop resistance against an enemy occupation. If they had followed their ideas to a logical conclusion, the authorities would have had to develop a doctrine of revolutionary warfare akin to that applied by the Vietminh and the Algerian Nationalists. Indeed, some elements in the armed forces tried to do this, thereby hoping to save France from herself, but such ideas never found full acceptance with the highest civil and military authorities.[29]

The series of colonial wars which raged almost without interruption until 1962 provided a new influence on defence policy. They were to have an important bearing on military thinking which we shall examine later. In the 1940s, however, the French were concerned with regaining their empire. Operations in Syria, Indochina and Madagascar were not conceived as crusades to liberate or protect the people from an alien ideology, but as a reassertion of French authority and its civilizing mission. There were some who saw the profound changes which had occurred in the world and the impossibility of returning to the *status quo ante*. . . . Among them was General Leclerc, French commander in Indochina, but his wisdom went unheeded and France embarked upon a long campaign to restore her dominion which was to have disastrous consequences.[30]

In its early years the war in Indochina was not taken very seriously in France. The first major warning about its effect on French economic strength and the danger of its prolongation came from M. Mendès-France in the budget debate of 1950. In spite of the lessons of Indochina, a similar gap in public awareness of the existence of a major conflict occurred during the Algerian war. Not until two years after its outbreak did it become an important issue in the debates on the defence budget.

Notwithstanding the pressing needs of the colonial wars, Europe continued to dominate French defence policy after the war. In this area, two related fears were uppermost in French minds. The first was the fear that France would be called upon to provide the cannon-fodder for the Anglo-Saxon powers. The second was the fear that, in the event of war, Britain and the United States would withdraw behind the seas. France would be overrun by the enemy, while they prepared for the liberation of the Continent in their own time, with all the horror of preliminary bombardment and subsequent land battles.

The first anxiety had its roots in the First World War when, apart from Germany, France had suffered the greatest number of casualties.* This drain on her manhood, coupled with a declining birthrate, haunted Frenchmen in the years between the wars and after 1945. The fear was given further impetus by the belief that while the Anglo-Americans wished to exercise freedom of manœuvre in the world at large, France was expected to concentrate on holding the line in Western Europe. British activities in the former French protectorates of Syria and Lebanon at the end of the war and American scheming in Indochina in March 1945 confirmed this idea. Finally, the weakness of the French forces and their dependence on American matériel accentuated the feeling of inferiority in relation to the allies.

The debate on the military budget in 1949 reflected these anxieties in the light of NATO's existence. Its main features were the general unease at the lack of a clearly defined defence policy, which was attributed to the imprecision of the Western Alliance, and the conviction that France was providing the manpower for the Anglo-Saxons. Naturally, the Communist Party was quick to seize this line. However, the view was widely shared. In the budget debate of 1950 the Minister of National Defence, René Pleven, said that he would not remain for one moment longer at

* It is possible that Russian casualties exceeded those of the French, but it is very difficult to obtain precise information on this subject.

his post if American policy conformed to the suggestion of General Lucius Clay, who no longer held an official position, that in the Western Alliance France and Germany should provide the infantry.[31]

The issue was of course related to the question of armaments. French weakness in this field placed the government at a disadvantage in discussions with its allies. It was natural that the French should suspect the Americans of offering them the second best, asking them to fight under a serious handicap in circumstances when the quality of weapons would be decisive. There arose a strong concern to develop the French armament industry in which United States off-shore purchases would play an essential role.

At the root of these anxieties and criticisms lay the wish to see America and Britain firmly committed to the defence of Europe. Even the Brussels Treaty of 1948 and the North Atlantic Treaty of 1949 could not appease the suspicion that when it came to a show-down on the Continent, the Anglo-Saxons would quickly retreat to the safety of their homelands and leave the French to face the aggressor alone. That fear was, of course, powerfully reinforced by memories of 1940 and the painful experience of liberation in 1944.

A clear analysis of this peripheral strategy is contained in General P. E. Jacquot's *La Stratégie Périphérique devant la Bombe Atomique*,[32] at the end of which he argues against its usefulness in the face of weapons of mass destruction. According to the author, peripheral strategy has its origins in the needs of the maritime powers after the collapse of the land barrier to a Continental aggressor and was intended to tide over the interval until new forces could be brought into play against him. Examples of this type of strategy are to be found in Wellington's Peninsular Campaign of 1808 to 1814; in the Greek campaign, the bomber offensive, the commando raids, the fostering of resistance movements and the North African and Italian campaigns of the Second World War; and, since 1945, in the Korean war.

However, in General Jacquot's view, peripheral strategy was not really a matter of choice, but was a solution imposed by the vicissitudes of war and by itself could never lead to victory. Moreover, since the Second World War the concept of peripheral warfare had lost its principal uses: modern weapons, especially atomic bombardment, would make peripheral bases such as Britain, the Iberian Peninsula and North Africa useless; there was no third force left to restore the balance against an aggressor. Thus, the purpose of peripheral strategy, which was largely based on the assembly of new forces, had been lost.

General Jacquot's conclusion was not as convincing as his analysis. He insisted that the lesson of his argument was the continued validity of a peripheral strategy, provided the Western Powers were determined to hold the European continent, by which he meant France and Italy. Apart from making a number of concrete suggestions, with particular reference to the organization of the armed forces and the tactics to be used against an invader, the author emphasized that the Anglo-Saxon powers must be determined in defending Western Europe and that the Continental states would accept the inevitable suffering, provided they did not feel abandoned. France was an essential corner-stone of defence with her African hinterland.

These informed and sophisticated arguments had their echo in the parliamentary debates of the early and middle fifties. In 1952 there was widespread apprehension that if the 'bataille d'arrêt' were not gained on the Continent, the eventual liberation of France would leave the country in ruins. Hence France must insist on an Anglo-American commitment to defence in Europe and on the continued presence of Anglo-American forces there, even after the creation of a European army.

The campaign against the dangers of an Anglo-Saxon peripheral strategy reached its crescendo during the important budget debate in the spring of 1954. The debate hinged upon the problem of preparing for new types of warfare. M. Triboulet summed up the issues on which the government's European defence policy had to be decided. It was a question of peripheral strategy versus the defence of Europe; atomic war versus traditional war; heavy armament versus light armament; a 'corps de bataille de couverture' versus 'la nation-armée'. The government and the deputies had rejected the idea of a peripheral strategy. As they saw it, the Americans, while committed to the defence of Europe, thought in terms of a possible rearguard action. In the opinion of Max Lejeune this called for 'une stratégie et une tactique adaptées à notre sol', failing which, France would be trapped in ' . . . la doctrine d'un Pentagon adepte de la conception industrielle d'une guerre de destruction totale'.[33]

On the military plane, the fear of France as a reservoir of man-power for the Anglo-Saxons and of her exposure to an enemy onslaught while the allies retired into their natural fortresses, reinforced the arguments for a national nuclear force. Only when she disposed of the ultimate weapon could France feel secure by threatening to inflict unacceptable damage on an aggressor. According to one witness, this view was expressed forcefully by M. Mollet in discussions with Belgian ministers at the end of 1956 or in early 1957.[34]

There were, however, other reasons which impelled Frenchmen to insist on the Anglo-American defence of the Continent. They not only reflected the military weakness of France and her pre-occupations elsewhere, notably in Indochina–though it is im-portant to remember that for France Europe was always the most important sector of national defence–but they derived from the priority which successive governments of the Fourth Republic gave to economic recovery. The more firmly the United States was anchored in Europe, the more easily could France concen-trate on rebuilding her economy and she would no doubt have made more rapid progress in this field if she had not borne the strain of the exhausting conflict in Indochina.

(iii) The turning-point in French defence policy and planning: 1954-5

An element of superficiality must always attend any attempt which tries to fix on a given moment in history as the decisive turning-point in the course of events. Thus it would seem rash to claim that the year 1954-5 was a watershed in French defence policy. On the one side were the preoccupation with the eastern frontier, the debate over the type of army best suited to defend it, the conception of extra-European operations as mere colonial campaigns. On the other side were the new doctrine of war arising out of the Indochinese experience and applied in Algeria and the emergence of a nuclear strategy which has transformed the army into its present shape.

This arbitrary division must, however, be qualified. The defence of the eastern frontier continued to be a serious pre-occupation, though that frontier was on the Elbe and the initial brunt of an attack would be taken by the armies of several countries and not by France alone. The principal point of the ideas about the nature and effect of warfare involving tactical nuclear weapons was not to make the use of conventional weapons ineffective, but to make it likely that the conflict would be fought across wide spaces and thereby destroy the traditional linear warfare. Conscription remained in force, but the conscript–leaving aside Algeria–had a less important role to play than the highly trained and technically equipped soldiers of an army pre-pared for nuclear war. The idea of revolutionary war with its political, strategic and tactical applications was not fully worked out until the Algerian rebellion was well under way. Indeed, at first the authorities handled it as if the lessons of Indochina had no relevance to the problem. Finally, the significance of a French army backed by tactical and strategic nuclear weapons was not seriously considered until the end of the decade and did not become apparent until the 1960s.

In spite of these reservations, the period from 1954 to 1955 is a good time in which to take stock of the changes which affected French defence policy since the war. Two important though unrelated events took place during this time: one marked the end of a colonial war and the beginning of another; the other concerned developments in NATO. The war in Indochina came to an end with the disaster at Dien Bien Phu, which had a far greater psychological than military effect. The fall of the camp only involved a small overall loss in the strength of the French expeditionary force, though it included some of its best fighting men. However, French hopes that the Vietminh would have exhausted and broken its best units in the assault on the fortress proved to be exaggerated. The psychological effect of the defeat was immense. It affected the expeditionary force which had striven for eight years to seek out the Vietminh in open battle only to be defeated in the one major encounter of the war. Although for some years before 1954 French officers in Indochina had pointed out the essentially different features of this war when compared with traditional modes of conflict, the final defeat gave a further impetus to new ideas about the nature of strategy in the war against communism. At the end of the war the returning army included not only those who had learnt lessons from the harsh experience of the battlefield and the fight against an invisible enemy, but a number of officers who had spent the last years or months in Vietminh prison camps and who had discovered that in revolutionary war the population is the principal target and that there is no clear distinction between military and political action in such a struggle.

Three months after the cease-fire in Indochina the nationalist rebellion in Algeria broke out. For a variety of local reasons the French government reacted quickly and did not hesitate to mobilize the full military strength of the country, including the conscripts, to meet the challenge. Very soon the highest military authorities adopted the ideas which younger men had begun to evolve out of the experience in Indochina and to insist that the two forms of conflict facing the world today were nuclear and revolutionary. These were the manifestations of the perpetual war between the western and communist worlds. The former depended on a series of politico-diplomatic manœuvres which rested on the concept of deterrence, while the latter was a psycho-military conflict in which the communists sought to outflank the western world by isolating it from Asia, Africa and Latin America, using propaganda, sabotage, subversion and open warfare as their means, fighting for the control of populations by persuasion or intimidation.

Much of this, of course, was a rationalization of French experience since the war and the expression of frustration at repeated failure to maintain one's positions in spite of unchallenged command of the air and superior equipment. Nonetheless, this view appeared more justified and received convincing support as a result of the decision to arm NATO forces with tactical nuclear weapons. In 1955 the NATO Council decided that tactical atomic weapons might be used in an emergency and authorized future defence planning on this basis. In consequence, the original force goals decided upon at the historic NATO Council at Lisbon in February 1952* were considerably reduced, although the basic forward strategy was retained.

This important change was accompanied by a modification of the McMahon Act which had effectively blocked any communication between the United States and her allies about the manufacture and use of nuclear weapons since 1946. The change in the Act was caused by NATO's plan to use tactical nuclear weapons against conventional attacks. Marshal Juin, at the time commander of allied land forces in Central Europe, had pressed hard for this modification. A firm advocate of the use of nuclear weapons from the 'première minute de l'agression', he was not allowed to know the nature or number of the atomic weapons at his disposal. The amendments permitted the sharing of some information, but not any which might be useful in the 'design and fabrication of the nuclear components' of atomic weapons.

The fundamental change in NATO policy provided a convenient excuse to escape from French obligations towards the maintenance of allied ground forces and encouraged the French to intensify their efforts to develop a nuclear capability. They were spurred on by the realization that, in spite of the relaxation of the McMahon Act, France would not achieve equal status with

* It appears that press reports of the number of first-line divisions which were agreed upon ranged from 50 to 60, whereas the figures advanced by the military authorities, which envisaged a German contribution, had been 42, of which 25 were to be combat-ready and the remaining 17 to be available three days after mobilization.

Britain within the Western Alliance unless she made substantial progress in this area.

Another factor which made the years 1954-5 so significant in the evolution of French defence policy was the impact of American and Russian hydrogen bomb tests. The first American test had taken place on the 1st November 1952 and the Soviet Union followed nine months later on the 12th August 1953. These events and the United States test at Bikini on the 1st March 1954 had aroused two contradictory reactions. They undermined allied confidence in the effectiveness of the American deterrent and, simultaneously, they heightened fears lest the United States should defend Europe after all and thereby reduce it to a radioactive wasteland.

By this time, too, the debate about a French nuclear armament was beginning to achieve some sophistication. It was no longer only a matter of demanding nuclear weapons for France, but it was developing into a discussion of choices. Thus a well-informed but anonymous report of the government's intentions in early 1955 spoke of a debate within the administration between those who favoured the construction of two submarines with nuclear propulsion and the partisans—numerous in circles close to the army and the air force—of absolute priority for weapons of mass destruction.[35]

In all the discussions about French nuclear policy during 1954 the events in Indochina no doubt played their part. M. Pleven's consultation of the three secretaries of state of the armed services about a military programme of atomic energy* took place a fortnight after the fall of Dien Bien Phu. Contrary to some reports at the time, the French government had not asked the United States to intervene in the battle with atomic bombs.[36] Instead, American atomic power was thought of as a deterrent to Chinese intervention on the side of the Vietminh, once American bombers had joined in non-nuclear missions to save the beleaguered camp. This project was given the code name 'Vautour'.

The idea of American nuclear might acting as a deterrent in the

* See below, p. 142.

conflict was not born in 1954. Ever since the Chinese communist victory of 1950 the French military authorities were haunted by the fear of a massive Chinese intervention, similar to that of the Korean war. This preoccupation was at the centre of military and diplomatic thought in the last years of the war. In the end, Congress and the British Government saw to it that any American action would be out of the question, thereby reinforcing nascent French suspicions about the reliability of American support.

Although we can trace back the influence of revolutionary war and nuclear strategy on French military thinking and policy to earlier years, the period between the last months of the war in Indochina and the first months of the Algerian conflict can be clearly seen as a time of new orientation in French defence policy. The concluding events in Indochina and the failure to secure American intervention to save Dien Bien Phu had undoubtedly left their mark on the policy-makers. The changes in NATO strategy, coupled with the decreasing gap between the nuclear capabilities of the United States and the Soviet Union, also influenced the course of French atomic policy. It was no coincidence that the first definite steps in the militarization of the atomic energy programme – the various consultations of 1954, the secret protocol of 1955 and the first financing of the C.E.A. from the defence budget* – took place at that time. Other factors contributed to making this a pivotal moment. These were the last months of the ill-starred European Defence Community which were followed by efforts to give the cause of European unity a different direction. Finally, it was a period of respite when it seemed as if France at last could give undivided attention to her role in Europe, for the full meaning of the Algerian rebellion was not grasped until the middle of 1955.

It was fitting that M. Mendès-France should have presided over this time of change. His new and unorthodox style seemed to portend a break in the pattern of political life which had established itself since 1946. However, the Mendès-France approach was premature. The country had to wait until 1958 for a basic

* See below, pp. 140–1, 142, 145.

change in its political structure and then it went further than many Frenchmen had bargained for.

(iv) The Algerian war: the relationship between 'la Guerre Revolutionnaire' and nuclear strategy

The full impact of the changes outlined in the previous section became apparent as the Algerian war gathered momentum and France devoted more and more of her resources and attention to this problem. The emotional impact of the conflict is easily understood when one recalls the long association between France and Algeria with its large European population, North Africa's strategic role in the Second World War and in the liberation of France, and the strong physical and emotional ties between the French army and that region. These factors account for the difference in French reactions to the wars in Indochina and Algeria. Having just returned after defeat in a revolutionary war, the professional army, which had felt isolated and forgotten in Indochina, threw itself into the new revolutionary conflict, determined to benefit from the bitter lesson and this time to be sure of the country's support.

Although the majority did not go so far as the extremists in pushing the theories of 'la Guerre Révolutionnaire' to their logical conclusion and trying to remodel French society, the acceptance of this type of warfare as the most important in the struggle against world communism was widespread among French government and military circles.

From 1954 onwards a succession of soldiers and politicians preached the new doctrine of war in which the West, conceived in terms of a civilization, defended itself in a constant struggle against the forces of world communism. The perpetual war, commonly referred to as 'the Cold War', had several characteristics. It was dominated by a nuclear stalemate between the two chief protagonists. This balance prevented the outbreak of a conventional war in Europe. Hence the Soviet offensive was directed to the weak spots in the western position, notably in territories which had just been freed from colonial rule or were still under its control. The action of the enemy was primarily subversive and based upon the principles of revolutionary war which had been developed by Marxist thinkers from Lenin to Mao Tse-tung.

From this premise it followed, in the words of M. Pierrebourg, rapporteur of the National Assembly's Defence Commission:

> ... That we must have an organization which is able simultaneously to deal with the atomic peril and subversive activities. This means creating a nuclear retaliatory force and a system of territorial defence armed with helicopters, the whole complemented by a large fleet of transport planes ...[37]

It is noteworthy that in the same year the Minister of National Defence, Bourgès-Maunoury, writing about the 'Principes de l'Armée future', analysed three types of war: conventional, atomic and revolutionary; for which the armed forces must be prepared. He devoted most emphasis to the need to be prepared for revolutionary war.[38]

The conclusion to be drawn from these suppositions was that France must be prepared for revolutionary and nuclear wars if she wished to retain her national independence, keeping her conventional forces available to serve in both. This became the leitmotif of speeches and writings by the highest military authorities.

Marshal Juin, for instance, sent the following message to a regional meeting of young members of the Union Nationale des Officiers de Réserve (U.N.O.R.) at Arras:

> Atomic war or subversive war, the dangers which threaten the country have the dual character of permanence and totality. It is therefore essential to establish a system of national defence which is permanent and total.[39]

General Ely also analysed the two essential characteristics of the contemporary military scene as nuclear armament and ideological conflict and he urged that the French forces must be prepared for all kinds of conflict.[40]

Apart from the general influence of new ideas about revolutionary war, the Algerian conflict had some quite specific effects which, in turn, encouraged a greater French reliance on nuclear armament.

The Suez expedition in the autumn of 1956 should be regarded as a part of the French campaign in Algeria. For the French, the attack on Egypt was primarily an attempt to destroy the principal foreign base of the rebellion. The crisis over the Suez Canal provided an opportunity to do that which the French had not been able to do with the Vietminh–to cut off the enemy from his major source of outside support. For many Frenchmen President Nasser was the real enemy in Algeria and it was hoped that in humiliating him the Algerian nationalists would suffer a severe, if not fatal, moral defeat as well as lose some of their material support. In the words of Robert Lacoste, Minister Resident in Algeria: 'Une division française en Egypte vaut quatre divisions en Afrique du Nord.'[41]

This attitude largely explains why France, in contrast to Britain, seemed so much more united at the time of the Suez crisis and why the effect of failure was, again in contrast to Britain, to harden attitudes to the outside world and particularly the United States.

Many people in France saw in the events of the Suez crisis a powerful argument favouring the development of an independent nuclear force because American support could not be counted upon in a situation in which the vital interests of the United States were not at stake. The experience of Suez thus reinforced the misgivings which were born at Dien Bien Phu. These feelings were not based on a very profound analysis of the crisis. President Eisenhower countered the Soviet threat to Britain and France with a warning that the United States would protect her allies against a nuclear attack. The cause of the allied collapse did not lie in the withdrawal of the American nuclear cover but at least partly in American economic pressure.

It is noteworthy that the acceleration of preparations for a military programme of atomic energy, beginning with the second secret protocol signed between Bourgès-Maunoury and Guille on

the 30th November 1956,* followed immediately on the Suez
adventure. The crisis obviously reinforced a natural disposition on
the part of those responsible for national defence to call for the
newest and most effective weapons. Moreover, the events of the
autumn of 1956 led the French to stress the different problems
posed by the defence of the mother country and of the overseas
territories. The former was covered by the NATO guarantee, the
latter depended exclusively on French forces. Although French
military leaders paid lip-service to the efficacy of NATO, the
Suez incident had strengthened their doubts about the American
guarantee, even in Europe. Thus Marshal Juin concluded his
reflections on the question 'Que devons-nous penser de la sécurité
française?' with the exhortation that France should not remain
subject to one member of NATO as far as the manufacture and
deployment of nuclear weapons was concerned.[42]

Even more significant are the comments of General Ely, Chief
of Staff of the Armed Forces. While recognizing NATO's effectiveness as a deterrent to Russian expansion in Europe, he weighed
up this advantage against the problem of French preoccupations
in North Africa. He argued that France must be able to operate
militarily in the world at large, that she must be prepared for
different types of conflict and, thirdly, that she must plan and
provide for a means of atomic retaliation, ready at any time to
thwart an adversary. In this idea and in his proposals for the
organization of French forces, to include a 'capacité de dissuasion',
consisting of a strategic air force and nuclear submarines, a
'capacité de manœuvre et d'intervention', and a 'capacité de
défense permanente', Ely foreshadowed exactly the ideas of
President de Gaulle and their embodiment in the first Five Year
Plan for national defence, launched in 1960.[43]

The arguments, advanced by the highest military authorities in
France, were reinforced by M. Bourgès-Maunoury's policy statements in early 1957. On 12th May, the Minister of National
Defence publicized the broad lines of French defence policy
which had been laid down at a meeting of the Comité de Défense

* See below, p. 141.

Nationale on 30th April. They included the decision to create a nuclear force which alone would enable France to keep her place among the great powers and enable her to fulfil her obligations within the Atlantic Alliance.[44]

Although there is no doubt that the Suez affair greatly stimulated plans and preparations for the nuclear armament of France,[45] the public utterances of those closely associated with the formulation of French defence policy were guarded and confined to generalities. Indeed, one government spokesman expressed a contrary opinion. M. Guille drew unfavourable conclusions about the value of a few bombs. When the government was pressed in the Conseil de la République to increase defence expenditure on atomic energy and to take an open stand in favour of nuclear arms, he concluded his reply with an oblique reference to the British experience in November 1956 which had demonstrated 'Le peu d'intérêt qu'a présenté pour un grand pays européen, au cours des événements récents, la possession de quelques armes atomiques.'[46]

Official reticence was offset by comments in the press, whose gist was the urgent need to provide France with nuclear weapons so that she could in future meet an ultimatum of the Russian variety and earn the respect of her allies.[47]

It is not yet possible to know precisely to what extent the Suez crisis had influenced French nuclear policy. However, a contemporary historian asserts that America's reluctance to support her allies in this crisis was one of the principal reasons why the military staffs recommended and the Comité de Défense Nationale formulated the creation of a national nuclear striking force within its 'Plan de Politique Militaire à long Terme'.[48] Another and possibly more important influence was the orientation given to British defence policy in the White Paper published on 4th April 1957, less than a month before the meeting of the Comité de Défense Nationale. Its emphasis on the nuclear deterrent was not an innovation in British policy. While recognizing that there could be no adequate protection against an attack with nuclear weapons, British planners concluded that it was 'more than ever clear that the overriding consideration in all military planning must be to prevent war rather than to prepare for it'. Hence Britain would develop the hydrogen bomb and generally place a greater emphasis on nuclear weapons than on ground forces for her defence. Militarily, the experience of Suez did not support the rationale of a weak nuclear force, but politically and emotionally it strengthened its appeal, particularly as France was shaken less by the Russian menace than by a sense of being deserted by her American ally.

Other aspects of the Algerian war became apparent more gradually but had no less an influence in preparing the ground for the acceptance of a national nuclear strategy. We have noted how the military authorities tended to see the chief danger of armed conflict outside Europe where the nuclear balance prescribed the *status quo*. Frustrated in securing Western Europe, its principal objective, by frontal assault, the Soviet Union would try to outflank and eventually encircle the Atlantic world by a vast movement through the Middle East, North Africa and across the Atlantic into Latin America, using economic assistance, trade and the encouragement of nationalism as its weapons. This view of the strategic situation naturally involved attempts to formulate an appropriate French military doctrine. It was an incentive to abandoning the traditional posture on the eastern frontier and to its replacement by a highly mobile force backed by atomic weapons.

However, an excessive preoccupation with subversive warfare in general and the Algerian conflict in particular weakened the military demand for French atomic weapons. An interesting by-product of this was the identity of view of those opposed to the government's Algerian policy (and they included most of the military hierarchy) and those opposed to its European and NATO policies under the Fifth Republic. Thus the unveiling of the plans for a 'force de frappe' in 1960 was as bitterly attacked by the upholders of 'Algérie Française' as by the 'Europeans'. General Valluy has been aptly described as the theoretician of this movement and General Challe is reported to have suggested to M.

Debré, when asking for his premature retirement in 1960, that France should renounce the atomic bomb and accept Atlantic integration in return for American aid in preserving French Algeria.[49]

The degree to which Algeria took hold of some of the most intelligent and gifted soldiers is illustrated by the career of Colonel Argoud. One of the most promising officers in the French army, he had embarked upon a brilliant career as a staff officer and became one of the principal architects of the French light division, the 'Division Mécanique Rapide' (D.M.R.), created to deal with the effect of tactical nuclear warfare. He bitterly regretted the complete change wrought by the Algerian war on the structure of the military units so laboriously built up to fight a European war under atomic conditions. In the spring of 1956 he was sent to Algeria. Within months of his arrival he was wholly absorbed in the strategy and tactics of 'la Guerre Révolutionnaire'. Argoud is an outstanding example of what happened to many of his contemporaries who, like him, ended their careers in rebellion against the government whose atomic policy became in their eyes one more act in the betrayal of Algeria.

The war in Algeria absorbed the army to such an extent that one of its by-products was to leave the problem of a French nuclear armament to the military technicians and some elements in the air force. The Fourth Republic had known inter-service rivalries which often lay at the root of opposition to several abortive attempts at unifying the three arms. The particularisms of the air force and navy were accentuated in the face of the army's traditional preponderance in the French defence establishment. In some respects, however, this alleged domination was exaggerated. In their public relations as well as in policy formulation the air force and the navy had some advantages over the army which was more directly under the supervision of the Ministry of National Defence.*

* The Ministry of the Army and the Ministry of National Defence, respectively in Boulevard Saint-Germain and Rue Saint-Dominique, adjoined through their courtyards, whereas the Navy (Rue Royale) and the Air Force (Boulevard

In the mid-fifties there were distant rumblings of the kind of squabbles over the control of nuclear weapons which were characteristic of relations between the armed services in the United States. Compared with the more sophisticated disputes involving strategic and tactical doctrines of the 1960s, these were confined to the relatively simple assertion by the air force of the right to handle the new weapon. After detailing a long list of attributes which had been taken away from the air force and distributed among its rivals, one advocate of that arm, a former air commander, suggested that only the air force could provide an effective defence against atomic and hydrogen bombs. It should, therefore, preoccupy itself with atomic weapons and the means of their delivery. Instead, he noted that a technical organ of the army was exclusively occupied with nuclear weapons and that the air staff seemed singularly uninterested in the problem.[50]

The navy, too, labouring under the handicaps of its Vichyist past and a chronically insufficient budget which made it appear as the cinderella of the three services, had been inspired to enter the nuclear field by copying the example of the first American atomic submarine, the *Nautilus*, launched in December 1954. The technically foolish project of fitting a natural uranium reactor into the ship may well have helped M. Guillaumat in his successful stand to retain the C.E.A.'s control over the atomic armaments programme.*

These interesting manifestations of things to come should not, however, be over-emphasized. The impulses behind the orientation towards atomic weapons came principally from within the C.E.A. and a small group of military specialists and politicians. The armed forces as a whole were so busy with the immediate tasks in hand that they were less open to long-range planning, such as was involved in the atomic energy programme. The

---

Victor) enjoyed a greater physical independence. For a general discussion of relationships between the three services and the characteristics of each one, see Jean Planchais, *Le Malaise de l'Armée*, pp. 97–102.

* See footnote on pp. 142–3 for a brief account of this incident.

situation changed after the establishment of the Fifth Republic when officers like General Ailleret were rewarded for their prescience by appointment to the highest positions.

The real controversy between the army and the air force did not burst until France had established some sort of nuclear capability and after the end of the Algerian war, when the services could give their undivided attention to the new weapons.

Although the military authorities played a secondary part in the decision-making process which, during the years 1954–8, turned the French atomic energy programme towards military purposes, their interest had been aroused and received its first serious expression in the period between the end of the war in Indochina and the beginning of that in Algeria.

In spite of its hold over the military mind, the Algerian war had an important if often indirect influence over the orientation towards atomic armaments. In 1958, the Minister of National Defence, discussing the broad basis of the French armament programme, declared that the possession of nuclear weapons and defence against subversion had equal priority.[51] The general change in strategic thinking at this epoch and the particular experience associated with the Suez crisis undoubtedly played a great part in providing these priorities for a defence policy.

(v) The reorganization of national defence: 1960–

French nuclear policy passed two milestones in 1960. On 13th February France exploded herself into the 'nuclear club' and henceforth the world had to accept France as a nuclear power. In the autumn the government introduced the first Five Year Plan for the development of national defence. Although forward planning had been an important ingredient of French economic policy since 1945, defence policy appeared to have little rhyme or reason during the first fifteen years after the war. This was due to domestic political instability and to the fact that France was almost continually at war during this period so that defence planning was subject to the frequent distortions which accompanied the changing fortunes of colonial campaigns. Only the militarization of the atomic energy programme continued at a more or less regular and accelerating rhythm, partly no doubt because it was outside the control of the defence establishment.

The first 'loi-programme à certains équipements militaires' incorporated many features which had been introduced in the last years of the Fourth Republic. However, it established a complete pattern of defence organization which has basically remained the same ever since. In this pattern the 'Force Nucléaire Stratégique' was the centre-piece and all other aspects of national defence served to complement it.

In order to reap the full advantage of the new programme it was necessary first to bring the Algerian war to an end. That conflict was a handicap for two reasons. It tied up a large proportion of French military resources and prevented France from full freedom of manœuvre in a world dominated by the strategic equilibrium between Russia and the United States. It also engaged the emotions of the French army to such an extent that the soldiers challenged the government's authority. While it would be an exaggeration to suggest that de Gaulle placed his emphasis on nuclear weapons in order to distract the army from its Algerian obsessions, there is no doubt that the new orientation towards nuclear power provided a most welcome means of turning the soldiers away from the theology of revolutionary war. The weapons programme was not developed because of this need but it provided a focus for a return to military professionalism in which the instrument rather than the policy became the centre of attention. The Minister of the Armed Forces, M. Pierre Messmer, told the Defence Committee of the National Assembly on the 18th May 1967 that an army which is technically developed is unsuited for 'coups d'état'. By giving back to the French army its real vocation the government's military policy had restored it to its proper place in the state.[52]

The need to have his hands free for pursuit of the grand design in Europe, which in turn depended on the possession of an instrument of deterrence, was therefore a most important reason why de Gaulle was so eager for a settlement in Algeria. He did not wait until 1962, however, to embark upon the reconstruction of the armed forces. The first 'loi-programme' (1960–5) laid the foundations. The second 'loi-programme' (1965–70) introduced necessary revisions and accentuated the general direction which was taken since de Gaulle came to power.

The French armed forces were organized in three tiers: the 'Force Nucléaire Stratégique'; the 'Forces d'Intervention'–tactfully renamed 'Forces de Manœuvre' in 1964; and the Défense Opérationnelle du Territoire (D.O.T.). It was apparent from the beginning that the nuclear striking force would be the centrepiece of French defence, but only with the second Five Year Plan did it become obvious that the other elements in the defence establishment would, if necessary, be sacrificed for its sake.

The nuclear force was envisaged in three generations. The first consisting of 62 Mirage IV bombers, now fully operational, whose life-span was to be extended beyond 1972 by various technical improvements and a capacity for carrying bombs of 80 to 90 kilotons. The second generation were to be the medium-range land-based solid-fuel ballistic missiles (S.S.B.S.). The first missile unit, with a range of about 2,500 kilometres carrying a warhead of 150 kilotons, is, at the time of writing, expected to be operational by 1971. The whole system of twenty-seven units, located in Haute Provence, may be ready around 1972. The missile-carrying atomic submarines provided the third generation. The first of these, the *Redoubtable*, was launched at Cherbourg on the 29th March 1967 in de Gaulle's presence and should be in commission by the end of 1970. The second submarine, the *Terrible*, is now under construction and may be operational by 1972. It was planned to lay down the third submarine at the time of the *Terrible*'s launching. Each ship has a displacement of nine thousand tons and a speed of twenty knots under water. Its sixteen missiles can be fired when submerged and cover a range of about 2,000 kilometres with a warhead of 500 kilotons. There were also plans for building a fourth submarine. The submarines were originally to have replaced the S.S.B.S. and to have provided

France with the ultimate in deterrence. However, in keeping with the evolution of strategic planning elsewhere, the government decided to retain the S.S.B.S. and no longer regarded the system as a bridge between the Mirages and the submarines. Moreover, the development of ballistic missile defence systems could make the submarine-based missiles more vulnerable under certain conditions.

The fulfilment of this ambitious timetable is largely dependent on French progress in developing suitable warheads to fit the means of delivery. An enormous effort was put into the completion of the gaseous diffusion plant at Pierrelatte which will produce the enriched uranium 235 necessary for both miniaturization and the development of thermonuclear weapons.

French nuclear armament was to be completed by tactical nuclear weapons with which the army should equip its first regiment after 1972. These weapons will be carried by Pluton missiles with a range of about 120 kilometres carrying 10 to 25 kilotons of explosive power, to be reinforced by tactical nuclear bombs carried in the Jaguar strike plane with a range of 500 to 1,000 kilometres. The whole panoply of the French nuclear force was expected to be fully operational by 1975 and to have an explosive power of thirty megatons.

When the first 'loi-programme' was launched in 1960, the 'Forces de Manœuvre' and the D.O.T. looked impressive on paper. The former were designed for frontier defence, for NATO operations and for use overseas in defence of the French Community. They were to consist of five mechanized divisions and one light division 'd'intervention outre-mer' with corresponding naval and air forces. According to the second 'loi-programme' the army was to have only three fully armoured divisions equipped with AMX thirty-ton tanks and two equipped with 'matériels moins récents' by the end of the decade. Since then it is expected that only two divisions will be modernized by 1970 and some observers predict that the five mechanized divisions will not be ready until 1975.

The real measure of the declining importance of conventional forces was to be found in the reduced resources devoted to their equipment. Under the second Five Year Plan 377 million Francs' worth of 'autorisations de programme' disappeared from the army estimates. Obsolescence may also overtake the tactical air force. In the debate on the military budget for 1968, the reporter for the Finance Commission of the National Assembly, M. Jean-Paul Palewski, a Gaullist deputy, speculated that by 1980 the number of squadrons, including transport planes, at the disposal of the air force will equal those of the Swiss air force today. As for the navy, by 1970 it will be reduced to providing the services and support required by the nuclear submarines.

Internal defence suffered a similar fate. In spite of extensive organization and reorganization, the forces for this purpose were reduced from one hundred regiments in the first 'loi-programme' to twenty-five and one alpine brigade in the second.

In 1960 the government claimed with some justice that its defence plans aimed at a balance between nuclear and conventional forces. In 1965 it became obvious that there was a serious and growing imbalance. The conventional forces were seen increasingly in the role of support and defence of the strategic nuclear force. After 1970 the principal mission of the navy will be to protect the nuclear submarines; air defence will cover the strategic nuclear force; the 'Forces de Manœuvre' and the forces of the interior will defend the S.S.B.S.

Should nuclear deterrence fail after all and France be invaded, then the armed forces must be prepared to organize national resistance. In this way General de Gaulle hoped to avoid the experience of 1940, but the importance of the D.O.T. was denied by the facts of the national defence programme. According to the official thesis, France would be most vulnerable to attack and invasion in the years before she had acquired the thermonuclear deterrent. However, internal defence was starved of the means necessary to become truly effective during this period.

The budget for 1968 continued to mark the trend which gave absolute priority to nuclear armament and which pursued the modernization of one service at the expense of another. For the

first time the navy disposed of greater credits for nuclear equipment than the air force. The army credits continued to lag far
behind those of the other two services. Even credits for the
development of the Pluton missile had to be postponed. The
economic and social crisis of the spring and summer 1968 caused
further postponements and cuts in a programme whose fulfilment
receded steadily into the future.[53] The salary and wage rises which
followed the Grenelle Agreement between M. Pompidou and the
strikers meant that running costs took a greater share of the
defence budget for 1969 than equipment costs. They accounted
for the increase in the global figure over the 1968 budget but left
little to spare for the maintenance and replacement of equipment.
The build-up of conventional forces therefore continued to lag
and, significantly, only the Gendarmerie showed an increase in
effectives while those of the air force and the army registered a
decline. Plans for the nuclear force marked time. A reduction in
its costs reflected the completion of some programmes, technical
delays in missile development and the abandonment of the 1969
series of thermonuclear tests. The whole problem of whether to
accelerate or modify the military programme was thus put off
until 1970.[54]

The contemporary structure of French defence has wrought
profound changes in the military tradition of modern France.
The National Service Law of the 9th July 1965, which took effect
in the following year, broke the institution of universal military
service which had since the Great Revolution become part of the
hallowed republican tradition and embodied the second of the
trinity of republican principles. Under the new law the army
moved into a position half-way between an 'armée de métier' and
an 'armée de conscription'. Of 415,000 men in the conscription
age group only 280,000 were actually required in 1966 and it was
hoped that the proportion called up would continue to decline as
the number of enlisted men increased. Universal military service
was still maintained in principle, but the number of exemptions
and the different forms of service open to those eligible made the
whole scheme more like a system of selective service.[55] Everything

thus pointed to an eventual abandonment of universal service.

The serious decline in the conventional element of French defence has meant that the pre-eminence of the land army is no longer the hallmark of French military strength. The emphasis on strategic weapons has reduced French conventional capability to the extent that military intervention in those areas where it might be most likely and justified, as in some West and Central African states, may turn out to be ineffective.[56]

Having embarked upon the nuclear adventure, the French are faced now with the problem of whether they will be able to keep up the development and quality of the national deterrent force so that it will not lose all credibility. The question of credibility is partly answered, as we have seen,* in the theoretical framework of the F.N.S., in which the French go to considerable length in circumscribing its use in a confrontation with a super-power.

There is more doubt over their ability to continue these developments independently. The first question that springs to mind concerns the cost of this ambitious programme. Can France afford it? The French claim that their defence expenditure has declined from 5·6 per cent of the Gross National Product and 28 per cent of the National Budget in 1961 to 4·43 per cent of the G.N.P. and 20 per cent of the National Budget in 1967.† The 1968 budget maintained these proportions although the figures of expenditure showed a 6 per cent increase over the previous year. The most significant feature of the budgets is that until 1969 more than half the total sum was devoted to equipment and of this amount about half was spent on the procurement of nuclear arms, although the exact amount is difficult to determine as some of the funds were 'hidden' in other budgets.

When we turn to a consideration of the national resources spent on defence, the problem becomes more complex. It is estimated that about 10 per cent of the French scientific labour force is engaged upon nuclear weapons research. Arms research

* See above, pp. 78–85.

† According to the method of calculation used by NATO, these figures would be somewhat higher.

and production account for 60 per cent of the electronics industry, 70 per cent of the aerospace industry and 55 per cent
of the expenses of the Commissariat à l'Energie Atomique.
The apologist for these figures usually argue that without the
resources of national defence the civilian sector would not have
benefited from the tremendous technological advances in these
fields. Yet, there are signs that the diversion of resources into
defence work is having a serious effect on national education and
technological progress.

Doubts must also be raised about the ability of the French to
develop very complex weapons systems on their own. The
government's policy of self-reliance has meant that the French
aerospace industry ranks third in the world. Nevertheless, France
depends on outside help for some developments and for the
effectiveness of her defence. Thus the American refusal of a
licensing agreement over the Minuteman and Polaris missiles in
1960 may well have delayed the deployment of French missiles by
four to five years. Similarly, France has had to buy American
computers to help overcome technical problems in the making of
nuclear warheads. Lastly, French defence depends very much on
the NATO Air Defence Ground Environment system (NADGE).
France also remains a member of various organizations within the
Atlantic Alliance which further demonstrates that modern defensive systems are more effectively conceived in regional than
national terms.

Technological and economic factors may well have proved to
be the Achilles' heel of the French policy of autonomy in national
defence. To offset this weakness France has so far preferred
bilateral co-operation to Atlantic or general European co-operation. But the need to provide wider markets to balance research
and development costs may force her to turn increasingly to
multilateral projects. De Gaulle's foreign and military policies
may have pulled France in one direction, economic realities will
encourage his successors to move in the opposite direction.[57]

In spite of this weakness, the scale and depth of development
make it very difficult to see how the nuclear programme can be

easily reversed. It was obviously President de Gaulle's intention to set the organization of national defence in a direction from which there would be no easy–if any–return. The Gaullist conception of military policy may well prevail in a modified form after the General has departed from the scene, just as Gaullist ideas gradually came to dominate nuclear policy before he arrived on the scene. To understand the influences and pressures which encouraged technicians, administrators and politicians to embark upon the course of nuclear armament years before General de Gaulle's advent to power, we must turn to the history of the French atomic energy programme since 1945.

References

1. For a lucid discussion of French defence policy between the two world wars, see Richard D. Challener, *The French Theory of the Nation in Arms: 1866–1939* (Columbia University Press, New York, 1955), pp. 137–256.
2. General Charles Ailleret, 'Défense "Dirigée" ou Défense "Tous Azimuts"' (*Revue de Défense Nationale*, December 1967), pp. 1923–32.
3. Planchais, *Le Malaise de l'Armée* (Paris, Plon, 1958), p. 23.
4. Interview with General de Lattre de Tassigny in the Swiss Journal *L'Illustré*, quoted in *Combat*, 21st–22nd July 1946.
5. Pierre Barjot, 'Stratégie Atomique', *Le Figaro*, 5th March 1946.
6. Colonel Ailleret, 'L'Arme Atomique: Arme à bon Marché' (*Revue de Défense Nationale*, October 1954), pp. 316–19, 321–3.
7. Colonel Ailleret, 'L'Arme Atomique: Ultima Ratio des Peuples' (*Revue de Défense Nationale*, December 1954), pp. 561–2.
8. Maréchal Juin, *Mémoires: Vol. II* (Arthème Fayard, Paris, 1959), p. 257.
9. J.O., *Débats Parlementaires*, No. 22, A.N., session of 17th March 1954, pp. 941–5.

10. *Le Monde*, 18th March 1954.
11. *Le Figaro*, 3rd March 1955.
12. *J.O., Débats Parlementaires, No. 22, A.N.*, session of 17th March 1954, p. 946 col. 2.
13. *Le Monde*, 9th October 1954; *Combat*, 9th–10th October 1954.
14. Discours prononcé par le Général de Gaulle, lors de sa visite au Centre des Hautes Etudes Militaires et aux trois Ecoles de Guerre, p. 3.
15. At a press conference on 11th July 1960, quoted in Jouve, Vol. I, p. 639.
16. *Ibid.*, pp. 641–2.
17. XX, 'La Dissuasion Française' (*Revue de Défense Nationale*, June 1965), p. 991.
18. Eric Muraise, 'Coalitions d'Hier et d'Aujourd'hui: II, l'OTAN et ses Crises' (*Revue de Défense Nationale*, August–September 1967), pp. 1466–7. See also General R. de Saint Germain, 'Regards sur une Politique de Défense' (*Revue de Défense Nationale*, July 1967), p. 1171.
19. Address of President de Gaulle during his annual visit to the Ecole Militaire and the Institut des Hautes Etudes de Défense Nationale, 20th January 1967 (*Le Monde*, 22nd-23rd January 1967).
20. See General André Martin, Chief of Staff of the air force, 'L'Armée de l'Air dans le Contexte Nucléaire' (*Revue de Défense Nationale*, October 1964), pp. 1499–1517, and the reply by General Le Puloc'h, Chief of Staff of the army, in a preface to an article by a group of officers on his staff, 'L'Armée de Terre et l'Armement' (*L'Armée*, January 1965). See also 'Die Prioritäten bei den französischen Rüstungen', *Die Neue Zürcher Zeitung*, 20th January 1965.
21. General Ailleret, 'Défense "Dirigée" ou Défense "Tous Azimuts" ', p. 1931.
22. Published under the title 'Emploi des différents systèmes de forces dans le cadre de la stratégie de dissuasion' by General M. Fourquet (*Revue de Défense Nationale*, May 1969, pp. 757–767).

23. Jean Planchais, *Le Malaise de l'Armée* (Librairie Plon, Paris, 1958), p. 15.
24. Press Conference, *Combat*, 14th May 1947.
25. Article signed J.S., *Le Monde*, 25th October 1947.
26. Speech by François Billoux, Minister of National Defence, before a congress of 'Anciens Francs-Tireurs et Partisans Français' (F.T.P.F.), at Issy-les-Moulineaux, on the 25th April 1947. (*Le Monde* and *L'Humanité*, 26th April 1947.)
27. Charles de Gaulle, *Vers l'Armée de Métier* (Editions Berger-Levrault, Paris, 1934), pp. 93–7.
28. Interview with Léon Boutbien by Claude Delmas, *Combat*, 31st December 1953.
29. For an interesting criticism of D.O.T. see Alexandre Sanguinetti (Vice-Chairman of the National Assembly's Defence Commission), *La France et l'Arme Atomique*, pp. 62–73.
30. For the role of Leclerc in Indochina during the years 1945–6, see Philippe Devillers, *Histoire du Viêt-Nam de 1940 à 1952* (Editions du Seuil, Paris, 1952).
31. Speech in Conseil de la République, *Le Monde*, 11th May 1950.
32. Gallimard S.P., Paris, 1954.
33. *Le Monde*, 17th, 18th, 20th March 1954.
34. Raymond Bousquet, 'La Force Nucléaire Stratégique Française' (*Revue de Défense Nationale*, May 1966, p. 809). M. Bousquet attended the meetings as French ambassador in Brussels.
35. *Le Monde*, 18th March 1955.
36. According to M. Bidault, however, the United States Secretary of State, Mr. Dulles, made two offers of intervention with atomic bombs when they met in Paris in April 1954. The first was for their use against the Chinese supply lines to the Vietminh and the second was for their use against the Vietminh around Dien Bien Phu. M. Bidault claims to have rejected both offers: the first because it might lead to a 'world-wide holocaust' and the second because the French and Vietminh were too closely enmeshed. (Geoffrey Warner,

'Escalation in Vietnam: The Precedents of 1954', in *International Affairs*, Vol. 41, No. 2, April 1965, pp. 273–4).

37. Speech in debate on defence budget for 1957; *Le Monde*, 8th December 1956.

38. Bourgès-Maunoury, 'Principes de l'Armée future' (*La Défense Nationale*, France Documents, Revue d'Etudes Politiques, Sociales, Economiques & Financières, Nouvelle Série No. 98, Paris, 1956, pp. 3–5).

39. *Le Monde*, 16th April 1959.

40. Paul Ely, *L'Armée dans la Nation* (Arthème Fayard, Paris, 1961), pp. 69–77.

41. Quoted by Grosser, *La Quatrième République et sa Politique Extérieure*, p. 370.

42. Maréchal A. Juin, 'Que devons-nous penser de la sécurité française' (*Revue de Défense Nationale*, January 1957), p. 16.

43. Général d'Armée Ely, 'Notre Politique Militaire' (*Revue de Défense Nationale*, July 1957, pp. 1040–3).

44. Claude Delmas, 'La France et sa Défense Nationale' (*Revue de Défense Nationale*, October 1957, p. 1446).

45. Scheinman, *Atomic Energy Policy in France under the Fourth Republic* (New Jersey, Princeton University Press, 1965), pp. 171–4.

46. J.O., *Débats Parlementaires*, No. 1, C.R., *1957*, session of the 16th January 1957.

47. See article by Paul Gérardot in *Combat*, 13th November 1956; the statement by Roger Duchet, Secretary-General of the Indépendants et Paysans, reported in *Le Monde*, 13th November 1956; Félix Gaillard in 'Libres Opinions', *Le Monde*, 7th December 1956.

48. J.-R. Tournoux, 'Force de Frappe' (*La Revue de Paris*, Paris, December 1960), pp. 111–12.

49. De la Gorce, p. 659.

50. Paul Gérardot, *Combat*, 4th October 1954. *Combat*'s columns were particularly open to this kind of advocacy. Partly, of course, because Gérardot was one of its principal contributors. However, it supported him editorially and became a persistent

champion of the case for a French nuclear armament. See its
issues of 25th January, 15th and 29th March, 10th May, 2nd
and 3rd August, 5th October, 22nd and 23rd November 1954.
51. M. Chaban-Delmas at a press conference. *Le Monde*, 9th–10th
February 1958.
52. *The Times*, 20th May 1967.
53. Wolf Mendl, 'Perspectives of Contemporary French Defence
Policy' (*The World Today*, February 1968, pp. 51–4); Jacques
Isnard, 'La France disposera en 1975 d'une capacité nucléaire
égale à celle d'un B-52 américain' (*Le Monde–Sélection Hebdomadaire*, 11th–17th July 1968).
54. Contrôleur Général Heidt, 'Le Budget des Armées pour
1969' (*Revue de Défense Nationale*, February 1969, pp. 203–13).
55. Georges Marey, 'Les Forces Armées Françaises en 1966'
(*Revue Militaire Générale*, January 1966, pp. 7–21).
56. Mendl, p. 57.
57. Mendl, pp. 55–6.

4 · The civil and military development of the French atomic energy programme

From the beginning, the French atomic energy programme was conceived in the broadest terms, in which its scientific, industrial and military uses all had their place. Until 1950, the emphasis was on the scientific and technological aspects of the work and on the need for the indispensable raw material. The years 1950 to 1952 were crucial in the history of the programme. Administrative changes in the Commissariat à l'Energie Atomique covered the decision to move forward to the industrial exploitation of nuclear energy, in which military considerations played a major–if not the most important–part. Henceforth an option had been created and successive governments had to face it. That of M. Mendès-France in 1954 was the first to consider it at cabinet level. The following year saw the beginning of substantial though secret military participation in the programme. The government admitted publicly for the first time in 1957 that France was working on the construction of an atomic bomb. The second Five Year Plan of 1957 for the development of atomic energy left no doubt about its ultimate intentions. The full implications of this policy on French military strategy did not become the subject of a major public debate until the end of 1959, after President de Gaulle's speech at the Ecole Militaire. Of course, the problem had been considered by military experts and technicians for some years previously, though chiefly in theoretical and academic terms. However, in the 1950s the general public had only been spasmodically exercised over the related questions whether France should possess nuclear weapons and whether she should make an atomic bomb.

(i) The origins: 1939–45

The origins of the French effort in the nuclear field go back to the years immediately preceding the Second World War and to French collaboration with the allies during the war. French scientists played a distinguished part in the experiments which opened the way to uranium fission, beginning with Becquerel's discovery of the radioactive properties of uranium in 1896,[1] followed two years later by the discovery of radium by Marie and Pierre Curie and their first isolation of it in 1902. French scientists had a less prominent part in laying the basic theoretical foundations of nuclear science.

In the 1930s, Frédéric and Irène Joliot-Curie's discovery of artificial radioactivity '. . . allait permettre à la science de passer du stade de l'alchimie naturelle à celui de l'alchimie dirigée'.[2] This, coupled with Chadwick's discovery of the neutron in 1932, prepared the ground for uranium fission. The demonstration of uranium fission by Joliot-Curie, Hans von Halban and Lew Kowarski in March 1939, at the Collège de France, made the experiment of a controlled explosion only a matter of time and resources. Frédéric Joliot-Curie had already foreseen this event in his Nobel Prize speech in 1935. The military authorities were equally alert to the potential of this development. According to General Beaufre, the students at the staff college in 1932 were told that an atomic bomb was within the range of possibility.[3]

Immediately after the war Joliot-Curie asserted that in 1940 France needed less than a year to complete research which would have enabled her to consider making a nuclear weapon,[4] thus reflecting the state of progress in French nuclear research up to the time of the surrender and occupation. As early as May 1939 there had been some consideration of a secret experimental explosion in the Sahara.[5]

When war broke out, those responsible for scientific matters showed much greater energy and foresight than were shown in other areas of the war effort. This was largely due to the persuasiveness of the team of scientists around Joliot-Curie and to the vision of the minister of armaments, Raoul Dautry, who was to become the first administrator of the Commissariat à l'Energie Atomique after the war. Dautry played a very important part in the French atomic effort before and after the war. He was more of an industrialist and 'animateur' than a politician. He was a *Polytechnicien*, like other key figures in the development of the atomic energy programme. The French scientists were working on the problem of securing the fission of U235, contained within natural uranium, by the use of moderators to reduce the speed of the fast secondary neutrons which would otherwise be absorbed by the commoner U238 before provoking the required fission of U235. The two moderators best suited for this purpose were graphite and heavy water. The work led to the taking out of patents in May 1939; one concerning the explosive use of uranium and the others with reference to machines for creating nuclear energy, later to be known as atomic reactors or piles. After 1945 the patents were to become a source of dispute and helped to embitter relationships between France and the United States.

In March 1940, Dautry sent one of his colleagues, Jacques Allier, on an adventurous mission to Norway in order to secure the only existing supply of heavy water for France. He also signed a contract securing for France the total future output of this material. At the same time he shared the details of French achievements in nuclear research with the British. An agreement with Belgium to assure the entire uranium production of the Congo for French use was initialled but never signed and concluded. In addition, Joliot-Curie received six tons of oxide of uranium from Belgium. These international moves were accompanied by measures giving Joliot all the facilities he required, including limitless credits and the right to recall any colleague from the armed forces who was needed for this work. The French remembered this vigorous start when they had to begin again after the war. Recalling how far advanced they had been and their willingness to serve the allied cause, French officials and scientists were conscious of the apparent disregard of their efforts and the ingratitude shown particularly by the United States.

During the war, allied collaboration in the nuclear field was bedevilled by the emotional and political undertones of the triangular relationship between the United States, the United Kingdom and the Free French.

In June 1940, Joliot's closest collaborators, Hans von Halban and Lew Kowarski, fled to England with Joliot's blessing and the precious stock of heavy water. Joliot himself chose to stay behind and take care of his laboratory.

British research in the nuclear field, based on the Cavendish Laboratory, had concentrated on the problem of fission by fast neutrons. The French scientists were welcomed and set up in Cambridge. The work of the MAUD Committee in 1940 and 1941 had envisaged a twofold programme in which a bomb should be made with U235, while Halban was to proceed with work on a uranium powered boiler, based on fission by slow neutrons.

The enormous industrial effort which would be required to produce sufficient quantities of U235 and the great amount of heavy water needed for an industrial boiler combined to make the project impracticable as far as the British government was concerned, particularly as the leading scientists were engaged on more pressing work for the immediate war effort.

It became clear that only the immense resources of the United States would be able to support such an effort. This point of view was pressed on American government officials in the autumn of 1941 by Marcus Oliphant, among others, and was made more urgent by fears of German progress. The entry of the United States into the war thus opened the way to Anglo-American co-operation in this field.

American progress had up to that time paralleled that of the French, oriented as it was to working on fission by slow neutrons. At the end of 1940, however, Glenn Seaborg had discovered plutonium, a new element formed by irradiation of uranium with slow neutrons, which was as fissile as U235 and easier to produce. Until 1940 the teams in the United States and France had been moving in the same direction independently of each other. During the war, the British effort owed a great deal to the French scientists, particularly through the knowledge and equipment brought over by Halban and Kowarski, but American progress had been made more or less independently and the scientists on the other side of the Atlantic, many of them refugees from Europe, felt no special obligation to their French colleagues.

This largely explains American indifference towards French efforts in the nuclear field since the Second World War. The French claim for credit in laying the groundwork has never been fully acknowledged in the United States. Experiences in inter-allied relations during the war helped to deepen the wound in French pride.

The policy of secrecy and the clash of personalities played their part in the chequered story of Anglo-American collaboration. In the summer of 1942 it was decided to move the work of the teams around Halban and Kowarski to Canada in order to enjoy better facilities and benefit from American efforts in Chicago. A heavy water reactor was eventually constructed in 1945 at Chalk River.

The presence of French scientists in the Anglo-Canadian team added to the difficulties of the Anglo-American wartime partnership which was broken off for nearly a year in 1943, between the date of an American decision to stop all assistance to the Anglo-Canadian project and the resumption of co-operation following a new agreement. Bertrand Goldschmidt had participated in the work at Chicago on chain reactions in uranium, using graphite as moderator and a chemical method for the separation of plutonium. He had been seconded to the British atomic group by the Free French forces and had been sent by it to Chicago in 1942. He eventually joined the French scientists in the Anglo-Canadian team and brought valuable experience and information with him. Indeed, the work at Montreal and Chalk River owed a great deal to the presence of a group of Frenchmen in the team. Until May 1944, when he was replaced by John Cockcroft as a result of American pressure, Halban directed the group. Pierre Auger was director of physics; Jules Guéron and Goldschmidt were directors in the chemistry department; Lew Kowarski, who had remained in Cambridge as a result of disagreements with Halban, joined the team under Cockcroft and built the first small heavy water reactor to function outside the United States.

The British authorities were much embarrassed by their commitments to the French scientists. Not only were they complicated and unique to the individuals concerned,[6] but they had not been fully explained to the Americans who, of course, had no such obligations to the French and who were particularly concerned that information about the atomic bomb project should not be passed to countries other than the three (U.S., U.K. and Canada) involved in the enterprise.

Matters came to a head when, one after the other, the French scientists engaged in the project at Montreal wanted to pay visits to liberated France. General Groves, in charge of the American bomb project, saw this as a threat to security. The Quebec agreement of October 1943, which had put an end to the interruption of Anglo-American co-operation, stipulated–on Churchill's suggestion–that neither partner should share information with a third party without the other's consent. It was known that Joliot-Curie had joined the Communist Party and it would be natural for the returning French scientists to inform him of their work.

Although inter-allied relations in this respect were eventually clarified, the entangled relationships between the French scientists, the British authorities and, indirectly, the American authorities, further envenomed subsequent Franco-American differences over patents in nuclear technology.*

* At the end of 1954 the C.E.A. claimed compensation from the United States Atomic Energy Commission for the use of patents lodged with it. This was the first claim of its kind. In 1939 Joliot-Curie, Lew Kowarski and Hans von Halban had lodged an application with the United States Patent Office for their work on the uranium fission process. No patent was issued, however, because the outbreak of the Second World War had brought about the suspension of patent rights on atomic inventions. Subsequently, the three scientists made over their claim to the C.E.A. which held that the Americans had used the French invention. Le Monde, 28–29 November 1954; The New York Times, 26 November 1954. The suit dragged on in spite of repeated American refusals to recognize the claim. Le Monde, 3 and 16 July 1958; The New York Times, 2 July 1958. It was finally

The years immediately preceding the war and the war itself provided the basis from which the French could develop their atomic energy programme. The work of French scientists until 1940 had assured their country's place among the leaders in this field. The acquisition of heavy water supplies from Norway had assured the valuable contribution of French scientists to allied research during the war. The six tons of oxide of uranium, hidden in Morocco during the occupation, as well as the accidental discovery of a wagon-load of sodium uranate at Le Havre station assured sufficient raw material for a start. Above all, France possessed a small, highly trained and able group of scientists whose experience bridged the gap in the national programme between 1940 and 1945 and whose natural ambition to continue their work would provide an added impulse to the development of nuclear energy in France.

At the same time, the war had left its mark of suspicion and bitter feelings. American attitudes towards nuclear research only added to the resentment felt by General de Gaulle and his followers over the way in which they had been treated. Though cut off from American co-operation by the Act of 1946, the British were as much involved in the policy of secrecy to make unlikely any serious co-operation between Britain and France. The Free French had made their first attempt to establish a formal co-operation with the British at the end of 1942. Colonel Jean Morin tried to persuade them to share all information about 'Tube Alloys' (the code name for the British atomic programme) after the war. However, he only extracted a vague oral undertaking from Sir John Anderson.[7]

France did not start on her work with a *tabula rasa*, but her allies made no effort to extend a helping hand, even when the

---

rejected by the United States Court of Customs and Patent Appeals on the grounds that the specifications for a nuclear reactor were too vague and theoretical to enable anyone to make use of them in practice. It did not assuage French feelings that Enrico Fermi was awarded a patent. *Le Monde*, 25 July 1959; *The New York Times*, 23 July 1959.

French insisted that the primary purpose of their programme was the development of nuclear energy for peaceful purposes.

(ii) Laying the foundations: 1945–51

On his visit to Ottawa in July 1944, the attention of General de Gaulle was first drawn to the revolutionary changes about to be effected through the use of atomic energy. Three of the French scientists in the Anglo-Canadian project, Pierre Auger, Jules Guéron and Bertrand Goldschmidt, with Guéron as their spokesman, secretly urged the head of the Provisional French Government to take the measures necessary for the earliest possible resumption of atomic research in France and pointed out the importance of Madagascar's uranium resources.[8] They had also drawn his attention to the immense advantage which the United States would derive from possession of the new weapon.

In March 1945 Dautry took the matter up and pressed for a speedy resumption of the French effort, reminding the General of French progress up to 1940 and the usefulness of Norway's supply of heavy water. Finally, in May 1945, Pierre Auger and Frédéric Joliot-Curie convinced de Gaulle of the need to establish a Commissariat à l'Energie Atomique. It is noteworthy that the pressure on General de Gaulle was exercised by scientists rather than by politicians.

The new enterprise was launched in October 1945 and the 'exposé des motifs', which preceded the ordinance setting up the Commissariat à l'Energie Atomique, clearly outlined the objectives and methods of its work. These were doubtless governed by the problems which faced the government in trying to set up such a programme at a time when France was in ruins as a result of defeat, occupation and military campaigns that had ravaged the country.

To lay firm foundations for a successful atomic energy programme it was necessary to have a sufficient number of trained scientific and technical personnel, to dispose of the necessary raw materials, to develop an adequate infrastructure and, of course, to provide funds.

A nucleus of qualified personnel was, as we have seen, available in 1945, but it was totally inadequate for a rapid expansion of the work. The shortage of trained staff was slowly overcome as the facilities of the Commissariat expanded, particularly after the acquisition of a centre for experimental research at Saclay.

Right from the start, the search for raw materials was actively undertaken. One of the principal tasks of the newly established Commissariat was to organize and control, in agreement with the interested government departments, the search for and the exploitation of the necessary raw materials. The prospecting for uranium was most important, since the resources of the Belgian Congo, exploited by L'Union Minière du Haut Katanga, were now reserved for the United States and Great Britain. In 1948 the search revealed large uranium resources at Crouzille and at the beginning of 1954 one of the largest mines was discovered at Limouzat near Vichy. The control of uranium resources in the French Union was firmly placed under the state by a decree published in the *Journal Officiel* of the 7th April 1946.

The problem of building up an adequate infrastructure to realize the industrial exploitation of atomic energy was closely related to the availability of sufficient funds. The first credits in 1946 amounted to no more than five hundred million francs, enough to enable the High Commissioner and the Government Administrator of the new organism to establish themselves in two flats on the same floor of an apartment house in Avenue Foch, but leaving little scope for more.

In spite of the modest beginnings, the Commissariat developed steadily. In addition to the annual credits, it was empowered to receive gifts and could raise a public loan with the approval of the minister of finance. Notwithstanding the great problems of reconstruction in the immediate post-war years, the credits increased steadily until 1950.*

*CREDITS In thousand million frs.	1946	1947	1948	1949	1950	1951	TOTAL
	0·5	0·6	1·6021	3·4368	4·7438	3·813	14·6957

La France et la Puissance Atomique, p. 7.

However limited its material basis during the early years, the Commissariat's work was greatly favoured by a statute which gave it the advantage of state support while enjoying a rare independence. Ever since the autumn of 1944 Dautry had prepared for its birth. With his customary vision he set the stage for unobtrusive and effective work beneath the troubled political surface of the Fourth Republic.

The Commissariat had a unique status in France, being a public institution under a management governed by private law, enjoying administrative and financial autonomy. Two characteristics distinguished its administration. Unlike other nationalized establishments, the C.E.A. was not placed under the traditional civil service and was not, therefore, under the tutelage of any one ministry. This meant that its budget was a purely internal affair and did not have to be submitted to the minister of finance. External control was exercised by reports to parliament, submitted by a 'Mission de Contrôle' which was an internal organ of the Commissariat.[9]

Supervision of the C.E.A. was placed in the hands of a committee under the authority of the President of the Council of Ministers. After 1947 he usually delegated his responsibilities to a secretary of state attached to his office. The committee included the High Commissioner, responsible for the scientific and technical work; the 'Administrateur Général délégué du gouvernement', responsible for administration and finance; three atomic scientists and the chairman of the Comité de Co-ordination des Recherches concernant la défense nationale. In addition, there was a Conseil Scientifique which had no powers and rarely met. Until 1951 the committee provided a kind of guarantee for the good conduct of the establishment, whereas the real authority was wielded by the High Commissioner and the Administrator General. Until his dismissal in 1950, Joliot-Curie occupied the

---

In 1948 the credits for the Commissariat amounted to 1/1,000 of the national budget. The United States was spending 100 times as much as France on atomic energy, the United Kingdom was spending 10 times as much, the Argentine somewhat more than France and Sweden about the same amount. *Combat*, 7 July 1949.

post of High Commissioner and by virtue of his prestige, his personal charm and his dynamism exercised an unchallenged pre-eminence within the Commissariat. The scientific and technical management was thus controlled by him and a team of his closest collaborators. Every year they went into retreat for several days at L'Arcouest in Brittany where they elaborated the next year's programme.

So the C.E.A. began its work endowed with a remarkably independent constitution, led by an able and enthusiastic team of scientists and technicians, provided with limited funds and a small quantity of raw materials, to be augmented by a vigorous programme of prospecting and mining.

Six objectives were laid down in October 1945: the Commissariat was to pursue scientific and technical research 'en vue de l'utilisation de l'énergie atomique dans les divers domaines de la science, de l'industrie et de la défense nationale';[10] to provide protection against the harmful effects of atomic energy; to organize and control prospecting for sources of raw material and their exploitation; to build reactors; to provide information for the government and to advise it in negotiations of international agreements; finally, to do everything to help France benefit from this branch of science.

Work started immediately on some of these objectives. Others, such as the development of atomic energy on an industrial scale, had to be postponed for seven years. The achievement of a chain reaction was the necessary first step and all efforts were bent on constructing an experimental pile at the fort of Châtillon, in whose gloomy vaults physics and chemistry laboratories were set up, while machine tools were brought in from the occupation zone in Germany. On the 15th December 1948 at 12.12 p.m. the first French uranium pile went into action–the first on the European continent, excluding the Soviet Union. Christened ZOE,* it served for research on chain reactions, the study of neutrons and the preparation of isotopes.

* Zero energy–not more than 5 kilowatts at most; Oxide of uranium was the activating material; Eau Lourde–about 6,000 litres were used as moderator.

(iii) The years of transition: 1951-2

An important decree of the 3rd January 1951 modified the constitution and organization of the C.E.A. The Comité de l'Energie Atomique was increased from six to ten members, headed by the Administrator General, who became its chairman in place of the High Commissioner who was to be one of the four scientists on the committee. Military participation was assured through the representative of the Comité d'Action Scientifique de la Défense National, which had replaced the earlier Comité de Co-ordination des Recherches concernant la défense nationale in 1948. The newcomers included the director of the Centre National de la Recherche Scientifique (C.N.R.S.) and three high officials to be chosen by the prime minister from his own office, the foreign ministry and the treasury. All members, except those serving ex officio, were nominated for a term of five years. The Conseil Scientifique was given greater importance and had to be consulted over the Commissariat's study and research programme.

Francis Perrin succeeded Joliot-Curie as High Commissioner. Like his predecessor, Perrin was connected with a distinguished scientific family. Born in 1901, he was the son of the physicist and Nobel Prize winner, Jean Perrin, who had succeeded Irène Joliot-Curie as Minister of Scientific Research in Léon Blum's Popular Front Government of 1936 and had founded the C.N.R.S. After a brilliant academic career Francis was awarded the doctorate of mathematical sciences in 1928 and that of physics in 1929. At the age of thirty he occupied a chair of theoretical physics and had made an important contribution to the study of nuclear chain reactions. The war found him visiting professor at Columbia University and in 1944 General de Gaulle appointed him delegate of the French in the United States to the Consultative Assembly in Algiers, whence he returned to Paris in 1945. Apart from being a member of the Comité de Direction of the Commissariat, he was professor of nuclear physics at the Collège de France from 1946. Perrin was essentially a theoretician. He was also known as a socialist.

Raoul Dautry died on the 21st August 1951 and was replaced

by Pierre Guillaumat as Administrator General. Some years younger than Perrin, he represented the post-war generation of technocrats who quietly laid the foundations for the brilliant French recovery. The son of a general, he became Director of Fuel after the war and played an important part in opening up the Saharan oilfields. At the Commissariat he prepared and carried out the two great development plans of 1952 and 1957 and was particularly associated with the construction of the plutonium factory at Marcoule. In spite of the military background of his family and his brilliant career at the Ecole Polytechnique, Guillaumat probably played a decisive part–for personal as well as public reasons–in keeping the C.E.A. free of military control during these years.

The arrival of Perrin and Guillaumat within a few months of each other at the head of the Commissariat not only meant that a new team was at work but, together with other events, clearly marks the end of one stage in the Commissariat's development and the beginning of a new one. Before the appointment of Perrin and Guillaumat there was a lengthy and bitter battle for the succession. The period between Joliot-Curie's dismissal in April 1950 and Perrin's appointment a year later saw Dautry in charge of the C.E.A. under the growing influence of its Secretary-General, René Lescop, who strongly favoured a military orientation of the atomic energy programme. The confused manœuvres which preceded the appointments of the new High Commissioner and Administrator General reflected a clash of personalities, political rivalries and a struggle over future atomic energy policy.[11]

It took nearly three months to settle the appointments of the new Comité de l'Energie Atomique and the new Conseil Scientifique.* On the publication of the list of members of the

* COMITE DE L'ENERGIE ATOMIQUE: Apart from Guillaumat and Perrin.
Louis Leprince-Ringuet (Professor of Physics at Polytechnique)
Yves Rocard   (Professor of Physics at Univ. of Paris)
Pierre Ailleret   (Director of Studies and Research at E.D.F. and brother of Charles Ailleret)

two committees, it was immediately noted that Irène Joliot-Curie had been dropped from the Comité de l'Energie Atomique. In fact, of the original six members only Perrin, General Bergeron and, for a few months, Raoul Dautry remained. One of the newcomers, Yves Rocard, later played an important part in elaborating the detonator mechanism of the first French bomb and in establishing a network of posts to detect the effects of the atomic explosion.* Jean Thibaud, director of the Institute of Atomic Physics at Lyons, joined the Conseil Scientifique. He had been a controversial figure during the war, having replaced Paul Langevin under Vichy. Of all scientists he had not only been the most outspoken in his criticism of the lack of means devoted to work on atomic energy, but had often raised the question of its military use.[12]

M. Belin	(Maître de Requêtes, Conseil d'Etat)
M. Gregh	(Inspector of Finances)
François de Rose	(Deputy Director of the Foreign Ministry)
General Bergeron	(Chairman of the Comité d'Action Scientifique de la Défense Nationale)
Gaston Dupouy	(Director of the Centre National de la Recherche Scientifique)

CONSEIL SCIENTIFIQUE:

René Anxionnaz, Louis de Broglie, Maurice de Broglie, Bugnard, Georges Chandron, Léon Denivelle, Donzelat, Jean Goguel, Hirsch, Joseph Pérès, Maurice Ponte, Maurice Roy, Jean Thibaud, *Le Monde*, 22–23 April and 8 November 1951.

* Professor Yves Rocard was a specialist in vibrations and thermodynamics and was director of the laboratory of the Ecole Normale Supérieure. He first attracted attention as the author of a short memorandum on the thermonuclear bomb. It has been written of him that '... il était ... connu comme le seul scientifique français de quelque classe qui fût "de droite" ' (de Lacoste Lareymondie). The same author suggests that when Rocard became Scientific Director of the Bureau des Etudes Générales under General Buchalet in 1955, '... il avait sans aucun doute espéré devenir une sorte de Haut-Commissaire Militaire'. However, Francis Perrin refused to share his authority in the technological and scientific field. 'Ainsi petit à petit, le professeur Rocard n'eut qu'une participation de plus en plus lointaine aux travaux du B.E.G. ...' (de Lacoste Lareymondie, pp. 25-6).

The new leaders of the C.E.A. considered two sets of questions. The first related to policy: should the Commissariat concentrate on research and industrial reactors, or should it embark on a programme of fissile material production? The former course might have meant rapid strides in the industrial utilization of nuclear energy, but would have depended on imports of fissile materials from the United States, the United Kingdom or possibly Russia. In view of the prevalent climate of suspicion and secrecy this might have been difficult to negotiate and would have implied technical and political dependence on other countries. The latter course would have meant a wait of several years before France would be in a position to exploit her home-made fissile material for industrial purposes, but would have assured the country's independence in this field.

The second set of questions flowed from the answer to the first. If, as was to be the case, the decision was to make France an independent producer of fissile materials, then one had to choose between plutonium and enriched uranium (U235) as nuclear fuel. The available knowledge at that time indicated that plutonium would be easier to produce, though its industrial applications were little known. U235 could only be produced in a factory for the separation of isotopes which would involve a long and costly construction.[13] Moreover, in 1951 it was estimated that the total annual production of natural uranium in France would be around one hundred tons. In view of the limited resources, the production of plutonium was the obvious choice as it would have required five to ten times more natural uranium to produce an equivalent amount of enriched uranium. The discovery of new sources of natural uranium in 1956 made plans for the production of U235 feasible and therefore strengthened the case for building a gaseous diffusion plant.[14]

Since the plutonium policy was adopted, the question arises whether the decision-makers had its military uses foremost in their minds. Plutonium can be applied for peaceful as well as military purposes; the former do not demand such a high purity of plutonium 239 as is required to make an explosion. Thus military plutonium is more expensive to produce, since over-irradiation causes the plutonium 239 to be contaminated with plutonium 240. To avoid this, the uranium bars must be replaced more frequently than is necessary if military-grade plutonium is not required. In the early fifties there was little practical experience of the industrial uses of plutonium, though a good deal of thought had been given to it as a source of electricity and as a fuel for breeder reactors. While not excluding its eventual use as a source of industrial energy, the choice indicated the production of an explosive for military purposes with electricity as a mere by-product.

There is no doubt that the scientists were aware of the political and military implications of this decision. Francis Perrin feared that a programme for the production of large amounts of plutonium would inevitably arouse military interest and threaten interference on the part of the defence establishment in the running of the C.E.A. M. Gaillard, the Secretary of State responsible for the atomic energy programme, was, however, ambitious for a large programme and was encouraged in his view by the shadowy figure of M. Lescop. Perrin was eventually persuaded to co-operate in carrying through the policy, but Lescop left his post as Secretary-General in 1952. Gaillard had become convinced that whereas the C.E.A. could be run harmoniously under dicephalous administration, it was essential to avoid a 'ménage à trois'.[15] Nevertheless, some of the scientists were not happy at this orientation of the atomic energy programme and it is interesting to note that Lew Kowarski not long afterwards left the Commissariat and found his way into the Centré Européen de la Recherche Nucléaire (C.E.R.N.), founded largely under the inspiration of Pierre Auger for fundamental research into a branch of nuclear physics which is remote from the field of nuclear energy.

Once the decision was taken, it received body and form from the first Five Year Plan launched in 1952. Of this plan there could be no doubt. Although military objectives were not mentioned at that time, they were predominant in the minds of its sponsors.[16]

Years of preparatory work and build-up of its potential had enabled the French atomic energy programme to reach the industrial take-off stage in 1952. The time had come to move into a more massive programme. Alongside the shift from research and experiment to production, there was a change in control. The purely experimental stage was over and with its passing went the predominance of the scientific element in the Commissariat. Management and control were now in the hands of technicians, administrators and politicians. The changed constitution ensured a firmer, though still discreet, government hold over atomic policy.

The early years also witnessed the emergence of some military interest in atomic energy and the establishment of embryonic services to deal with the matter. In 1951 the Ecole Militaire de Spécialisation Atomique de l'Armée de Terre at Lyons began on a programme of speeded training for officers of the three services in nuclear physics and the effect of nuclear weapons. In the following year the Commandement des Armes Spéciales, attached to the chief of staff of the army, began studies of the use of nuclear weapons on the field of battle as well as 'les conditions générales de réalisation d'armes atomiques'. The ground was thus prepared for an ever greater military concern over the work of the Commissariat.

(iv) The first Five Year Plan: 1952

At ten years' distance it may have seemed clear that the first Five Year Plan implied an orientation towards the military use of atomic energy. At the time it was by no means so obvious and the officials chiefly responsible, whatever their private thoughts, did not stress this possibility and only admitted it under pressure.

The Plan was the special child of Félix Gaillard, the young Radical Secrétaire d'Etat à la Présidence du Conseil et aux Finances. It was first outlined in public at the end of 1951, was approved by the cabinet in June and adopted by both houses of parliament after brief debates in July 1952. It was an ambitious plan in the light of the previous work and resources of the atomic

138

energy programme, but it remained very small compared with the total amount of national expenditure.

It contained two basic elements: the first was a continuation and intensification of the previous programme. This involved completing the search for radioactive minerals; further programmes of training research workers, engineers and technicians; the encouragement of fundamental research in physics, nuclear chemistry, metallurgy and related sciences; and the manufacture of indispensable equipment. The second gave a new orientation to the work and aimed at the production of plutonium from two major piles of 50,000 and 100,000 kilowatt capacity and its extraction from the irradiated uranium by a highly complex chemical process in a factory largely run by automation. The new piles and the plutonium factory were located at Marcoule near the Rhône in the north of the Département de Gard. Thirty-seven thousand million francs, spread over six years, were to provide the financial sinews of the Plan.*

In later years M. Gaillard explained in greater detail the objectives he had in mind when launching the first Five Year Plan, but he never denied that it made possible an eventual decision to give the atomic energy programme a military orientation. He told the Conseil de la République in 1952 that although France remained faithful to her unilateral commitment not to use atomic energy for warlike purposes, she might not always desist from making atomic bombs if others continued to manufacture them on both sides of the Iron Curtain.[17]

The consequences of the new legislation were immediately felt in the expansion of the Commissariat's services. Work on the first reactor (G1) at Marcoule began in the summer of 1954. It did not work at full strength and various technical hitches compelled its temporary closure. An official statement from the Commissariat heralded the entry into function of the second pile (G2) on

---

* Although the total was almost double that of the previous six years, it compared with an annual outlay of five hundred thousand million Francs for the American and eighty thousand million francs for the British atomic energy programmes. *Le Monde* and *The New York Times*, 19 June 1951.

the 21st July 1958. The automatic factory for the separation of plutonium, begun in 1955, was ready in 1958.

Such large-scale technical achievements were accompanied by advances in other sectors. A third research reactor became operational at Saclay in 1957 and at the end of 1958 President Coty inaugurated a proton synchrotron, for fundamental research, the most powerful in the world until the completion of the one in Geneva belonging to CERN. In 1955 it was decided to found another nuclear research centre at Grenoble.

All these developments in the scientific, technical and industrial fields owed a great deal to the close and expanding relationship between the Commissariat and industry, particularly the Electricité de France (EDF) which was associated with the enterprise at Marcoule. Such progress could not, however, have been maintained and speeded up if the Commissariat had not received financial support from other sources.

Less than three years after the Plan's adoption, Francis Perrin showed that its provisions had been surpassed and he called for an increased budget.[18] A month later his call was answered by a decree which more than doubled the appropriations for the Five Year Plan, raising them to one hundred thousand million francs. Issued on the 20th May 1955, it apportioned the new credits among various projects and gave the lion's share to the extension of the Marcoule centre with the view to the construction of a third pile (G3). Substantial sums were also devoted to a study of the prototype of a marine nuclear engine and for the extension of experimental work, including the third research pile at Saclay. The minister responsible, from whom the revised plan got its name, was Gaston Palewski, a loyal Gaullist.*

On the day on which this plan was published, a secret protocol

* When Palewski was director of Reynaud's cabinet he met de Gaulle for the first time. Subsequently he became one of the General's earliest and closest collaborators. It is suggested that his entry into Faure's cabinet (he resigned after eight months) caused him to fall from favour with the General. In 1962 he was appointed Minister of State, responsible for atomic energy and rocket development. Pierre Viansson-Ponté, *Les Gaullistes: Rituel et Annuaire* (Paris, Editions du Seuil, 1963), pp. 162–3.

was signed, providing for a substantial contribution from the defence budget to the work of the Commissariat.* In return, the Commissariat had to share the results of its research and experiments with the Ministry of the Armed Forces which could make suggestions and requests through its representatives on the various organs of the C.E.A. The defence budget of 1955–6 included for the first time substantial credits for the atomic programme, though these figures were not published under such a heading. The protocol was signed by Gaston Palewski, General Koenig, Minister of the Armed Forces, and Pierre Pflimlin, Minister of Finance. The first two were Gaullists and M. Pflimlin belonged to the M.R.P. The protocol formally established and sealed the relationship between the C.E.A. and national defence.

Eighteen months later, on the 30th November 1956, a second protocol was signed between Mm. Bourgès-Maunoury, Minister of National Defence, and Georges Guille, Secrétaire d'Etat à la Présidence du Conseil, responsible for atomic energy. It defined the roles of the Commissariat and the Defence Ministry in the projected second Five Year Plan. Pending a final decision of the government, the Commissariat was to undertake preparatory studies for an experimental atomic explosion; to provide the plutonium necessary for such studies; to prepare the assembly of a device to effect the explosion; to draw up blueprints for the construction of a factory for the separation of isotopes which would produce enriched uranium. The armed forces had the task of organizing the test and preparing the site for it. An additional protocol was signed with the Minister of Finance to elaborate the discreet methods of subsidizing the projects. Military participation in the French atomic energy programme was hereby cemented. The reference to the need for the government's final decision over the go-ahead for an atomic explosion could not in effect have meant much more than setting a target date. Preparations were so far advanced, the financial stakes were so considerable, that it had become most unlikely that the government would alter course.

* The military authorities were to contribute towards the construction of G.3 (Scheinman, p. 122).

Two important features mark the relations between the Commissariat à l'Energie Atomique and the defence establishment under the Fourth Republic. The first was their rivalry over the control of the military aspects of the atomic programme and the second was the minor role played by the military authorities in their elaboration.

Military interest in atomic energy had indeed grown steadily since 1952 and had been reinforced by the first British atomic explosion in October 1952. During the following year there appeared to have been something of a take-over bid by the Ministry of National Defence. The motives and personalities involved remain obscure. In spite of the ordinance of 1945, which gave the C.E.A. a monopoly over all matters affecting the development of atomic energy, some enthusiasts in the Defence Ministry wanted to set up a separate organ for its military applications. Pierre Guillaumat effectively protected the Commissariat's prerogatives and at the same time drew the government's attention to the need for reaching the first decisions relating to the military uses of atomic energy.

Henceforth, from the beginning of 1954, we find a steady advance on the executive and technical levels towards the manufacture of the first atomic bomb. On the 20th May of that year the Minister of National Defence, M. Pleven, officially consulted the three secretaries of state of the armed forces '. . . sur un programme atomique de défense nationale'.[19] As a direct result of this preliminary examination of the problem, a secret decree, dated the 26th October 1954, established under the authority of the Ministry of National Defence a mixed Commission Supérieure des Applications Militaires which never met, but from which emanated a Comité des Explosifs Nucléaires which met periodically. Military personnel were also seconded to the Commissariat. However, in these and subsequent arrangements the administrators of the C.E.A. exercised a dominant influence.*

* According to Lacoste Lareymondie, Guillaumat '. . . venait sans doute de subodorer que les militaires pourraient fort bien arriver à la création d'un organisme plus ou moins rival du C.E.A. Il ne pouvait en être question, car dans

Following the protocol of 1955, the effort of the military authorities divided into two branches. At the policy-making level, the Minister of National Defence set up a Cabinet Armement which was responsible for the atomic programme for national defence, as outlined in the protocol. In 1959 its functions passed to the Bureau Technique de l'Etat-Major Général des Armées.[20] At executive level, the minister established on the 13th February 1956 an inter-service organ known as the Groupe d'Etudes des Expérimentations Spéciales under the chairmanship of the Commandant des armes spéciales de l'Armée de Terre. Its principal functions consisted of the study of the technical problems posed by nuclear explosions and of organizing such tests, especially by training the necessary personnel.

Parallel to the organizational structure developed under the Defence Ministry, the Commissariat elaborated its own department responsible for military research. In December 1954 a Bureau d'Etudes Générales was established, which became the Direction des Etudes Nouvelles in 1956 and was finally transformed into the Direction des Applications Militaires (D.A.M.) in September 1958, with the threefold task of making an atomic bomb, preparing the test and carrying it out. It is important to note, however, that the Bureau d'Etudes Générales was not officially subordinate to the C.E.A. and that its Director was technically responsible to the Prime Minister. As it turned out, he enjoyed very close relations with some of the C.E.A.'s administrators, notably Guillaumat, and had an excellent understanding with them. General Albert Buchalet* was

---

son esprit l'atome ne se divise pas: volonté de puissance? réalisme technique? Sans doute les deux à la fois . . .' He also suggests that Guillaumat's concern was quickened by the navy's inspiration to build a nuclear submarine (the ill-fated Q244) after the successful construction of the first American submarine, the *Nautilus*, launched in December 1954. The navy had embarked upon the technically impracticable enterprise of placing a natural uranium reactor into the ship (pp. 22–3). In 1958 the project was written off at a loss of eight billion francs (Scheinman, p. 123, note 61).

* Born on the 2nd October 1911, General Buchalet is a Saint-Cyrien and served in the infantry. During the war he worked for the intelligence service of the

143

put in charge of the programme, assisted by Professor Rocard.

Since the spring of 1954, and possibly earlier, there had thus been a steady and accelerating orientation towards the first French nuclear explosion. It was clear to the initially small number of technicians, administrators and military personnel involved where they were going and they were eager to get there. However, this collaboration was essentially on the surface. Underneath were cross-currents of bitter rivalry, the echoes of which reverberated into the parliamentary debates of the Fifth Republic. The military compensated for their failure to control the atomic energy programme by bitter accusations that the C.E.A.'s tactics and the attitude of some of its officials seriously hindered the progress of French atomic armament.[21]

With the advent of the Fifth Republic, the relationship between the Commissariat à l'Energie Atomique and the military establishment was clarified after M. Guillaumat's appointment as Ministre des Armées in 1958.

While it is possible to sketch an outline of the technical and administrative measures which preceded the final decision to go

---

resistance and saw action in North Africa, Italy and Germany. In 1946 he was in the cabinet of the Minister of the Armed Forces under the Gouin and Bidault governments. There followed a six years' spell as services attaché in Brazil and in 1953 he was transferred to a North African command until he took over the Bureau d'Etudes Générales in March 1955. In November 1957 he was appointed Conseiller Technique of Félix Gaillard who, as Prime Minister, took the final decisions about the tests.

General Buchalet gave the following account of how he had been appointed to become the French equivalent of General Groves: 'A l'origine de cette affaire, nous a-t-il déclaré, nous étions en pleine clandestinité. Pas de tapis vert au départ, mais un petit guéridon autour duquel se trouveraient trois personnes: Mm. Guillaumat, alors à l'Energie Atomique, Villemer et Marc Boegner, représentant M. Gaston Palewski. Je passais par hasard dans le couloir, et je n'étais au courant de rien. J'ai été harponné.

' "Vous êtes militaire, vous arrivez d'Afrique du Nord, vous n'êtes pas technicien, et vous connaissez rien aux questions atomiques. Vous êtes donc l'homme qu'il nous faut." '

From a report of his press conference before L'Association des Journalistes Savoyards, *Combat*, 19–20 March 1960.

ahead with the manufacture of an atomic bomb, it is less easy to trace the course of deliberations at the political level during these years.

M. Pleven's consultation of the three secretaries of state in charge of the armed services is the first indication that the problem of French nuclear armament was being formally considered by the government. About six months later the question was put to the cabinet for consideration.

Some time in the late autumn of 1954 Pierre Mendès-France instructed his secretary of state for scientific research, M. Henri Longchambon, to ask the experts two questions: given the existing state of the French atomic programme, how long would it take to manufacture an atomic bomb and two atomic powered submarines? For how long would it be possible to continue on the present lines without a clear distinction between the programme's civilian and military aspects before one had to separate them in order to achieve the objectives set out in the first question? The answer to the first question was five years—which proved to be wildly inaccurate as far as the submarines were concerned, that to the second was three years, which meant that until 1957 governments could maintain that work in the field of atomic energy was as necessary for its peaceful development as for its military potential.

In December the whole issue was raised at cabinet level. Apart from the ministers directly concerned, a number of officials took part in the discussions, including Francis Perrin, Jules Moch, French delegate to the United Nations Atomic Energy Commission, and Etienne Hirsch, Commissaire-Général of the Economic Plan. Opinion was divided. Henri Longchambon and Jules Moch opposed any military orientation of the atomic energy programme. This view was largely shared by Francis Perrin who was, however, in favour of the submarine project. M. Edgar Faure, the Minister of Finance, sat throughout the meeting without saying a word. At length, Mendès-France decided to launch a secret programme of preparations for both a nuclear weapon and an atomic submarine, though the fall of the government cut short his initiative.[22]

The next two years were, as we have seen, particularly important in laying the groundwork for a military programme of atomic energy. Although there was no lack of official statements during this time, they were ambiguous and contradictory until the pressure of events forced the government to take the final steps which confirmed France upon the path to nuclear armament.

(v) The second Five Year Plan and the final decision to make the atomic bomb: 1957–8

The budget of the second Five Year Plan dwarfed all previous financing of the French atomic programme and is a good example of the comparative costs of creating an option and then taking it up. The sum set aside for the work and administration of the C.E.A. amounted in round figures to 200,000,000,000 francs. A further 73,000,000,000 were to come from contracts with other government departments, notably that of National Defence, while extraneous sources, chiefly the Electricité de France, were to provide an additional 76,000,000,000 to finance mining and industrial development, especially the production of electricity.[23] The C.E.A. would concentrate during this period on continuing and extending its work in the production of uranium, on research and on the development and equipment of prototypes.

The great expansion envisaged in the plan did not, however, excite public debate. The real controversy centred on the authorization of an additional sum of 25,000,000,000 francs to make a start on the construction of a factory for separating isotopes and thus produce uranium 235. This material is only rivalled as an explosive by plutonium and is a valuable supplement to natural uranium as a fuel. Since the exploitation of plutonium as a fuel was still not within sight at that time and since natural uranium cannot be used as an explosive, U235 has the great advantage of serving both purposes. The three existing nuclear powers had kept the method of producing U235 a closely guarded secret, although it had been outlined in the Smyth Report of 1945.[24]

U235 could have been bought at a much cheaper rate from the United States via the International Atomic Energy Agency or

EURATOM, but it would have meant surveillance of its use and the threat of a cut-off at a critical moment. Above all, it would have curtailed its application for military purposes.

The decision to go ahead with the construction of the plant implied willingness to make enormous sacrifices in order to ensure national independence in the production and use of fissile material. The projected factory was to be located in the communes of Pierrelatte and Saint-Paul-Trois-Châteaux in the Drôme and took its name from Pierrelatte.

Official interest in this development was not new. Scientific and technical studies had already started in the year 1948-9 when three classmates from the Ecole Polytechnique, who were employed in the Service des Poudres, formed themselves into a team to work on the separation of isotopes. In 1955 they chose another contemporary of their class, M. Besse, to be their leader and they set to work seriously. M. Besse became Director-General of La Société pour la Construction de l'Usine de Séparation Isotopique (S.U.S.I.) in 1959. By the end of 1957 an experimental chain had been built at Saclay by a consortium which grouped the C.E.A., the Compagnie Générale de Télégraphie sans Fil (C.S.F. and Ugine et Rateau. The effort had been co-ordinated by M. Pierre Couture, who succeeded M. Guillaumat as Administrator General *ad interim* in June 1958 and was later officially confirmed in that post on the 4th February 1959.*

Regardless of technical progress it was not clear before 1957 whether the government would actually want to embark on the construction of such a factory. In 1960 Pierre Guillaumat revealed that prior to the negotiations over EURATOM the French government had asked the British whether they would co-operate in building the plant at French expense. This request had been refused in 1955. A similar approach had been made to the Federal

---

* Pierre Couture is a good example of the close links between industry and the C.E.A. A *Polytechnicien*, he was trained as a mining engineer and was director of mines in the Saar from 1950 to 1957, after which he became director of the Charbonnages de France and represented that industry on the C.E.A. He was especially interested in the factory for the separation of isotopes.

German Republic but was not pursued after the start of discussions on EURATOM. Following the decision to set up EURATOM, a study group under the chairmanship of Bertrand Goldschmidt examined the possibilities of building the factory as a common enterprise. The project was finally abandoned after the report of EURATOM's 'three wise men' (Messrs. Armand, Etzel and Giordani) on their return from the United States. They pointed out that American supplies of U235 would be much cheaper and available in ever-growing quantities by the time European production was under way. Furthermore, the need for enriched uranium would become more questionable with the increasing possibilities of the industrial use of plutonium.

When France was asked to report on her progress in November 1957, only Italy had shown any interest in being associated with the project, in spite of canvassing by the C.E.A.

Co-operation with the partners in EURATOM would have meant a peaceful orientation in the production of U235 and it seems that in this case French policy suffered from the same internal contradictions which affected the government's attitude to EURATOM as a whole. In fact, it appears that if EURATOM had gone into the business, France would have tried to construct a smaller factory in which she would have refined the product from the EURATOM factory, so that it could be used for military purposes.[25]

The proposal to authorize work on the factory was quite openly linked to defence needs.* U235 was an essential fuel for

* In the report of the Finance Commission of the National Assembly, on the second Five Year Plan, it was stated that since imports of fissile materials from America could not be used for national defence: '... la France devrait donc pouvoir disposer dans un délai aussi bref que possible, pour ses besoins énergetiques et militaires d'uranium 235 enrichi ...' (Rapport No. 5263 sur le projet No. 4789 présenté par M. Max Brusset, 26 Juin 1957, p. 6).

Speaking before the National Assembly, M. François Benard, Sous-Secrétaire d'Etat à l'énergie atomique, drew up a long list of needs for which U235 was required. It included '... la fabrication d'armes stratégiques et tactiques'. (Debate on Rapport No. 5263 at National Assembly; J.O., Débats Parlementaires, 1957, A.N., 2 July 1957, pp. 3118–19.) In the debate before the Conseil de la Répub-

the motor of a nuclear-powered submarine and it seemed unlikely that the United States would provide the fissile material for this purpose. However, the major reason for seeking an independent supply of U235 was the need for France to become a thermo-nuclear power. It was evident by 1957 that nuclear independence would be an illusion unless France could keep up with the technological race. This meant the development of thermo-nuclear weapons and an appropriate means of delivery. A fission device was necessary to trigger a thermonuclear explosion. U235 would help to solve the problem of miniaturization, so that a hydrogen bomb could become operational. The original sum proposed would not, of course, have got the process sufficiently far to achieve this objective and it seemed inevitable that the factory would have to be extended at enormously increased cost to be able to produce almost pure U235 for this purpose.[26]

Technically speaking, the decision to construct the factory at Pierrelatte was taken by General de Gaulle, who converted the 'l'autorisation de dépenses', voted by the National Assembly at M. Gaillard's request, into 'crédits de paiement'. Yet in the light of previous decisions this was a mere formality. The first official intimation of the government's intentions in this respect was contained in Francis Perrin's statement during the National Assembly's debate on EURATOM in July 1956.[27] As we have noted, the protocol of the 30th November 1956 included the construction of a factory for the separation of isotopes as part of the military objectives of the second Five Year Plan. The objective became a decision in March 1957 and M. Gaillard chose the site in April 1958.

It is true that the first two sections of the projected factory would have produced fissile material for civilian use and that the original budget certainly did not go further than that.[28] But there would have been no point in planning a factory for this purpose alone, since it was clear that U235 was available more cheaply

---

lique, M. Benard omitted all mention of the military uses of U235. (*J.O.*, *Débats Parlementaires*, 1957 C.R., 17 July 1957, session of 16 July 1957, p. 1549.)

through purchase from the United States and other foreign suppliers.

Thus, the last governments of the Fourth Republic were prepared to create an option for the construction of a hydrogen bomb which was likely to be taken up once the means were available and the time was ripe, just as they took up the option to make an atomic bomb, created for them in 1952.

The decision, which the experts had told the Mendès-France government must be taken in 1957, was not reached until 1958. Budgetary restrictions and the slow progress of the piles at Marcoule accounted for the delay.* However, in the last days of the Mollet government, on the 10th May 1957, the Minister of National Defence, Bourgès-Maunoury, drew up a list of priorities for nuclear studies in which the weapon of strategic reprisal was at the head. A meeting of the Comité de Défense Nationale, held in February 1958, endorsed the policy of creating an atomic striking force.[29] On the 11th April, a few days before the fall of his government, Félix Gaillard signed the decision that all measures should be taken to prepare for a series of military test explosions to take place from the beginning of 1960.[30] On the 22nd July, General de Gaulle finally fixed the technical date of the first atomic explosion within the first trimester of 1960.

(vi) The programme after 1960

After the military programme of atomic energy had come into the open under the Gaullist regime, the Commissariat continued to have responsibility for the production of nuclear explosives. Its expansion went on unabated. By 1968 it absorbed annually the equivalent of 5 per cent of the national budget and employed thirty thousand workers.[31] In 1963 Robert Hirsch had succeeded Pierre Couture as Administrator General and continued the tradition of administration by *Polytechniciens*. Like Mm. Guillaumat and Couture before him, M. Hirsch has the background of a technocrat. Trained as an engineer, he served in the air force

* G1 was functioning below its normal strength; G2 was not at full strength until October 1958; G3 would not be in operation until the middle of 1959.

and had administrative experience as a prefect on several occasions since the war.

The C.E.A. became one of several instruments which served the government's nuclear policy. Its officials executed policy but no longer inspired the military aspect to any significant extent. Pierrelatte was the focus of attention in its work. The constant upward revision of the plant's cost was an object lesson in the spiralling expenses of a national nuclear programme for military purposes. It became the most expensive factory ever to be built in France. In the spring of 1967 the final stage of the plant came into operation. Although the exact degree of enrichment has not been revealed, it is known to be between ninety and one hundred per cent.

The main shift of emphasis and interest since 1960 has been from explosives to the means of delivery. A programme for manned aircraft and missiles to carry nuclear weapons was under way by 1958. The Mirage IV had been conceived in 1957. The rocket programme had started immediately after the war, and, after slowing down in the 1950s, was resumed with great vigour at the end of the decade.

As in other fields, Gaullist governments pushed through policies of centralization and co-ordination amid the multitude of agencies and committees which had grown up around missile and space research. The Société pour l'Etude et Réalisation d'Engins Ballistiques (S.E.R.E.B.) was founded in 1959 to direct and co-ordinate the entire missile programme while space research became the business of the Comité de Recherches Spatiales, created in 1959, under the control of the governmental delegate for scientific research who was directly responsible to the Prime Minister. This organ became the Centre National d'Etudes Spatiales (C.N.E.S.) by the law of December 1961. Professor Auger chaired the Conseil d'Administration but its first director was General Aubinière from the air force.[32]

The pattern of civil-military collaboration which dominated the military programme of the C.E.A. in its period of clandestinity was repeated in the more open missile and space research programmes. In each case ultimate control was firmly in civilian hands although the programme served primarily military purposes.

The basic decisions to create and take up the military option in the nuclear energy programme as well as to provide suitable carriers for French nuclear weapons had all been taken in the days of the Fourth Republic. Yet those who held office under it were among the most vociferous critics of Gaullist military policy. We must therefore turn to the problem of policy formulation under the Fourth Republic in order to establish the true responsibilities for the decisions which gave France her nuclear force.

References

1. For the historical background and scientific explanation of the early stages of atomic science, see the excellent first chapter of Bertrand Goldschmidt's *L'Aventure Atomique*, pp. 13–24.
2. Goldschmidt, *L'Aventure Atomique*, p. 19.
3. General André Beaufre, *Bâtir l'Avenir* (Paris, Calmann-Lévy, 1967), p. 38.
4. *The Manchester Guardian*, 24th January 1946.
5. Goldschmidt, *Les Rivalités Atomiques*, p. 50.
6. Margaret Gowing, *Britain and Atomic Energy: 1939–1945* (London, Macmillan & Co. Ltd., September 1964), pp. 168 note 3, 209–15, 290–1, 293, 295–6, 342–6. Richard G. Hewlett and Oscar E. Anderson, *The New World, 1939–46: Volume I, A History of the United States Atomic Energy Commission* (the Pennsylvania State University Press, University Park, Pennsylvania, 1962), pp. 331–2.
7. Goldschmidt, *Les Rivalités Atomiques*, pp. 85–6.
8. *Ibid.*, pp. 88–9. The uranium resources of Madagascar were considerably exaggerated at the time.
9. Scheinman, p. 10, note 20.
10. *Le Monde*, 1st November 1945.
11. Goldschmidt, *Les Rivalités Atomiques*, pp. 188–93.
12. *Le Monde*, 14th August 1945, 28th September 1949, 8th November 1951; *L'Humanité*, 24th April 1951.

13. *La France et la Puissance Atomique*, pp. 8–9; Goldschmidt, *Les Rivalités Atomiques*, p. 193. A full discussion of the technical reasons why France could not concentrate simultaneously on the production of plutonium and U235 and why she chose plutonium, is to be found in the speech of M. Max Brusset, Rapporteur of the Finance Commission, during the debate on the second Five Year Plan. *Journal Officiel, Débats Parlementaires, No. 66, A.N., 1957,* Session of 2nd July 1957, p. 3114.

14. Jean Andriot, 'Le Problème de la Production des Matières Fissiles' (*Revue Militaire d'Information*, No. 331, October 1961), pp. 5–21.

15. Goldschmidt, *Les Rivalités Atomiques*, p. 194.

16. Goldschmidt, *L'Aventure Atomique*, p. 98.

17. *Le Monde*, 12th July 1952.

18. Interview with Claude Delmas in *Combat*, 14th April 1955.

19. *La Première Explosion Atomique Française* (Notes et Etudes Documentaires, Documentation Française, Paris, No. 2648, 21st March 1960), p. 10.
    The secretaries of state were:

War	...	Pierre de Chevigné (M.R.P.)
Navy	...	Jacques Gavini (Rép. Indép.)
Air	...	Louis Christaens (Rép. Indép.)

20. The principal sources of reference for the different organs set up by the Ministry of National Defence and the Commissariat are to be found in *La Première Explosion Atomique Française*, pp. 10–13, 25; *La France et la Puissance Atomique*, pp. 18, 21. J. Perret-Gentil has also written a useful article: 'La France Puissance Atomique: Histoire, Organisation et Infrastructure', *Revue Militaire Suisse* (Avenue Gare 39, Lausanne), No. 5, May 1960, pp. 234–46, in which he analysed the organizational structure of the military programme for atomic energy.

21. See particularly the speech by Pierre de Montesquiou in the debate on the 'Loi-Programme Relative à certains Equipements Militaires' in October 1960. (*J.O., Débats Parlementaires, 1960–61, No. 67, A.N., 19th October 1960,* session of 18th October, p. 2590.)

22. For an account of these discussions see *La France et la Puissance Atomique*, p. 13; Goldschmidt, *Les Rivalités Atomiques*, pp. 206–7; *Le Monde*, 28th December 1954, 31st December 1959.

23. *La France et la Puissance Atomique*, p. 23.

24. H. D. Smyth, *Atomic Energy–A General Account of the Development of Methods of Using Atomic Energy for Military Purposes under the Auspices of the United States Government: 1940–1945* (reprinted by H.M. Stationery Office, London, 1945).

25. Pierre Drouin, *Le Monde*, 5th and 10th April 1957.

26. 'Eléments d'un Dossier sur la Force de Frappe' by an anonymous group of 'jeunes savants' and 'officiers modernes' concerned with the French nuclear programme, *Les Cahiers de la République*, No. 54–5, April–May 1963, pp. 293–4. For lucid accounts of the technical problems involved, see 'Qu'est-ce qu'une usine de séparation isotopique?' by Nicolas Vichney, *Le Monde*, 4th November 1958; and for a more official point of view, 'La Force Nucléaire Stratégique Française' by Joël Le Theule, *France-Forum*, No. 47, March–April 1963, p. 6.

27. *J.O., Débats Parlementaires, 1956, No. 78, A.N., 6th July 1956*, session of 5th July 1956, pp. 3263–4. Lacoste Lareymondie, p. 27.

28. Jules Moch, *Non à la Force de Frappe*, pp. 72–4.

29. J. R. Tournoux, 'Force de Frappe', *La Revue de Paris*, December 1960, pp. 111–12.

30. *La Première Explosion Atomique Française*, p. 5; Ailleret, *L'Aventure Atomique Française*, p. 300.

31. Goldschmidt, *Les Rivalités Atomiques*, p. 279.

32. For descriptions of the development of the French missile and space exploration programmes see Judith H. Young, *The French Strategic Missile Programme*; Commandant L. Germain, 'La Recherche Spatiale en France' (*Revue Militaire d'Information*, No. 345, January 1963), pp. 33–9; General R. Aubinière, 'Le CNES et la Politique Spatiale de la France' (*Revue de Défense Nationale*, December 1968), pp. 1791–1800.

5 · The domestic political environment

Several characteristics distinguished the debate over atomic armament under the Fourth Republic. Official statements about the government's intentions were vague and sometimes contradictory. Public discussion of the issue was conducted in a fog of half-understood facts and was usually tangential to the core of the problem. With the exception of the communists and the Gaullists, the political parties and groups did not speak with one voice. Each included some enthusiastic partisans of a French nuclear armament, some equally fervent opponents and a mass of undecided or indifferent members. Finally, a small number of people, strategically placed in various organs of the government, in the C.E.A., in the military establishment and in industry, laid the foundations of a nuclear weapons policy and at the same time persuaded a significant section of political opinion to accept the premises of such a policy.

(i) The ambiguity of declared policy

The military orientation of the atomic energy programme was a well-guarded secret, although qualified observers were not slow to note the implications of various public decisions taken before 1957. Yet the issue whether France was to possess nuclear weapons and to make them, if she was unable to buy them from her allies, was not formally debated on the government's initiative. The question was usually raised by members of parliament, or was incorporated into debates dealing with rather different problems, such as French membership of EURATOM.

With some notable exceptions, government spokesmen took shelter behind the 'option' and, even when it was time to decide, made vague references to the needs of national defence. In a sense

155

they were justified. The time factor and technical limitations postponed a final commitment at the highest level until 1957, no matter what enthusiastic officials and technicians were up to in the meanwhile. However, not all ministers were discreet and consistent in their statements, so that we find not only differences in approach among members of the same government, but one minister might very well contradict himself during his usually short spell in office.

The attitude of M. Edgar Faure is particularly illustrative of these vacillations. He was Prime Minister from the 23rd February 1955 until the 23rd January 1956 and was rather garrulous on the subject of atomic energy. Speaking at a Foreign Press Association lunch in April 1955, he explained how the rate of technical progress imposed a delay of about two years before one could take a decision whether the programme should have an orientation towards military as well as civilian purposes. The premier did not disguise his own preference for a European pool of atomic energy, though he did not specify whether this should also apply to a military programme.[1]

A week later M. Faure told a press conference that the government had decided to eliminate research devoted specifically to military uses and that it had no intention of studying the creation of an H-bomb or of 'another bomb'.[2] In view of the movement afoot to take a new step towards European integration, following the setback over EDC and the subsequent initiatives of the Benelux leaders, it is most plausible that the decision Faure referred to reflected the French government's concern for European unity. Significantly, Faure's speech included an appeal for European co-operation in this field, though he affirmed: 'Il est nécessaire que la France devienne une puissance atomique.' There was, therefore, no question of halting the atomic energy programme, only a hint that the question of nuclear arms might be resolved within a European framework.

A great deal of attention was focused on Faure's renunciation of a military programme, less was paid to a statement he made on the 21st April after a lunch meeting convened to discuss the industrial development of atomic energy. On this occasion he affirmed the intention to make France a 'great atomic power'. At first the emphasis would be on the industrial uses of atomic energy, but that did not mean 'France will renounce the eventual use for her defence of the means which may become available from progress in research and in the atomic installations'.[3] These remarks bring us back to the position of wait and see which characterized his speech at the Foreign Press Association lunch.

In so far as the development of atomic energy for military purposes was concerned, we know now that the Faure statement did not reflect a basic change of course. The problem remains why he should have felt compelled to make a series of statements in short succession, thus breaking with traditional government reticence about the atomic energy programme. Clearly, the French position had to be explained in the light of the impending negotiations over EURATOM. No-one quarrelled with the existence and development of the French effort in the nuclear field, but Faure reflected indecision as to the ultimate objectives.

The year 1955 marked a considerable relaxation of tension in the relations between the Soviet Union and the Atlantic Alliance. Edgar Faure was assiduous in exploiting the new climate in international relations. He took a prominent part in promoting the summit meeting in Geneva and launched the idea of increasing aid to underdeveloped countries by a levy on the defence budgets of the major powers. The atmosphere of goodwill also extended to the realm of atomic energy with the summoning of the first United Nations Atomic Conference at Geneva in August.

Faure's statements must be seen primarily as a personal attempt to come to terms with the atomic problem in the light of his dual conviction that France should play a leading part in world affairs but that this role should be essentially peaceful and conciliatory. The Prime Minister was under pressure because politicians, administrators, and some military leaders had been inspired by both the American and British examples. The United States had launched the world's first nuclear submarine, the *Nautilus*, and the British had decided to make an H-bomb while at the same time launching a large programme for the production of electricity from nuclear energy.

Faure's successor, Guy Mollet, was caught in even more serious contradictions. The contrast between the progressive militarization of the atomic energy programme during his term of office from the 2nd February 1956 until the 21st May 1957 and his publicly declared opposition to a French nuclear armament programme is startling. The Prime Minister maintained a fairly consistent stand on this issue, but he was constantly forced to qualify it in face of pressures within and outside his cabinet. Some evidence suggests that his public utterances may no longer have reflected his real thought at the end of his term of office and that he was convinced that France should acquire a military capability in the nuclear field.

As a known and convinced 'European', M. Mollet sincerely wanted to see EURATOM succeed. Like many others, he doubted the political and economic wisdom of embarking on a programme leading towards a European bomb, let alone a French one. EURATOM, in the opinion of many, would not be able to get off the ground without Anglo-American technical help, which was unlikely to be forthcoming if it included a military programme.

European co-operation in atomic matters did not, of course, begin in 1955. Earlier moves in this direction had been made principally under the impulse of scientists. In 1949 Louis de Broglie had called for regional research centres in Europe which would tackle projects requiring greater resources than those available in any one country. The next year UNESCO convened a conference of scientists from which emerged C.E.R.N. and the decision to construct a giant accelerator.

Parallel to the negotiations which led to EURATOM another less publicized set of negotiations established a European Nuclear Energy Agency under the auspices of O.E.E.C. Twelve nations participated in this looser and more limited organization whose work centred on three technical programmes, located in England, Belgium and Norway.

We should also note the drawn-out processes which preceded the ratification of the International Atomic Energy Agency. Proposed in December 1953 by President Eisenhower, it received Russian support on the eve of the atomic conference held in Geneva in 1955 and was finally elaborated at the United Nations Headquarters in October 1956, entering into effect exactly a year later. It did not receive enthusiastic support from France, whose delegation was instructed to oppose certain proposed controls. From the French point of view the Agency was an American-inspired creation and the government was only authorized to ratify the statutes after it had accepted a proposition of the Conseil de la République that France would never submit a request for aid to the Agency without the approval of parliament.[4]

In all these moves towards international co-operation France was prepared to accept programmes confined to a precisely limited technical collaboration, but resisted any suggestion which would have affected the freedom to control and direct her national effort in this field. EURATOM threatened to do this and in the debate over the project the question of French nuclear armament, which had become increasingly entangled with the problem of the organization of Europe during the Mendès-France and Faure governments, was finally fused with the debate over Europe.

EURATOM was the twin of the European Economic Community. Both were launched at the Messina Conference of June 1955, representing a return to the charge by the 'Europeans' after their defeat over the European Defence Community, this time with the emphasis on the functional method of building a united Europe, as it had been with the European Coal and Steel Community.

It should be noted that on the 25th July 1955 French experts had submitted a report at Brussels which envisaged European co-operation in atomic matters, while safeguarding national military programmes. As far as France was concerned, the negotiations, which lasted for two years, were dominated by the problem of safeguarding French autonomy in the military uses of atomic energy. Apart from those to whom any supra-national project was anathema, however limited it might be, the 'Europeans' divided themselves into those in favour of using EURATOM as a means whereby to become more independent of the United States, and those who thought of a Europe very closely allied to America. Their opposition crystallized over the question whether EURATOM was to construct a factory for the separation of isotopes and thus seek independence in the use of U235.

As far as her freedom to pursue a military programme was concerned, France eventually received full satisfaction from the terms of the treaty. She retained the right to undertake the production of atomic energy for military purposes and the articles referring to the ownership of fissile materials, other than natural uranium, were drafted accordingly.* France undertook not to explode an atomic device before the 1st January 1961, which was no great sacrifice since it was expected to take four years before she would have such a device.

The government, therefore, avoided the pitfalls of the proposed European Defence Community, when deputies and senators were confronted with the choice of all or nothing. It was helped by the great disparity between French progress in this field and that of the other five member states. Thus, while France insisted on her sovereign rights, her partners were correspondingly anxious to avoid another failure. Although on the surface the issues did not appear to be quite so far-reaching as they had been in the debate over EDC, the government was more flexible and ready to swim

---

* Goldschmidt, *L'Aventure Atomique*, pp. 133–4, footnote 4. 'Ainsi, d'après le Traité, et à la satisfaction des juristes, un atome d'uranium 235 pourrait plusieurs fois changer de nationalité: extrait au Limousin dans de l'uranium naturel, il serait français; mais s'il était concentré dans la future usine française de séparation isotopique, il deviendrait européen, à moins que, se trouvant dans de l'uranium à plus de 95%, il soit envoyé dans un arsenal pour servir dans une arme, auquel cas il redeviendrait français.' In this respect, the essential articles are: Arts. 84, dealing with the ownership of fissile materials; 24 and 25, safeguarding secrets for defence purposes; 62, safeguarding the national supplies of fissile material. *Communauté Européenne de l'Energie Atomique (EURATOM)*, Journal Officiel, No. 1107, 1958.

with the current. The debate showed that differences were more over the extent of EURATOM's functions than its very existence.

Before he could offer EURATOM for public debate, M. Mollet had first to get agreement within the cabinet. Maurice Faure, the Radical secretary of state at the Foreign Ministry, was in favour of the position reached at Brussels in the summer of 1956, which stipulated that none of the contracting parties would explode a nuclear weapon within the next five years, at the end of which the Community would decide on any request to be allowed to make atomic weapons. Three of the six members would have to support such a request to ensure its acceptance.

M. Bourgès-Maunoury, the Minister of National Defence, and M. Chaban-Delmas, Minister of State, strongly opposed these terms on the grounds that France would be reduced to a second-rate power, that during the period of moratorium advances in nuclear technology might enable still smaller powers to embark on a weapons programme and, finally, that France could not put her trust in finding two fellow members of EURATOM to support a request to be allowed to explode an atomic bomb.

M. Mollet eventually found a compromise and the cabinet agreed to propose that at the end of the moratorium on test explosions the desire of a country to go ahead was to be subject to mere consultation among the members of EURATOM and not to their approval. This solution was written into the final draft of the treaty.

Pressure from within the cabinet, the administration and parliament had really given the government a much more definite orientation towards a French nuclear weapons programme. For Mollet the achievement of a new step towards a united Europe and the continuation of his ministry were probably more important than the problem whether France should make an atomic bomb. The question of M. Mollet's real intentions has pursued him down the years. On several occasions he has tried to dispel suspicions of having been an artful dodger over the issue in 1956. Exactly six years later he told the National Assembly during the debate of a censure motion on the government's revised budget for 1962, that he had always opposed a national nuclear force but that his government had been willing to leave the final choice open to its successors.[5]

A motion, suitably doctored at Mollet's behest to appease some of the critics,* was passed by a substantial majority and an analysis of the vote reveals how effective his compromise had been.†

* The motion was introduced by M. Depreux on behalf of the S.F.I.O. and read as follows: 'L'Assemblée Nationale, après avoir entendu les explications du gouvernement, lui fait confiance pour aboutir à l'institution, entre le plus grand nombre possible de pays européens, d'une coopération atomique efficace, (*tout en développant pleinement l'effort atomique français, condition primordiale d'une coopération féconde;*)

'Lui demande de poursuivre les négociations en vue d'aboutir à la rédaction du traité instituant l'Euratom en conformité des principes posés dans la déclaration d'investiture sur la base du rapport de Bruxelles (*et des déclarations du président du conseil et des membres du gouvernement au cours du présent débat;*)

'De s'employer parallelement à développer la coopération atomique au sein de l'O.E.E.C. tout en facilitant à chaque pays membre de cet organisme ou même à des pays non membres la possibilité de participer ou de s'associer à l'Euratom, et repoussant toute addition, passe à l'ordre du jour.'

The passages in brackets and italics are the additions to the original motion, inserted to mollify the critics. *La France et la Puissance Atomique*, p. 21.

† The analysis of the vote was as follows:

Groups	For	Against	Did not take part for various reasons
Communists (144)	—	144	—
Progressistes (6)	—	6	—
Socialists (100)	99	—	1
Radicals (61)	29	27	5
UDSR-RDA (19)	18	—	1
RGR (14)	12	—	2
Indépendants d'Outre-Mer (9)	8	—	1
Républicains Soc. (22)	15	3	4
MRP (74)	73	—	1
Indépendants (84)	61	—	23
Paysans (14)	12	—	2
Poujadists (42)	3	—	39
Non-inscrits (5)	2	1	2
(594)	332	181	81

La France et la Puissance Atomique, p. 21.

Whatever the difficulties in trying to find out what governments really intended in so far as the military application of atomic
energy was concerned, France had never formally denied herself a
military programme in this field. Ambassador Parodi's speech at
the United Nations in June 1946, during the debate on the Baruch
Plan, should not be interpreted as a permanent French commitment to refrain from making nuclear weapons. The essential
passage of the declaration reads as follows (referring to the
creation of the C.E.A.):

> There is one outstanding feature of all these studies, plans and
> uses: they are all directed towards peaceful undertakings and
> towards activities having as their principal aim the good of
> mankind.
> I have been authorized to say that the aims which the
> French Government has set for the research work of these
> scientists and technicians are purely peaceful ones. We hope
> that all the nations of the world may do likewise as soon as
> possible and it is with this aim in view that France will readily
> submit to the rules which may be deemed best for guaranteeing
> world-wide control of atomic energy, as soon as they are
> adopted by the United Nations.[6]

The statement was not accurate, since one of the specific tasks of
the C.E.A. was to pursue its work with a view to its use in national
defence. However, given the nature of the preliminary research
and the absence of any need to make a choice between the peaceful
and military uses of atomic energy, it probably reflected French
intentions and particularly those of Joliot-Curie.[7] The last sentence
emphasizes the importance of reaching international agreement
over the control of atomic energy. While France would hasten to
submit herself to any regulations, there is a conditional note in the
statement which provided one of the main justifications for a
turning to the military uses of atomic energy. In later debates
French spokesmen insisted repeatedly that the failure to establish
international control, in the sense of inspection and verification,
liberated France from any obligation to stick to peaceful research

only, once she was in a position to develop a military programme and her security demanded it.

(ii) The public debate

Official statements did not make for an informed discussion of French atomic policy. Other reasons also militated against a sustained public debate on the military aspects of the French nuclear programme under the Fourth Republic. At first it was wholly theoretical and in the realm of speculation. In the last years of the Republic, when military preparations were actively pursued, official discretion and the so-called option prevented the matter from assuming great urgency. Unlike its experience in other spheres of national defence, the Fourth Republic was remarkably successful in keeping the secret of the growing military orientation of the atomic energy programme. In this, of course, French governments were only copying the example of other nuclear powers. At a time when the United States began to ease restrictions on sharing atomic data and technology, the French programme was entering that phase of development through which the British had just passed in the greatest secrecy.[8]

In its early stages an atomic energy programme lacks dramatic appeal. Every now and then a national newspaper would run a series of special articles to describe progress to date, usually concluding with a peep at the future world of atomic plenty. Similarly, scientists would make public pronouncements in which they would alternate between rosy prognostications and warnings against excessive optimism. All this was not sufficient to stimulate debate over French atomic policy and to distract attention from far more absorbing domestic politics and, later, from the growing preoccupation with the war in Algeria.

Above all, the military financing of the programme was largely hidden from the public eye. In contrast, the official budgets of the C.E.A. until 1957, though increasing steadily, were small when compared with the total national budget, arousing only cursory attention and no serious controversy, except in so far as the sums were deemed to be insufficient. In any event, there was almost unquestioning approval of the principle that France should have her own atomic industry. Nevertheless, if atomic policy caused only a few ripples in the pool of public debate, it would equally not be true to suggest that there was no discussion at all.

The first major political debate which involved the C.E.A. focused on the position of Joliot-Curie at its head. Frédéric Joliot-Curie was undoubtedly the most distinguished nuclear scientist in France. Born in 1900, he became Madame Curie's 'préparateur particulier' in 1925. His doctoral thesis was on polonium, one of the two elements–the other was radium–discovered and isolated by Pierre and Marie Curie. He married the Curies' daughter, Irène, and with her won the Nobel Prize for chemistry in 1935 for their discovery of induced radioactivity. He became professor at the Collège de France and was director of the Centre National de la Recherche Scientifique before becoming High Commissioner of the C.E.A. In 1943 he was elected to the Académie des Sciences.

Politically Joliot had always been on the left, though of an independent turn of mind. In 1939 he had signed the manifesto of French intellectuals, expressing their 'stupéfaction' at the Nazi–Soviet Pact. He had chosen to remain in France under the occupation and became president of the Front National in 1941. He joined the Communist Party a year later and became a member of its central committee in 1944. After the war he was active in the communist-controlled Stockholm Peace Movement and in the 'Partisans de la Paix'.

Joliot-Curie had a complex personality. Beneath a brilliant exterior he appeared to be rather unsure of himself and wanted to be popular and appreciated by his colleagues. These characteristics may have accounted for his decision to remain in France during the war, rather than work in a strange country where he might not have stood out so much among other brilliant atomic scientists. After the war the Communist Party probably played upon his need to be liked and to belong. In 1950 he was forced to choose between his views and those of the party. He chose the latter and it cost him his job.[9]

DOMESTIC POLITICS

The effects of the Cold War had made themselves felt in the French atomic energy programme for some time before the events of 1950. There had been rumblings about communist infiltration into the Commissariat and there were hints that American help might be more forthcoming if the communists were eliminated from the French nuclear effort. The criticisms came from within and outside the country.[10]

The stage was therefore set for a major crisis over the position of an avowed communist at the head of the Commissariat. Curiously enough, the controversy broke as the result of differences between Joliot-Curie and the Communist Party. Answering criticisms in the foreign press that Russia would obtain atomic secrets via the French Communist Party, Joliot-Curie told an audience of the Anglo-American Press Association in January 1949 that the results of research which might possibly have military applications should be kept secret as long as nuclear weapons were not outlawed by the United Nations. A communist, like any Frenchman employed by the government, could not honestly think of sharing the fruits of his labours with a foreign power since they did not belong to him but to the collectivity which had permitted him to work.[11]

This statement, while revealing that Joliot-Curie was a patriot as well as a communist, led to confused reports of reprimands by the Communist Party. The climax came with Joliot-Curie's speech at the national congress of the party at Gennevilliers in April 1950, of which the essential passage reads as follows:

> Progressive scientists and communist scientists will never give one particle of their knowledge to make war against the Soviet Union. We shall stand firm, sustained by our conviction that in acting thus we serve France and the whole of humanity.[12]

Whether the speech was an attempt to make amends for his lapse in front of the Anglo-American Press Association, as was widely believed at the time, or whether it revealed serious differences with the government over the direction of nuclear policy, the government could not ignore the challenge. It announced Joliot-

Curie's dismissal on the 28th April 1950. Except for the communists, there was widespread political support for its action.

One might ask how far Joliot-Curie's dismissal was related to any thought of turning the work of the Commissariat to military purposes. Obviously, developments had not yet reached the stage where military production could be envisaged. Nor did the government show any signs of wishing to allot sufficient funds to make such an effort possible. This does not, however, rule out tentative discussions about a military programme in which Joliot-Curie might have taken part. Such a problem had already been raised in public from time to time. It is also interesting that national defence was among the principal reasons advanced for his dismissal and this not only by those who had made Joliot-Curie their target for some years but by the Prime Minister himself.

Although the question of security in the Commissariat continued to exercise parliament, from 1952 onwards there was a clear shift away from preoccupation with communist infiltration and betrayal to an emphasis on the military potential of the atomic energy programme. This was obviously related to the government's choice of plutonium production as the way in which to launch the programme's industrialization.

Apart from a brief discussion of the first Five Year Plan and from the debates on the defence budget, during which the government was under mounting pressure from the small number of deputies who took an interest in these matters to commit itself to a national atomic armament, the next major discussion over policy in the field of atomic energy occurred during the EURATOM debate. The subject caused deep division between parties and within parties because it combined the controversial question of European unity with that of an independent nuclear armament. In the end it was not always clear which of the two issues dominated individual votes.

Although Guy Mollet had achieved a satisfactory compromise over EURATOM within the government, the debate continued within the political parties and in the columns of the press. The

167

strongest attack against EURATOM came from some Gaullists, the extreme right and the communists. A few days before Mollet's investiture in January 1956, General de Gaulle had paid his first visit to the C.E.A. At the end of a tour of Saclay he warned the leaders of the Commissariat that the ongoing 'European negotiations' threatened the loss of national independence.[13]

The Social Republicans, who liked to think of themselves as Gaullists though they had been disowned by the General and did not always follow his line, were uncertain in their attitude. Some shared the extreme views of Michel Debré, who had severed his connection with the parliamentary group on account of his anti-European stand.[14] More moderate on the whole, the party expressed a firm conviction that France should make nuclear weapons and it was prepared to accept EURATOM on four conditions: France should have full freedom in military research; she should give priority to the construction of a factory for the separation of isotopes; she should retain separate membership in the International Atomic Energy Agency and not be represented by EURATOM; there should be no parallel between the organization of EURATOM and that of the European Coal and Steel Community.

The Radical Socialists held a party caucus where they had considerable differences over EURATOM, but agreed on one important item: the right of France to make atomic weapons. Their disagreements centred on EURATOM's role in this respect. Bourgès-Maunoury, as Minister of National Defence, viewed the treaty's provisions with some hesitation at first, but was reassured by the Mollet compromise. Gaillard, while in favour of EURATOM, wanted to eliminate the imposed period of delay before the first explosion. Mendès-France, true to his policy as Prime Minister, wanted to include the United Kingdom in EURATOM and to link it to Western European Union. His opposition was, however, more emphatically directed against the Common Market. In the division at the end of the debate in the Assembly the Radicals divided into almost equal halves.

Before the government's compromise proposals had become

clear there had been similar divisions among the Indépendants and the U.D.S.R., but the groups were overwhelmingly favourable when it became known that there was no danger of interference in the French defence programme. Because of their 'European' inclinations, the M.R.P. and the socialists were generally favourable to EURATOM. The two most notable pacifistic speeches came from members of these two parties. Félix Gouin, a former socialist Prime Minister, recalled Einstein's warnings, reminded the deputies of Parodi's statement at the United Nations, and asked whether this was the moment to talk in terms of French nuclear arms when there were signs of a relaxation of international tensions. In any event, he preferred French security to be based on NATO. M. P.-H. Teitgen (M.R.P.) spoke of the futility of concentrating on the construction of a few outdated bombs and thus running the risk of losing the economic war which would be waged against France.[15]

It has been suggested, despite Mollet's assertion to the contrary, that the vote really marked parliamentary approval of a French atomic bomb. This is an exaggeration. The substantial government majority could be assembled precisely because the motion and the tenor of government statements during the debate satisfied both 'Europeans' and 'anti-Europeans', 'nuclear armers' and 'nuclear disarmers'. If the issue had been more clear-cut with a definite commitment to a French nuclear armaments programme, the division might have been much more even and the outcome doubtful. Most of the M.R.P. and socialists might well have joined the communists, the Progressistes, a number of Radicals and possibly some Indépendants and others in opposition. Equally, some opponents, like General Koenig, and some abstentionists, like Pierre André and Jacques Soustelle, would have supported such a motion.

An examination of parliamentary attitudes towards the atomic energy programme must take into account the composition and functioning of the important committees which, as time went on, acquired considerable powers in shaping legislation. Working more on the American than British pattern, the committees of the

National Assembly examined all government and private members' bills, summoned ministers and permanent officials for private hearings and eventually prepared a draft report on the proposed measure to be submitted to the National Assembly. The subsequent debate took place on the bill as amended by the committee, thus placing the government at a disadvantage.

In theory, the committees were supposed to reflect the political composition of the National Assembly. In practice the members chosen from the various political parties and groups frequently represented a minority view within their own group. Max Lejeune, one of the few socialists convinced of the necessity of a national nuclear armament, was chairman of the committee of national defence from July to December 1954. Other chairmen of this body were equally ardent supporters of a French atomic weapons programme, notably the conservative deputy Pierre Montel and the Gaullist General Koenig.* All three at other times held government posts intimately concerned with the effect of atomic energy on national defence. Hence, those in government working towards this end were often ably seconded by the National Assembly's principal spokesmen on defence. The prestige and influence of committee chairmen and rapporteurs were further enhanced because, in the eyes of their fellow deputies, they were the experts possessing inside knowledge acquired at closed committee hearings. Their views were given special weight in press reports of parliamentary proceedings.

Under the Fifth Republic the importance of the parliamentary committees declined with the diminishing importance of parliament. Moreover, so far the government has had a solid majority which assured the smooth passage of its military programme. Thus the confusion which had marked the public debate under the Fourth Republic disappeared with the advent of the Fifth Republic. The debate over French defence policy was clear-cut. The government and its supporters openly affirmed their intention to create a small

* Pierre Montel held the post from January 1949 to July 1951 and from January 1955 to October 1957. General Koenig held the post from August 1951 to July 1954.

nuclear force which would sustain a vigorous and independent foreign policy. By the mid-sixties it became apparent that the object was to establish a policy which it would be impossible to reverse. M. Messmer has insisted that no-one would throw atomic bombs on the scrap-heap; no-one would convert nuclear-powered submarines to diesel-powered submarines; no-one would shut down Pierrelatte and no-one would make France re-enter the Atlantic Treaty Organization.[16]

Every five years the debate reached a crescendo during the discussions over the next 'loi-programme'. French nuclear policy also featured in periodic discussions of the government's European and Atlantic policies.

The arguments used by the various opposition groups may be summarized under the headings of economics, strategy and foreign policy. We shall take a closer look at the economic arguments later in this chapter. They had the most appeal because they appeared to be most relevant to the prevailing social and economic malaise which found its dramatic expression in the popular explosion of May 1968. The best chance of arousing public feeling against the government's military policy was by making it into a bread and butter issue. Lack of funds for social services and housing, a shortage of scientific and technical personnel, the hopeless inadequacy of the educational system–all these could be attributed to the government's atomic extravagance.

A handful of sophisticated people, including some military commentators, criticized the policy on grounds of military strategy. Apart from the obvious question about the effectiveness of the proposed strategic force, there were doubts about its credibility because of inadequate support from the conventional arms. With the unfolding of the second Five Year Plan the gap between French nuclear and conventional armaments became alarming. Opposition on purely military grounds was mixed with some special pleading on the part of those who represented particular service interests. During the debate on the military budget for 1968, M. Frédéric-Dupont, one of the earliest apostles of French nuclear armament, proposed to cut appropriations for the second generation of the strategic nuclear force in the interests of the conventional forces.[17] His amendment was narrowly defeated by 242 against 239.

In the last analysis, these and other criticisms turned on the question of the effect of French nuclear armament on international relations. Many feared the impact of the French example on potential nuclear weapon states in general and the Federal Republic of Germany in particular. The government's propensity for 'going it alone' alarmed the protagonists of European unity. The opposition divided into schools of thought at this point. One group wanted to see the 'force de dissuasion' as the nucleus of a European defence community which the British might eventually join, thus laying the foundations of a truly independent European policy. It seemed to them that this approach would offer a more effective guarantee that France and Europe would not fall under the control of the Americans or the Russians than would the creation of an inadequate national nuclear force.

The second school had a stronger Atlantic orientation and argued for a European nuclear force within the context of partnership with the United States. Various formulae were proposed. Some suggested a return to the system of allied command which was worked out in the last months of the First World War. Others wanted a continental European deterrent force within the NATO framework, which might deploy tactical nuclear weapons and thus complement the Anglo-American strategic forces. Still others sought the solution in some structural changes within NATO which would give the Europeans a greater say in the formulation of allied strategic policy and a greater control over whether or not American strategic power should be used in their part of the world.[18]

Except for those who believed that the national economy could not stand the strain of a nuclear military policy and those who considered an independent nuclear force as military nonsense, the quarrel of most opponents of the government's policy was less with the existence of some form of national nuclear force and more with the purposes it was intended to serve. This largely explains why some of those who had not strenuously opposed – to say the least – the military orientation of the atomic energy programme under the Fourth Republic were nonetheless determined opponents of the government's policy under de Gaulle.

The political and parliamentary scene we have described must be seen against the background of a public opinion only fitfully disturbed by atomic problems. The public was first exercised about these matters immediately after the war, following the impact of the bombardment of Hiroshima and Nagasaki. In the middle fifties there was further widespread discussion when a conjuncture of events and developments concentrated attention on the devastating power of the new weapons and the need for France to define her position towards the nuclear arms race. Finally, in 1959–60, when the manufacture of atomic weapons entered the realm of practical politics, the issue aroused some of the reflexes which were noticeable in Britain in earlier years.

A systematic sampling of public opinion was not undertaken until 1957, although an apparently random poll in 1946 revealed that 56 per cent of those asked wanted France to make her own atomic bombs.[19] In 1957 a majority believed that without atomic weapons a country could not play a major role in world affairs, but an even larger majority thought that France should give priority to the peaceful uses of atomic energy as against the making of atomic weapons. Only 3 per cent were of the opinion that the civilian and military programmes were equally important.[20] From then onwards the question of French atomic armament was posed more systematically and was frequently related to international negotiations for a test ban treaty. The replies showed that the public was influenced by the progress of international negotiations. In brief, as long as Britain and the United States – but especially Britain[21] – did not renounce or at least share their nuclear weapons, a strong current of public opinion supported French efforts at creating an independent deterrent. During the test ban treaty negotiations and after its signature, the number of those in favour of a French nuclear striking force decreased proportionately until they were outnumbered by those opposed to it, except for one occasion in November 1963.[22] Although the partisans of a national nuclear force were in the majority two years later, those who believed in its efficacy were in the minority.[23]

If we take the figures of all the polls cited, it is indeed remarkable that, apart from the sampling taken in 1946, on no occasion had the supporters of French nuclear armament a clear majority over those opposed or undecided. Regardless of this indication that the general public has been unenthusiastic, to say the least, over the military projects of the Gaullist Republic, the issue of French nuclear armament played an unimportant role in its electoral politics. One may perhaps infer from the evidence that it is very difficult to take a stand of outright opposition to a programme which has been pushed through at considerable expense and effort, however unpopular it might be. Whatever the conclusions to be drawn from these not always consistent trends in public opinion, it is clear that international developments in this field influenced public opinion even if they did not affect the policies of the governments under de Gaulle.

Unless political or moral considerations, as with communists or pacifists, dominated thinking on this problem, the positions for or against a French atomic striking force were principally dictated by assessments of the chances of creating the force and by analyses of the politico-strategic situation in which France found herself and about which there was room for differences.

The public lacked the technical sophistication to understand the problem in depth. Accordingly it had to rely upon the experts for their judgment as to whether a French nuclear force was a feasible proposition or not. Since the experts themselves were divided and official comment was ambiguous, it is not surprising that the whole question did not arouse much concern under the Fourth Republic. The fact that the Communist Party claimed to have monopolized the cause of peace was a powerful inducement to caution among independent-minded people before they committed themselves to campaigns against atomic weapons.

Under President de Gaulle, public concern over French nuclear armament and the international arms race was at first over-shadowed by the passions of the Algerian war. After 1962 it was lost in the phase of 'apolitisme' which came to an abrupt end in 1968. The great revival of political debate in the last year of the General's rule did not include significant discussion of military policy. However, the circumstances which gave rise to the debate will undoubtedly have important consequences in the field of national defence.

(iii) **The role of economic arguments in the public debate**
The arguments advanced in support of setting up the C.E.A. at the end of the war were mainly concerned with the need to ensure for France the position of a great industrial nation. No-one believed that France would be able to make a bomb without years of effort and some doubted whether she would ever have the capacity to make such a weapon. The potential military interest of nuclear energy could not, however, be denied and was embodied in the presence of the chairman of the Comité de Co-ordination des Recherches concernant la Défense Nationale on the Commissariat's board.

The discussions about the military applications of atomic energy might have lacked reality in the early post-war years, but it seems that the industrial potential of the atomic programme, particularly as a source of energy, provided the immediate justification for launching it in the straitened circumstances of post-war France.

The only two references to the C.E.A. in the last volume of de Gaulle's war memoirs explicitly link its creation to the need for developing national sources of energy.[24] This emphasis on atomic energy as a source of industrial strength did not, of course, preclude its use to enhance France's position in world politics. In whatever he did, the General's basic objective was to restore France to her place in the concert of powers from which she had been excluded during the war.

The concern over supplementing sources of energy during the first ten years of the C.E.A.'s existence is easily understood in the light of the country's historic industrial weakness when compared with its neighbour across the Rhine. French industrialization had lagged in the latter half of the nineteenth century partly because of the shortage of iron and coal. Although the possession of Alsace-Lorraine and, until 1935, of the Saar had largely remedied this position after 1919, French industrial progress had been relatively slow throughout the period between the world wars. The war of 1939 to 1945 had underlined more than ever that a strong industrial base was a prerequisite of a powerful nation. By 1945 the growing importance of oil as a source of energy and the possibility of using atomic energy to produce electricity reflected themselves in the French search for oil and uranium which offered an escape from a traditional industrial inferiority.

The problem of developing new sources of energy was one of the principal reasons advanced in support of each major step in the national atomic energy programme. It lay at the basis of the measures which set up the C.E.A. in 1945.

During the discussions over the first Five Year Plan in 1952 there were those who wondered at the unusually high credits which seemed to be contrary to the government's traditional makeshift policies as far as the budget was concerned. Félix Gaillard has, however, insisted that his motives were governed by the prospect of the industrial exploitation of nuclear energy.[25]

The necessity of developing new sources of energy was the principal reason advanced in support of French membership of EURATOM. It was heavily underlined in the declarations of Francis Perrin and Louis Armand before the National Assembly in July 1956. The government had resorted to the rare expedient of inviting the two experts to address the deputies and thereby to lend weight to its policy. According to Louis Armand, of all members of O.E.E.C. France imported the largest amount of energy.[26] The whole of his speech was a plea for the speedy ratification of EURATOM as the enormous complexity of the atomic industry required a larger unit to be effective and efficient than France could provide by herself.

The arguments of the specialists were seconded by other

speakers in the debate, one of whom, M. Pierre July, calculated that in 1955 France had an energy deficit equivalent to thirty-nine million tons of coal and that within ten years it would be between fifty-two and sixty-five million tons.

The official 'exposé des motifs' of the second Five Year Plan of 1957 again emphasized the importance which the government attached to the search for new sources of energy. The intention was to free France from the strain imposed on her balance of payments, particularly with the United States, as a result of having to import her sources of energy. Neither national coal nor oil resources had so far proved sufficient to meet her needs in this respect. Even when the full extent of the Saharan oil and natural gas reserves became known by the end of the 1950s and in the early 1960s, it was still thought necessary to develop nuclear sources of electricity to meet the ever-growing demands of French industry.

There has never been a serious dispute that France should develop a nuclear capacity in order to meet her energy needs. The controversy has, however, centred on the method in which to meet them. In simple terms, those who defend the chosen course insist that the increasing emphasis on a military programme has served two functions. It has provided the stimulus and financial support which would not otherwise have been forthcoming and it has provided the uneconomic and complex industrial infrastructure on the basis of which the French nuclear industry could become competitive.

It is significant that these arguments were first developed around 1954-5 at a time when some military circles were beginning to show a serious interest in the French atomic programme and when the first sustained arguments for a French nuclear armament began to appear in the press. Colonel Ailleret wrote with reference to the peaceful and military applications of atomic energy that, as in other instances, military applications were opening the way to the pacific uses of atomic energy.[27] He went on to argue that only the military establishment could afford the expense involved in starting an atomic industry, especially as it took much longer to put nuclear energy to profitable peaceful use than to develop it militarily. He pushed home his thesis by pointing to the examples of the United States, the Soviet Union and the United Kingdom, all of which were on the threshold of using nuclear energy for industrial purposes after having exploited it first for military ends. Ailleret's arguments were echoed in the press and in parliament.

During the debate over the second Five Year Plan the military emphasis of the programme was apparent to all observers, but was never admitted by official spokesmen. Thus it was asserted that the object of the plan was twofold: the production by the Electricité de France (E.D.F.) of electricity from atomic energy and the development of the central programme of the C.E.A.[28] Notwithstanding, it was freely admitted that military backing, the extent of which was 'difficilement chiffrable', made an important financial contribution to the programme. The hint was thrown out that precisely because of this factor, France had risen to fourth rank among the nuclear powers, surpassing Canada whose programme was wholly oriented towards civilian uses.

When the military programme was at last in the open with the 'loi-programme', which covered the years from 1960 to 1964, it was argued that without the military interest funds would not have been found to finance Pierrelatte. The same was held to apply to aeronautical and ballistic studies.[29]

With remarkable consistency, therefore, the supporters of a military programme from 1954 onwards held that such a programme was essential to lay sound foundations on which to build an industrial programme. Until 1960 the argument was so phrased as to imply that the civilian objectives of the French atomic energy programme could only be fulfilled with military help. After 1960, when the priority of military objectives was officially admitted, it was claimed that a military orientation was necessary so that later an industrial programme could be built on its successes.

Both these arguments were vigorously challenged as soon as they were presented to the public. Following M. Pleven's speech

178

in the budget debate of 1954, foreshadowing a military programme of atomic energy, the military correspondent of *Le
Monde* warned that French resources were too small, so that a
programme of nuclear armament would seriously handicap a
programme for the industrial exploitation of atomic energy.[30]
This view was subsequently repeated many times by experts,
politicians and private individuals.

The confrontation of the two viewpoints crystallized in the
debate over the second Five Year Plan, the main issue of which
was the decision to go ahead with plans for building a factory to
separate isotopes. Broadly speaking, the arguments advanced in
support of this enterprise rested on four assumptions: plutonium
was only useful for nuclear explosions, U235 could also be
applied to the propulsion of submarines; the production of
plutonium under the existing programme was too limited and too
small for the build-up of a stock of bombs; the United States
would never sell U235 for military use; France must be independent in all aspects of her nuclear policy.

Each of these points was countered by the opponents of the
project. In fact, Francis Perrin had provided them with their
ammunition in his speech during the debate on EURATOM a
year earlier. After he had reviewed the uses of U235 he concluded
that it was only in the first stage of industrialization that the
production of U235 could play an important role and was
clearly distinguished from the method which only used the
natural uranium-plutonium cycle. He did not disguise the limited
interest which such an undertaking had in his eyes, especially as
France was only two years behind Britain in the industrial
production of atomic energy.[31]

In 1957 the critics argued that France should concentrate on
developing the use of plutonium for industrial purposes, on
building breeder reactors and on fundamental research. They
insisted that it would take at least four to five years to build a
factory for the separation of isotopes and that in the meanwhile
the development of breeder reactors would make its product less
interesting. Since they opposed the military application of U235

they pointed out that the fissile material could be bought from the United States at half the price compared with the cost of production. Finally, with the Suez adventure fresh in their minds, they emphasized that a small nuclear power could not operate independently of the nuclear giants.

These arguments assumed greater substance as the years went by and since 1960 there has been an ever heavier barrage of criticism raising serious doubts whether the French economy could stand the strain of nuclear armament. The thesis that military needs help industrial development has been powerfully challenged. Thus, France had to buy foreign plutonium to activate its first experimental plutonium reactor at Cadarache. The factory at Pierrelatte, built at enormous cost, is too small and limited to serve a civilian programme. Plans for its extension exist but if the government balks at the cost, which it might well do after the events of 1968, then all the effort and resources poured into the enterprise will have yielded no benefit to the national economy. The problem is not confined to the production of nuclear explosives, but applies as much, or possibly more, to the means of their delivery. For example, the engines for the Mirage III and IV are of no use in developing the super-Caravelle, for which Rolls-Royce provided the engine. The insatiable demands of the military programme caused even those who were not wholly unsympathetic to the aims of government policy to question the wisdom of its extent.

While it is possible, therefore, to maintain that military needs often provide a fillip to scientific and technological progress, there soon comes a time when work on the military application of atomic energy is far removed from its civilian uses.

(iv) The pressures within the machinery of government

If we were to set side by side organizational charts illustrating the formal policy-making machinery of the Fourth and Fifth Republics, we should see at a glance the essential difference in the two systems of government. The one of the Fourth Republic would represent a profusion of committees, councils and authorities linked to each other by many and devious strands, the whole spreading horizontally across the page. The one of the Fifth Republic would have a vertical aspect, all lines from the various bodies and authorities converging at the apex of a pyramidal structure.

The formal machinery of government is, however, only of marginal interest in a study of the origins of the nuclear weapons programme and its subsequent development. Under the Fourth Republic a comparatively small and scattered group of men exercised pressure at key points in the governmental apparatus and thus furthered decisions at the highest political level which led to the establishment of a nuclear weapons programme. A number of these men occupied important positions in the first eleven years of the Fifth Republic and thus became the executants of a policy whose outlines were decided by President de Gaulle.

From 1945 until 1957 a handful of permanent officials and private individuals exercised a profound influence over the long-term formulation of nuclear policy. They included those in charge of the C.E.A., civilians and military men who held key positions in state organs primarily concerned with national defence, and some industrialists. Their position *vis-à-vis* the politicians was strengthened because they were sheltered from the buffetings of the ever-changing political wind, because they were the experts, and because they did not have to answer to the National Assembly for their views and actions. The points of intersection between them and their political masters were in the Prime Minister's office and in the Ministry of Defence.

The C.E.A. was particularly favoured as its special statute kept it well away from public scrutiny. After 1951 it was hardly affected by the turmoil of the political arena. The personnel of its highest posts presented a picture of remarkable continuity. During the first twenty-three years the C.E.A. had two High Commissioners and four Administrators General.* The first High

* *High Commissioners:*

               Frédéric Joliot-Curie   1945–50
               Francis Perrin   1950–

Commissioner, Joliot-Curie, steadfastly opposed the military application of the French atomic energy programme. His successor,
Francis Perrin, was much more 'nuancé' in his expressions of
opinion, but there is substantial evidence that he did not like the
militarization of the programme.[32]

In contrast to the attitude of the two men who presided over the
scientific work of the C.E.A., the Administrators General were
much more favourable to its militarization. Raoul Dautry died
too soon to be intimately involved in this development, though
early on he had understood the importance of atomic energy for
the nation. After leaving the C.E.A. Guillaumat first became
Minister of the Armed Forces and then minister responsible for
atomic energy, thus retaining his close association with the
military side of the programme.* His successor, Pierre Couture,
was an example of the technicians who worked so effectively on
the execution of the programme.

The 'eminence grise' of the administrator-technicians was M.
Lescop, whose appointment to the ill-defined post of Secretary-
General of the C.E.A. in 1948 was hardly noticed. A *Polytechnicien*, he came from the Direction des Etudes et Fabrications
d'Armements (D.E.F.A.). He occupied a key position as a kind of
liaison officer between the different branches of the C.E.A. and
was principally responsible for the planning and execution of its
reorganization in 1951.

One writer has described the nationalist spirit of the men who
worked on the technical aspects of the military development of
the atomic energy programme, noting that their feelings were
related to their wartime experiences when they had seen France

---

Administrators General and Governmental Delegates:

Raoul Dautry	1945–51
Pierre Guillaumat	1951–8
Pierre Couture	1958–63
Robert Hirsch	1963–

* He was Minister of the Armed Forces from June 1958 until February 1960 and
minister for atomic energy from March 1960 until 1962 when he was succeeded
by Gaston Palewski.

humiliated not only at the hands of her enemies but by her allies as well.[33] On the other hand, even after the purge of communists in 1950–1, many of the scientists of the C.E.A., like their chief, appear to have been much more reserved towards the military programme.

Among the military a few men were most intimately concerned with the work aimed at creating a French atomic armament. Apart from General Buchalet, another officer closely associated with the planning was Colonel Charles Ailleret who became Chief of Staff of the Armed Forces in 1962 and remained in that post until his death in an air crash in 1968. Ever since he was appointed Commandant des Armes Spéciales in 1952, he was interested in the military exploitation of atomic energy and became a vocal and influential advocate of a national nuclear force.* With the help of a small band of collaborators, Ailleret hammered away at official indifference and caution in order to persuade the political and military leadership of the need for a national nuclear armament. He met with limited success as he operated from the narrow base of a technical organ attached to the army. The President of the Comité d'Action Scientifique de la Défense Nationale accused him of meddling in affairs which were outside his competence. The service staffs were absorbed in colonial wars or the French membership of NATO. In the military schools there was a reluctance to embrace new strategic and tactical doctrines. Among the scientists only Jean Thibaud was sympathetic to his ideas because, as Ailleret suspected, it might serve his career and place him in the position of taking over a weapons production programme when the time was ripe. Only the Army Chief of Staff, General Clément Blanc, gave him and his colleagues full support

* Charles Ailleret was born on the 26th March 1907. A *Polytechnicien*, he specialized in artillery. From 1942 he played a distinguished role in the resistance. After a brief and unhappy spell at S.H.A.P.E., Ailleret was appointed Commandant des Armes Spéciales in January 1952. Five years later, on the 1st February 1958, he became Commandant inter-armées des Armes Spéciales. It should be noted, however, that the Commandement des Armes Spéciales in its early years was principally concerned with studies of the effects of nuclear weapons and that it was a small operation.

183

and encouragement. Ailleret provided ammunition for the speeches of various parliamentary advocates of a national nuclear armament and during the debate over EURATOM may have influenced Reynaud in taking a stand favourable to keeping open the military option. The Commandement des Armes Spéciales was also behind the plan to establish a military division of the C.E.A. which was unsuccessfully espoused in the Conseil de la République by Mm. Edgard Pisani and de Maupeou in June 1956.[34]

The career of Charles Ailleret was, however, an excellent example of the secondary role which the military played in the first eleven years of the atomic energy programme. Until 1960 his chief activities were to publicize the advantages of a national nuclear strategy and to organize the first test explosions. He was only indirectly associated with the decisions which led to the creation of a French atomic armament.

Thus the technicians and administrators, notably M. Guillaumat, kept firm control over the whole field of atomic research and technology. For example, the first major committee created by the Defence Ministry to deal with French atomic armament, the Commission Supérieure des Applications Militaires, did not include Colonel Ailleret, but M. Guillaumat. The latter's task was much facilitated by his good working relationship with General Crépin, at that time Inspecteur Général des Fabrications et Programmes des Forces Armées, one of the few members of the military hierarchy who actively supported a military programme of atomic energy.

The influence of private industry is at first sight obscure. In its relations with industrial concerns the C.E.A. occupied a half-way house between the co-ordinating functions of the American Atomic Energy Commission and the virtual monopoly of the United Kingdom Atomic Energy Authority. The research establishments and the plutonium producing plant were directly under the control of the Commissariat, as were all matters relating to the study and manufacture of nuclear weapons. The exploitation of nuclear energy for purely industrial purposes, which meant the

184

production of electricity, was left to other enterprises, notably the Electricité de France. The search for and mining of raw materials was originally in the hands of the C.E.A., but its policy of purchasing minerals at guaranteed prices encouraged private mining which, by 1962, accounted for about one-fifth of the national production.

The construction of the factory at Pierrelatte was placed in the hands of an industrial group. In 1958 several leading banking houses formed la Compagnie de Financement de l'Industrie Atomique (CONFINATOME) and were joined by several more in the following year.* The importance of their role became apparent when the charges for the French effort in the nuclear field amounted to three per cent of the national budget by 1962.

The participation of private and nationalized industry increased further after the decision in 1960 to create a 'Force de Dissuasion Nationale' with its consequent shift in emphasis from the manufacture of nuclear explosives to the means of their delivery. When parliament voted the first slice of the credits for aeronautical construction under the 'loi-programme' creating the nuclear striking force, more than three-quarters of the sum went to the firms controlled by Marcel Dassault.

The power and influence of this man as a result of his control over an industrial and commercial empire ranging from banks and aircraft production to supermarkets, cinemas and bowling alleys symbolize the role of industry in the affairs of state in general and in the nuclear programme in particular. He had

* The founder members were: L'Union Parisienne
L'Union Européenne
Rothschild Frères
Banque Mobilière Privée
They were joined in 1959 by: Banque d'Indochine
Comptoir National d'Escompte
Crédit Industriel et Commercial
Lazare Frères
The Société Générale and L'Union des Mines were co-opted on to its administrative council. D. Ollivier, 'La Force de Frappe et les Sociétés Financières', *Economie et Politique–Revue Marxiste*, January 1961, p. 75.

backed the Gaullist Rassemblement du Peuple Français (R.P.F.) from its earliest days, entering the National Assembly under its mandate in 1951. Those associated with him and his enterprises include General P.-M. Gallois, ardent propagandist for the national nuclear striking force, Guillain de Bénouville, who directs *Jours de France* (owned by Dassault), M. Chalandon, one-time secretary-general of the Union pour la Nouvelle République (U.N.R.), and many technicians and officers, principally connected with the air force.

The ramifications of M. Dassault's interests provided a link between technicians, military men, industrialists and politicians who favoured the development of the French nuclear striking force. It is not surprising, therefore, that his brother, General Dassault, administrator of the Commercial Bank of Paris, the financial hub of the Dassault industrial empire, was an eloquent advocate of nuclear weapons in early 1956.[35]

The ideas and aspirations of the various interest groups were fed into the political level of government through the Prime Minister's administrative organ, the Secrétariat Général du Gouvernement, and through the 'cabinets ministériels', particularly those of ministers and secretaries of state responsible for national defence.

The importance of the secretariat's role[36] was enhanced by the Prime Minister's key position in the cabinet. Under the constitution of the Fourth Republic he was recognized as the official leader of the ministerial team and certain important governmental responsibilities were permanently in his keep and could only be delegated by his authority. These responsibilities included national defence, which he usually delegated by special decree to one of his colleagues. The Prime Minister was also responsible for the C.E.A. Moreover, all secretaries of state, including those responsible for administering departments which fell under another minister's province, derived their authority from the Prime Minister. Hence, in theory at least, the Prime Minister enjoyed considerable power in the cabinet and was in a position to formulate general policy. In practice, of course, the extent of his power and influence depended a great deal on his personality and political strength.

The secretaries of state attached to the Prime Minister's office were thus in a particularly influential position and some of them acted simultaneously as administrators and collaborators, having direct supervision of a department and advising their chief over policy related to it. Such a position was frequently occupied by the secretary of state responsible for atomic energy. It was a short step from being the Prime Minister's collaborator to being the initiator of government policy in one's field of competence. Occasionally, a secretary of state's importance was further enhanced by attributions which gave him influence in a field concerning several ministries. In 1954, for instance, M. Mendès-France appointed Henri Longchambon as Secretary of State 'à la Recherche Scientifique et aux Progrès Techniques'. The ministries concerned delegated their responsibilities in this field to him and one had the makings of an entirely new ministry. M. Long-chambon's role was accordingly described as one of 'pure impulsion'.[37]

Although secretaries of state did not, as a rule, participate in the Conseil des Ministres, the central policy-making organ of the government, except by special invitation, and then merely as consultants in matters affecting their field, those attached to the Prime Minister's office participated regularly.

Within this institutional framework it is easy to see that the secretary of state or minister responsible for the C.E.A. could play a role of prime importance in shaping policy relating to atomic energy. Looking at the list of those occupying such a position* it is noticeable that until November 1947 the Prime Minister retained direct responsibility for the atomic energy programme–possibly as a safeguard against a communist slipping into the position of political control under the system of 'dosage'. For the following ten years the responsibility was invariably delegated to a secretary of state or minister attached to the Prime Minister's office. After 1957 it reverted to the Prime Minister.

* See Appendix.

Five men held this position at crucial periods of the C.E.A.'s development. First, Maurice Bourgès-Maunoury from July 1950 until August 1951, followed by Félix Gaillard until June 1953. Henri Longchambon was in charge during the Mendès-France cabinet. Gaston Palewski was Ministre délégué à la Présidence du Conseil, responsible for the C.E.A. during the relatively short but fruitful period between February and October 1955. The fifth was Georges Guille who held the oversight under the Mollet government from February 1956 until May 1957.

These five men between them covered the time which included the decision to concentrate on the production of plutonium, the reorganization of the C.E.A., the launching of the first Five Year Plan, the extension of the Plan, the secret protocols of 1955 and 1956, the decision to go ahead with preparations for the first atomic explosion and the beginning of the programme to build a factory for producing U235. Four of them were closely involved in formulating policy relating to atomic energy at other times in their careers. M. Bourgès-Maunoury held the posts of Assistant Minister for National Defence in 1951, Minister of Armaments in early 1952, Minister of National Defence in M. Mollet's government, and Prime Minister from June until September 1957. M. Gaillard was a keen supporter of the whole programme in and out of office. Since 1949 he had been the champion of the atomic energy programme in the Finance Commission of the National Assembly and had helped to push through the mounting annual budgets for this work. In 1954 he was associated with moves which led to the creation of a Commission de Coordination de l'Energie Atomique et des Recherches Nucléaires at the National Assembly. He was one of the principal French delegates at the negotiations which led to the establishment of EURATOM. As Prime Minister in November 1957 he resumed direct control of the programme without a secretary of state as intermediary. M. Longchambon held no other ministerial post, but from May 1955 until the end of 1958 he was Président du Conseil Supérieur de la Recherche Scientifique et du Progrès Technique, of which M. Gaillard was also a member in 1955. M. Palewski, after exile as ambassador in Rome, became minister responsible for atomic energy and rocket development in April 1962. He had a long-standing interest in atomic energy and in 1955 had asked M. Faure to give him charge of the programme.

There is little doubt that at least three of these men exercised a considerable influence over the development of the atomic programme and its military application, not only when they were directly responsible for the C.E.A. but also when they occupied other positions of influence and power under the Fourth and Fifth Republics. Their careers are a good example of the small turnover of personnel at the highest political level. That is not to say that their interests and intentions were identical. M. Bourgès-Maunoury, for instance, was very much interested in the military side of the programme, no doubt partly because of his own background as a *Polytechnicien*. M. Gaillard, on the other hand, did not have a military or scientific training. As the former Inspecteur des Finances he was closely connected with business and financial circles. An early associate of Monnet, Gaillard believed in long-range planning and was convinced that atomic energy should play an essential part in providing new sources of industrial power. His interest in the programme was, therefore, much broader, though he played an important part in creating its military potential.

It would be misleading to over-emphasize the roles of these political appointees. Because of their interest in and sympathies for certain policies they became the midwives of measures conceived within the C.E.A. and other centres of bureaucratic power which were the real sources of atomic energy policy under the Fourth Republic. However, the help of the Secrétaires d'Etat was essential to make these plans acceptable at the political level.

The other area of influence in shaping atomic policy was that covered by the legally ill-defined but politically important 'cabinets ministériels'. Traditionally described as 'l'ensemble de collaborateurs personnels du ministre',[38] their numbers were circumscribed by decree, though they often included undeclared members, 'les clandestins', whose importance sometimes grew in proportion to their obscurity. Ministers or secretaries of state in charge of a military department were also authorized to set up an Etat-Major Particulier whose officer members were limited in number and were unpaid.

Cabinets served as organs of liaison and communication for the minister and for the elaboration and preparation of his policy. As time went on, the most interesting and significant development was their increasingly intimate relationship with the highest grades of the permanent civil service. Ministers very largely relied upon high officials to staff their cabinets. This, in turn, led to a continuity of membership so that, on the average, civil servants remained in a cabinet under more than three successive ministers. Thus, on the one hand, highly placed officials influenced ministerial policy and, on the other hand, cabinets became more and more involved in departmental administration. This blending of functions can be seen as a precursor of the much more developed government by technocracy under the Fifth Republic.

An example of the part played by officers in ministerial cabinets is provided by General Lavaud. After a distinguished career as staff officer and a period of command in North Africa, M. Bourgès-Maunoury appointed him 'conseiller technique' in his cabinet when he took over the defence ministry in 1956. General Lavaud was responsible for all questions related to armaments and, on account of this, was a member of the Comité de l'Energie Atomique. In this position he was involved in the establishment of the various committees and departments set up under the C.E.A. and the Ministry of National Defence–sometimes under their joint supervision–during M. Bourgès-Maunoury's term of office. Upon the establishment of the Fifth Republic he was appointed to assist the Minister of the Armed Forces, Pierre Guillaumat, in handling all the technical aspects of armament. In February 1959 he became Chief of Staff of the Armed Forces.*

---

* General Lavaud's first association with M. Bourgès-Maunoury was as 'chef' of his Etat-Major Particulier when he served as Minister of Armaments in 1952. Before that he had been director of the army's Technical Section. Lavaud was a *Polytechnicien*, like others associated with the modernization of the army and with the military applications of nuclear energy.

Two other military figures closely concerned with the military applications of atomic energy also served in ministerial cabinets at one time or another. General Buchalet, then colonel, served as technical adviser to the Prime Minister in the Félix Gaillard government from November 1957 until April 1958.* Colonel Charles Ailleret had a brief spell as Chef d'Etat-Major Particulier to M. Laforest, the Radical Secretary of State for Armament from November 1955 until February 1956. Ailleret also co-operated with Colonel Stagnaro of M. Pleven's cabinet at the time of the latter's important speech on the defence budget in March 1954.[39]

We may therefore conclude that the basic pressures for a rapid expansion of the atomic energy programme and its militarization under the Fourth Republic came from the technocrats, some military circles and certain sectors of industry. All represented the younger generation which had come to positions of responsibility during and since the war. In this connection one should not draw too sharp a distinction between permanent officials, technocrats and industrialists on the one hand and politicians on the other. In background and outlook, men like Bourgès-Maunoury and Gaillard had much in common with the new managerial élite. Many of the technocrats had a brilliant educational background. They were profoundly marked by their wartime experiences and they had seen enough of the world to want France to shake herself free from old habits of thought and management. They were ardent nationalists who differed from others of their compatriots in refusing to be satisfied with the contemplation of past glory and the unquestioning acceptance of their superior civilization. They were acutely conscious of the stiff competition awaiting any country which wanted to keep its place among the technologically advanced nations and they were convinced that nuclear energy provided the key to economic and political power, the best guarantee for French independence and greatness.

---

* Referring to Gaillard's order in April 1958 for all necessary preparations for the first series of atomic explosions, de Lacoste Lareymondie writes that it was '... due, en grande partie, à la présence du général Buchalet, comme conseiller technique au Cabinet de la Présidence du Conseil' (p. 31).

Among the military a group of young and technically minded officers shared this outlook. Sheltered by their skills and duties from too much exposure to the absorbing passions of colonial wars, they were anxious to equip the armed forces to fight wars in the nuclear age and were as convinced as the technocrats that atomic energy was essential for national independence and power. At a time when one generally deplored the decreasing number of *Polytechniciens* who found their way into the armed forces, many of the officers closely concerned with the atomic energy programme were *Polytechniciens*, like many of the leading technocrats.

After 1958 the military orientation of the French atomic energy programme was in the open. France had the means with which to make nuclear explosives and she was on the way to providing herself with the means to make thermonuclear weapons. Attention therefore shifted from the purely explosive aspect of the new weapons to the weapons themselves. The effect of these weapons on national security, on strategy and on the structure of the armed forces became the centre of a formal debate on French defence policy.

With the 'lois-programmes' the government opened a full examination of French military policy. A 'loi-programme' covers a period of five years and is concerned with capital expenditures.[40] These include the estimated costs of research, development, production and the infrastructure of the weapons systems. The capital expenditures are spread over the annual budgets and are therefore constantly revised. However, the discussion of the annual budget tended to focus on operational costs (pay, training, maintenance, etc.) because they lay closest to the hearts of most deputies under the Fifth Republic, as they did under its predecessor, for the simple reason that votes were to be won or lost on such issues.

Hence a grand inquest on national defence policy only took place once every five years which was at least some improvement over the situation under the Fourth Republic when it never took place at all. The reasons for military policy in the nuclear field became the currency of public discussion while the centre of policy formulation shifted from the administrative-technical circles in and around the C.E.A. to those in and around the defence establishment. This did not mean, however, that the military hierarchy had an unduly important share in taking decisions.

When Charles de Gaulle came to power in May 1958 he did so under pressure from the army–admittedly, an army prompted by Gaullist politicians–and as a man of the army, though not loved by it. For him there had never been any doubt about the subordination of the military to the civil power. Disobedience in the face of surrender to an external enemy was legitimate, but not disobedience against the policy of a legally constituted authority. With the end of the war in Algeria, the military establishment became once more the tool of state policy in the hands of a government whose dominating figure directed national policy in the same way a general would command an army in battle. The nerve centre of the government was essentially in the secretariat around General de Gaulle and this was particularly true of the realms of foreign and defence policy.

References

1. *Le Monde*, 7th April 1955. See also *The New York Herald Tribune*, 6th April 1955.
2. *Combat*, 14th April 1955.
3. *Le Monde*, 23rd April 1955.
4. See Goldschmidt, *L'Aventure Atomique*, pp. 124–7, and *Les Rivalités Atomiques*, p. 172, for an account of the French position during the negotiations, in which the author took part as his country's delegate.
5. *J.O., Débats Parlementaires, 1962, A.N., 17th July 1962*, session of 16th July, p. 2482.
6. *United Nations Atomic Energy Commission*, official records, N. 3, Third Meeting, 25th June 1946, pp. 36–41.

7. Parodi's statement had been prepared by the Atomic Energy Committee (Scheinman, p. 36).

8. For an interesting account of the public debate–or rather, lack thereof–in Britain over the policy leading towards a nuclear deterrent, see Alfred Goldberg, 'The Atomic Origins of the British Nuclear Deterrent', *International Affairs*, Journal of the Royal Institute of International Affairs, Oxford University Press, Vol. 40, No. 3, July 1964, pp. 423–5.

9. Goldschmidt, *Les Rivalités Atomiques*, pp. 20, 186–7.

10. Scheinman, pp. 40–5. Dr. Scheinman gives a very thorough account of the issues involved in Joliot-Curie's dismissal as seen from inside the C.E.A.

11. *Le Monde*, 6th January 1949.

12. *Le Monde*, 29th April 1950. According to the *Daily Worker* of 6th April 1950, he added: 'We know that the Soviet Union will never start the use of the atom bomb and we also know that she and her allies would inevitably win a world war.'

13. Goldschmidt, *Les Rivalités Atomiques*, p. 216.

14. For a discussion of 'De Gaulle et les Gaullistes', see Grosser, *La Quatrième République et sa Politique Extérieure*, pp. 136–41.

15. *J.O., Débats Parlementaires, 1956, No. 78, A.N., 6th July 1956*, session of 5th July, pp. 3256–7, 3261.

16. Pierre Messmer, 'L'Atome, Cause et Moyen d'une Politique Militaire Autonome' (*Revue de Défense Nationale*, March 1968), p. 402.

17. *Le Monde*, 26th October 1967.

18. For illustrations of these ideas see General M. Carpentier, 'Déclarations et Réalités' (*Revue Militaire Générale*, March 1962), pp. 404–9; 'Chronique d'Actualité' (*Revue Militaire Générale*, December 1965), pp. 696–7; General M. E. Béthouart, 'L'OTAN et les Evolutions Nécessaires' (*Revue Militaire Générale*, March 1961), pp. 287–99; 'Les Problèmes de l'Alliance Atlantique', the Report of the Association Française pour la Communauté Atlantique (*Revue Militaire Générale*, November 1965), pp. 431–44; General André Beaufre, *L'O.T.A.N. et L'Europe* (Calmann-Lévy, Paris, 1966).

19. The question was asked in 1946: 'Etes-vous d'avis que la France devrait fabriquer des bombes atomiques?' The replies were divided into the following percentages:

OUI	56
NON	32
SANS OPINION	12

Institut Français d'Opinion Publique (hereafter referred to as I.F.O.P.), N.S. 28, 16th January 1946, p. 18.

20. An extensive poll of public attitudes to nuclear weapons was taken in August 1957. It included the following questions: *Question 38:* 'Estimez-vous que, désormais, une nation peut jouer un rôle de premier plan dans la politique mondiale, sans posséder des armes atomiques?'

REPLIES:		
	OUI	25%
	NON	51%
	UNDECIDED	24%

Question 39: 'Est-il plus urgent pour la France . . .

d'intensifier la mise en application de l'énergie atomique à des usages pacifiques?	64%
ou de procéder à la fabrication d'armes atomiques?	15%
les deux?'	3%
UNDECIDED	18%

Question 40: 'Croyez-vous que la France peut assurer sa sécurité si elle ne possède pas de bombes atomiques?'

OUI	58%
NON	42%

'Si "oui", croyez-vous qu'il soit suffisant que ses alliés la possèdent?'

OUI	24%
NON	34%

I.F.O.P., N.S. 122, 30th August 1957.

21. The following question was put in a public opinion poll in July 1959: 'Si la Grande Bretagne renonçait à la possession

d'armes atomiques croyez-vous que la France pourrait accep-
ter d'y renoncer aussi?' 44 per cent replied in the affirmative,
25 per cent in the negative and 31 per cent did not know or
did not reply. *I.F.O.P.*, Question 6, S.3210, 'L'Actualité vue
par le Public', No. 4, July 1959, Rapport 1243.

22. A series of samplings were taken at fairly regular intervals in
1962 and 1963. The question was always the same: 'Estimez-
vous que la France doit avoir sa propre force de frappe
atomique?' The replies were as follows:

Date	OUI	NON	UNDECIDED	(REF.)
16th July 1962	39%	27%	34%	(Q.20, S.4265)
22nd January 1963	* 42%	31%	27%	(Q.35, S.4475)
16th July 1963	37%	38%	25%	(Q.16, S.4831)
21st August 1963	34%	37%	29%	(Q.21, S.4901)
November 1963	39%	37%	24%	(*Sondages*,
April 1964	39%	40%	21%	1964, No. 3, p. 53)

* The rise in the percentage of those favourable coincided
with the NASSAU Agreement and de Gaulle's veto of
Britain's entry into the European Economic Community.

A direct question on the Test Ban Treaty brought the
following results: 'Un traité a été signé à Moscou par la
Grande Bretagne, les Etats-Unis et l'Union Soviétique pour
arrêter toutes les expériences nucléaires à l'exception des
expériences souterraines. Pensez-vous que la France devrait
signer cet accord, même si cela devait interrompre son
programme d'armement nucléaire?'

OUI, devrait signer	53%
NON, ne devrait pas signer	18%
UNDECIDED	29%

I.F.O.P., S.4901, 21st August 1963, E.R. 96.

23. 'Estimez-vous que la France doit avoir sa propre Force de
Frappe Atomique?'

	OUI	NON	UNDECIDED
7th–23rd April 1966	46%	42%	12%

'D'après vous, la force atomique dont la France dispose maintenant est-elle efficace?'

	OUI	NON	UNDECIDED
23rd July–4th August 1965	31%	37%	32%

(*Sondages, Revue Française de l'Opinion Publique*, 1966, No. 2), pp. 22–3.

24. *Mémoires de Guerre, Vol. III, Le Salut, 1944–1946*, pp. 96, 237.
25. *La France et l'Energie Atomique dans la Paix et dans la Guerre*, p.15.
26. As Président du Comité de l'équipement industriel and Commissaire du Gouvernement at the C.E.A., Louis Armand had played a key role in the direction of the Commissariat's work. In his own words, his '... responsabilités datent de 1951, lorsque M. Félix Gaillard, au nom du Gouvernement, me fit l'honneur de me consulter sur l'orientation à donner au commissariat à l'énergie atomique ... il a été décidé de créer au commissariat une division industrielle et un comité de l'équipement industriel. Le rôle de ce comité, dont j'ai suivi les activités, a été défini en quelques mots: il devait être l'organe mobilisateur de l'industrie française ...' *J.O., Débats Parlementaires, No. 78, A.N. 1956, 6th July 1956* session of 5th July, p. 3267. Gaillard had in fact offered him the post of Administrator General in succession to Dautry. Armand declined and suggested Guillaumat instead.
27. Colonel Ailleret, 'Applications "Pacifiques" et "Militaires" de l'Energie Atomique' (*Revue de Défense Nationale*, November 1954), p. 431.
28. Speech by M. Max Brusset, Rapporteur of the Finance Commission, *J.O., Débats Parlementaires, No. 66, A.N.*, session of 2nd July 1957, p. 3113.
29. 'Avis présenté au nom de la commission de la Défense Nationale et des Forces Armées sur le projet de loi de programme (No. 784) relative à certains Equipements

militaires' by M. le Theule. (*No. 882, Assemblée Nationale, Première Session Ordinaire de 1960–61*, Annexe au Procès-Verbal de la séance du 13 Octobre 1960, p. 13.)

30. Jean Planchais, *Le Monde*, 14th April 1954.
31. *J.O., Débats Parlementaires, No. 78, A.N. 1956, 6th July 1956*, session of 5th July, pp. 3263–4.
32. *Le Monde*, 19th and 20th November 1959, 16th and 19th February 1960.
33. Pierre Lyautey, *L'Armée: Ce Qu'elle Est, Ce Qu'elle Sera* (René Julliard, Paris, 1963), pp. 251–2. Since Gaullism, if it represents any political philosophy, is identified with nationalism, it is not without interest to note that the C.E.A. under the Fourth Republic has been described as: '. . . un des derniers bastions gaullistes dans le régime', Viansson-Ponté, *Les Gaullistes: Rituel et Annuaire* (Editions du Seuil, Paris, 1963), p. 131.
34. Ailleret, *L'Aventure Atomique Française*, pp. 97–111, 164–77, 183–94.
35. *Le Monde*, 31st May 1956. General Dassault was, incidentally, the first representative of National Defence to sit on the board of the C.E.A.
36. For the development of the cabinet secretariat, see Roy C. Macridis, 'The Cabinet Secretariat in France', *The Journal of Politics*, published by the Southern Political Science Association in co-operation with the University of Florida, Vol. 13, No. 4, November 1951, pp. 590–6.
37. J. C. Groshens, 'Les Secrétaires d'Etat de la Quatrième République' (*Revue du Droit Publique et de la Science Politique*, Vol. 71, No. 2, April–June 1955), p. 368.
38. Jean-Louis Seurin, 'Les Cabinets Ministériels' (*Revue du Droit Publique et de la Science Politique*, Vol. 72, No. 6, November–December 1956), pp. 1207–94.
39. Ailleret, *L'Aventure Atomique Française*, p. 165.
40. For a definition and description of 'loi-programme', see H. Dofing, 'Programmes des Armées' (*Revue Militaire D'Information*, No. 351, July–August 1963), pp. 45–51.

6 · Conclusion

[The problem of building an atomic industry on the basis of the limited resources available in 1945 made it inevitable that for a long time its military uses would remain an open question.[Until 1957 there was no need of a formal commitment to nuclear armament and it was only in the preceding year that the government took steps which made such a course inevitable. No matter what their previous decisions, governments had been justified in treating the matter as undecided.] The peculiar budgetary and administrative arrangements enabled the authorities to avoid having to seek formal parliamentary approval for the growing investment of defence funds in the programme.[The civilian sponsorship of the two Five-Year Plans of 1952 and 1957 and the civilian control of the C.E.A. partly explain why the government could avoid taking the initiative in any formal debate on the military application of atomic energy before 1960. Nevertheless, for twelve years France pursued a course which laid the foundation on which President de Gaulle could build his independent foreign and defence policies] Although all the major decisions had been taken by May 1958, their implications had never been openly debated. Furthermore, these decisions were taken against the declared policies of at least two prime ministers and followed a direction which many of the responsible leaders of the Fourth Republic were to oppose vigorously under the Fifth Republic.]

An explanation of this state of affairs has to be sought equally in the institutional machinery of the Fourth Republic and in the role of the men who manipulated it.

[A variety of factors favoured a continuous atomic policy oriented towards military uses. The C.E.A.'s attachment to the prime minister's office kept it out of the politically controversial activities of the ministry of national defence. The constitution of the Commissariat gave it a guarantee of stability and provided for access to funds which were not subject to parliamentary control. The political instability of governments gave the permanent officials a decided advantage. Every change of government provided an interruption at the top–even though a minister might return to the same post held under the previous government–while the administrative machine ticked on below.

Although we only have fleeting glimpses of the debate behind the scenes, there is sufficient evidence that while the programme's orientation was the subject of fitful public discussion, a small group of influential men was pushing steadily for a military development of atomic energy. They included some in key positions within the C.E.A., some in the circles around the ministry of national defence, some industrialists, some politicians in office and some out of office, all supported by a small number of publicists.

The relationship between these groups was partly personal and partly political. A considerable number of those who most actively furthered the military side of the programme were *Polytechniciens* and thus had the advantage of close association brought about by membership of an extensive old-boy network.[1] On the political level a surprising number were in one way or another associated with the Gaullist movement in its broadest sense. Some, like General Koenig, Mm. Palewski and Chaban-Delmas, were Gaullist politicians, others, though they may have had different or no known political affiliations, were sufficiently in sympathy with the General and his policies to have served under him in one capacity or another. Among these one must include M. Guillaumat and Generals Ailleret and Lavaud.

Gaullists played an increasingly important part in the later governments of the Fourth Republic and their influence was undoubtedly exerted in favour of policies which were to be more vigorously pursued under the Fifth Republic. A number of the General's sympathizers also held important positions within the C.E.A. and the military establishment.

The small group of Radicals who had been associated with the atomic energy programme at one time or another under the

Fourth Republic included some like Mm. Mendès-France and Gaillard who vigorously opposed the Gaullists on the political level and others, such as Mm. Edgar Faure and Bourgès-Maunoury, who might be described as more sympathetic to the General's broad objectives. Finally, a few other political leaders, notably Mm. Pleven and Mollet, share responsibility for furthering a national nuclear armament. The role of M. Mollet is particularly ambiguous and there is some evidence that he accepted the reasons for pushing ahead with a military programme during the last months of his term of office as prime minister.

In parliament and the press the pressure for a national nuclear armament came from the same political quarters, reinforced by a miscellany of conservative politicians. They formed the spearhead in the drive for a nuclear force in the few debates which touched upon the topic.

[It is sometimes argued that, once started, the French atomic energy programme gathered a momentum of its own and that the progress towards a military orientation became inevitable. Each decision automatically led to the next. But decisions were not taken blindly without the knowledge and approval of responsible ministers, although the original initiatives may have come from other quarters. The reasons why they were taken were supported by elaborate arguments, some of which were developed for public consumption while others were a truer reflection of official thought.

The economic arguments for an atomic energy programme were in the forefront of publicly declared policy. Until 1957 the provision of new sources of energy was the *raison de'être* of the C.E.A.'s work. Nor can there be any doubt that this view was widely shared in and outside official circles, so that the value of an atomic energy industry was not challenged during this period. By the time the second Five Year Plan was launched it had, however, become clear that the purely industrial benefits of the programme were of secondary importance in the minds of some politicians and officials. The debate turned essentially on the question of priorities. Those who favoured a military programme insisted that, far from hindering the industrial development of atomic energy, it would act as a valuable stimulant. The opponents of nuclear armament maintained equally forcefully that the military emphasis had diverted valuable resources from the civil programme and was imposing serious delays on progress in this area. The debate continues though the military interest has so far won in practical terms.

Military concern with nuclear weapons passed through several phases after 1945. Because of the remoteness of a French-made nuclear force in the 1940s, military attention was principally turned to the effect of atomic weapons on conventional warfare. They were seen as new weapons to be fitted into the context of traditional strategic and tactical thought. Hence, in the first eight years after the war, French military planning tried to apply the lessons of the Second World War to the strategic objectives of an earlier period, although the campaign in Indochina raised doubts as to the validity of this line of approach.

From 1954 onwards there are two distinct developments in the military scene. First, the possession of nuclear weapons becomes a possibility, if not a probability, and a small but not uninfluential military lobby presses for the creation of a national nuclear force. Secondly, a much greater preoccupation with ideological warfare develops out of the Algerian war which soon absorbs most of the country's effective fighting strength.

The emerging nuclear balance between the two super-powers and the doubt it cast upon the credibility of the American deterrent influenced those who advised the government on its defence needs. This consideration was added to a more deep-rooted anxiety which had dominated discussions of French defence policy since 1945. Soldiers and politicians feared that in the event of an armed conflict with the Soviet Union, the British and the Americans would look upon France as the first line of defence and as the principal source of manpower while they retired behind their sea ramparts to mobilize their resources and to bomb the enemy at least cost to themselves. However, this point was stressed much less once it became clear that the Federal

202

Republic of Germany would provide the 'infantry' of the Alliance. Yet, by and large, there was no fear of a direct attack from the Soviet Union. The failure to secure American intervention in Indochina at the time of Dien Bien Phu and the experience during the Suez crisis were seen as decisive arguments in favour of a nuclear striking force. The Suez crisis, in particular, was not so much an indication of the unreliability of the American deterrent, as a warning that the United States would not support France in areas where their interests were at variance. After de Gaulle came to power and in the two years following the first atomic explosion, French nuclear power was often justified as necessary for the defence of the Franco-African Community.

The military authorities believed that the real conflict with communism was for the control of the Afro-Asian world, precisely because of the nuclear balance in Europe. The struggle for the defence of western civilization and values, of which Algeria was regarded as the beleaguered outpost, became the *leitmotif* of military propagandists and, for a short time at least, was half-heartedly accepted by the government. Since one was engaged in a mortal struggle with communism, it was not so important who controlled nuclear weapons within the Western Alliance as long as they provided an effective barrier to a direct attack in Europe. The full implications of the doctrine of 'la Guerre Révolutionnaire' may not have been shared by more than a handful of fanatics, but its strategic analysis was widely accepted.

The third phase of military thinking begins with the accession of General de Gaulle to power. From 1958 until 1962 he was preoccupied with the liquidation of the Algerian problem. The strength of the army's attachment to the cause of 'French Algeria' and to the philosophic and strategic ideas of the doctrine of revolutionary war dictated a certain caution in the government's approach. However, from November 1959 onwards it became clear that a nuclear striking force was to be the core of French military strength. This was not because de Gaulle saw it as a convenient toy with which to distract the army's attention from Algeria, although it was no doubt useful in this respect, but because he no longer believed in the need for large conventional forces as a prerequisite for national independence. The policy formulated in the 'loi-programme' of 1960 and continued in the 'loi-programme' of 1965, with its corollary of the gradual abandonment of conscription, may be seen by future historians as the end of a period in French military history which began with the Revolution of 1789.

Although purely military arguments of doubtful validity are advanced in support of a national nuclear striking force Gaullist governments saw it principally as an essential political and diplomatic weapon. This use of an atomic armament was foreshadowed in the debates under the Fourth Republic, in the same way that some of the military arguments of the 1960s were formulated in the 1950s. The political and diplomatic *rationale* was, however, far more important in the public mind and in some official pronouncements under the Fourth Republic.

One may, of course, try to see the reason for various policy decisions as French reactions to particular historical events. Thus the first Five Year Plan for atomic energy, with its hints of a military development, coincided with a period of high tension in the Cold War and with the formal emergence of Britain as a third nuclear power. The more definite military orientation in the years 1954 and 1955 coincided with the disastrous end of the war in Indochina, the defeat of E.D.C. and the prospect of German rearmament under the subsequent Paris and London Agreements. Simultaneously, the more hopeful atmosphere in international disarmament negotiations probably influenced the public declarations of Mm. Edgar Faure and Guy Mollet. Again, the increasingly open military orientation of the French atomic programme in 1956 and 1957 was undoubtedly encouraged by the Suez crisis and may also have been influenced by British defence policy in the period from 1955 to 1957, just as the plans for Pierrelatte may have been hastened by British progress in the field of thermonuclear power.

All these and possibly other events influenced French official thinking, although their exact impact on policy discussions at the highest level cannot be measured precisely for the time being. It may be argued, however, that the project for a European Defence Community and the negotiations to set up EURATOM marked the turning point. They forced the French government to come to terms with and promote a military programme of atomic energy. Nevertheless, an analysis of the political and diplomatic arguments for the creation of a national nuclear force must take account of a fundamental psychological factor as well as specific policy objectives more or less consciously pursued by governments. These two elements are certainly related, for policies are usually formed in pursuit of what is thought or felt to be the overall national interest.

The humiliation of 1940–4, post-war weakness and disorder, the drama of colonial wars, all combined to place France in a position of real and acutely felt inferiority *vis-à-vis* the Soviet Union and the principal Western allies. From the earliest days of the Liberation successive governments sought to restore France to her former greatness. After 1947 there emerged a second concern with the communist threat which was seen as internal rather than external.

Two alternatives presented themselves in pursuit of these aims. One was to seek an extension of French power through an integrated Western Europe, the other was to seek a return to a great-power status in which France would be the acknowledged leader of Western Europe. These two opposing policies were in fact pursued simultaneously under the Fourth Republic. French policy over EURATOM provides an excellent illustration of this combination. It was another step towards a United States of Europe and at the same time it gave France the opportunity to emerge as the only power with atomic weapons in the European Community.

A closer analysis of the context in which French aspirations to atomic power were discussed reveals that it was almost exclusively in terms of relations within the Western Alliance. Thus, while the military arguments for a national nuclear force were couched in terms of resisting an attack from the east, the political arguments dwelt on inter-allied relationships.

CONCLUSION

Foremost was the concern to build a new relationship with Germany. In the 1950s this took the form of a deliberate policy of rapprochement in which it was hoped that any aggressive tendencies of that country would be contained within a European union which Germany could not dominate. The opponents of this policy wanted to compensate for the weakness of France in conventional armaments with a potential nuclear force which was denied to Germany under the terms of the Paris and London Agreements. Both sides were agreed that the German threat must be laid once and for always.

Relations with the United States and Britain were ambivalent. On the one hand there were the traditional ties of friendship and the debt owed to the allies during the war as well as the knowledge of continued dependence on their economic, military and political support. On the other hand there was a feeling of resentment at the real or imagined way in which these powers had tried to relegate France to a second-class status in the last months of the war. This feeling expressed itself strongly in the realm of nuclear energy. Neither power had shown any desire to help France make progress in a field in which she had played an important part before the war, in which she had provided useful service to the British during the war, and in which achievement was the status symbol of a great power after the war.

This ambivalence was revealed in the persistent hope of material help from the United States, in the early efforts to bring Britain into the European Community and, more particularly, in the search for British co-operation in the development of atomic energy. The attitude of the Anglo-Saxon powers finally gave reason to all those who insisted that France could only return to great-power status through her own efforts.

Any attempt to measure the impact of the French nuclear force on French standing in the world or on the course of international relations is a daunting task for two reasons. The force has hardly more than symbolic status and is not likely to achieve military credibility before 1974 or 1975. Secondly, we have little evidence

206

CONCLUSION

of the impact of nuclear weapons on the policies and influence of lesser powers. After twenty odd years of nuclear confrontation between Russia and the United States we are in a position to analyse with some precision the effect of nuclear weapons on their mutual relationship. Thus we can talk about a limited adversary relationship and examine its implications. We do not yet have enough hard facts to reach similarly firm conclusions about the place of such weapons in the external policies of smaller nuclear weapon states.

The French, more than the British, the Americans and the Russians, think that the function of nuclear weapons is principally in the psychological field. They constitute a threat or counter-threat and as such serve to support or stultify diplomatic manoeuvre. The only way in which we may assess the relevance of the F.N.S. to the position of France under de Gaulle is by examining the part assigned to it in French policy and by observing the reaction of other states.

The essential psychological factor in French policy is the belief that the possession of nuclear weapons gives France a basic security and a freedom to act which is the privilege only of nuclear weapon states. When looking at the purely military aspect of French nuclear policy we notice a great divergence between the structure of defence as presented in government plans and the structure as it exists today and, taking into account present trends, is likely to exist in five to ten years' time.

On paper the French nuclear force is central to the French security system. It guarantees the inviolability of the national territory and covers French initiatives outside its borders. By the mid-seventies it should include a range of strategic and tactical weapons on a scale proportionate to the size and resources of France. In addition, French power is symbolized by five armoured divisions and one airborne division. Finally, to emphasize the determination of national self-defence after the nuclear deterrent has failed and France is invaded, a system of territorial defence will reinforce the army and, if necessary, provide the moles of national resistance and resurrection.

CONCLUSION

In practice the scheme is much less tidy. In spite of constantly rising costs, France has so far successfully contained her defence expenditure at a satisfactory level of the national budget. Indeed, the charges are considerably less when compared with earlier periods during this century.* This is only possible by giving the nuclear component half the total resources devoted to national defence. Hence the 'Corps de Manœuvre' will not be fully 'modernized' until 1974 or 1975. By that time some of its 'modern' equipment may have become obsolete, particularly if developments in anti-tank weapons give a new primacy to the defence in conventional warfare. The D.O.T. is little more than an administrative skeleton and the rate of progress makes it doubtful whether it will have acquired any flesh by the mid-seventies.

The concentration of resources on nuclear weapons at the expense of the other sectors has not saved the nuclear programme from serious embarrassment. Every now and then official spokesmen announced a delay in its fulfilment. M. Debré made the latest statement following the events of May and June 1968.[2] The Mirages, always a deterrent of doubtful efficacity, will continue to be the sole strategic force until the generation of silo-based missiles comes into operation; the first squadron of nine may not be fully in place until after 1971 when the first nuclear submarine should have made its appearance. The generation consisting of I.C.B.M.s mounted in submarines was intended to fit the doctrine of 'Tous Azimuts' and was destined to emerge by 1980. Financial pressures could postpone it to 1990 if the plan is maintained which is doubtful. It is estimated that if the policy of 'Tous Azimuts' receives full implementation, including more ambitious projects involving operations in space, military expenditure may rise by at least 10 per cent.[3] Since the summer of 1968 the proposed tactical

* Compare the following percentages of military expenditure in relation to the national budget:

1912–13	30%
1938	35%
1961	26·3%
1967	20·7%

nuclear armament has also been called into question and may eventually be abandoned.

Financial difficulties and technical obstacles in some sectors—there is no shortage of scientists but a shortage of technicians, notably in the computer industry—will continue to act as brakes on military plans. At best, therefore, France may acquire a small quality force which has a credible second-strike capability in its submarine component but whose credibility may be steadily eroded as the years pass by. The prospect of keeping up with the technological race is a daunting one. If the Gaullist government with all its enthusiasm for this kind of military policy was forced to retrench, postpone or even abandon part of the programme, a successor government, less endowed with such determination, may have to impose a halt on further progress.

For the moment France is only a nuclear paper tiger. The whole policy of deterrence at present rests in the last analysis on the probability that after the outbreak of hostilities one or two Mirages would be able to penetrate Russia. Even these calculations are subject to downward revision as the opponent's anti-aircraft defences improve.

When we compare the French effort with that of other military nuclear powers, we note that the Soviet Union and the United States are in a class apart. China has the potential to join that class. From the beginning the Chinese nuclear effort has aimed at a thermonuclear capability so that it seems almost to have by-passed the earlier stage with the result that while basic preparatory studies started six or eight years after those of France, China is ahead in the development of thermonuclear explosives. Moreover, a Chinese nuclear force is part of a much larger and formidable Chinese military posture based upon an almost limitless reservoir of manpower and a doctrine of revolutionary warfare.

Britain had a considerable start over France in the nuclear field and originally aimed at self-sufficiency. After fifteen years of increasing difficulties, the British government is in the process of abandoning this objective in both the conventional and nuclear spheres. This has led to the curtailment of strategic commitments, to an emphasis on joint projects for weapons development, to a reliance on the United States for nuclear weapons components. As a corollary, while Britain retains an independent second-strike capability for national defence in the last resort, her foreign and defence policies are firmly anchored in the Western Alliance. Britain, like France, is facing the possibility of reaching the limit of nuclear weapons development during the next few years. The problem may become increasingly one of phasing out of the nuclear arms race. Although the military aspect of such a policy has not so far been formally admitted, the political conclusions have been drawn some time ago. Through her alliance policy and commitment to Europe, the United Kingdom has demonstrated that full sovereignty is no longer the prerogative of any but the super-powers.

President de Gaulle set out to prove the contrary. Absolute national independence was the objective. It could only be achieved by the creation of a complete military panoply including a whole range of nuclear and other weapons. The ambition was obviously beyond the reach of France. At best she will have token forces in all spheres.

Nearly every independent commentator on contemporary French military policy analyses at great length its weaknesses and ultimate absurdity. Yet President de Gaulle conducted French foreign policy as if the French military posture were a reality and not just a neat blue-print for annual debate.

In 1968 the position of France was one of armed neutrality. Although a member of the Atlantic Alliance, France had withdrawn from its military organization. Association to meet specific contingencies; co-operation to cover special needs; these were the Gaullist concepts of alliance. The emphasis on 'Défense Tous Azimuts' could have meant defence against a Russian capability to attack France from any direction, by submarine for instance, or it could have been intended to ward off a hypothetical threat from the United States or even China.

In 1968 France claimed a leading position in Europe west of the Elbe. The British were kept out of the Common Market and their policy was identified with that of the United States. France was the only nuclear weapon state on the Continent outside Russia. If the United States were to have withdrawn her troops then France would have claimed to be the only serious military power in Western Europe. The European Economic Community was a valued vehicle for economic progress but at the political level France preferred bilateral agreements, such as the Franco-German Treaty of 1963, and the safeguard of her independence through insistence on the unanimity rule in international organizations.

Elsewhere in Europe and the world France was the apostle of national independence, always ready to throw her weight into the scales so as to obviate the dominant influence of one or other, or both, of the super-powers. In Vietnam and Latin America the French intervened to offset American domination. In Eastern Europe the French encouraged a spirit of national independence to resist a foreign ideological yoke. In the Middle East—unsuccessfully in 1967—France tried to replace the super-powers as arbiter between Israel and the Arab states. For years before the latest war in the region, President de Gaulle courted both Israel and the Arab states in the hope of eventually influencing the course of the conflict.[4] The basic objectives of these excursions was to resist the hegemony of the super-powers, to remind other peoples of their national vocation and to increase French influence. President de Gaulle was concerned, above all, that super-power rivalry should not take place at the expense of the other states, for he saw their hegemony less as an agreement to manage the world than as a subtle power game played out in well-defined spheres with the tacit understanding that the struggle should not be carried into their respective heartlands.

Since the establishment of the Fifth Republic France had played a more active and in certain respects a more impressive international role than at any time after 1940. Even before the end of the Algerian war France had shed the unenviable reputation of being the sick man of Europe. The attack on the structures of the Atlantic Alliance, the Franco-German entente, the opening of relations with the countries of Eastern Europe, the series of well-publicized excursions into the 'Third World', the launching of an independent policy in the Middle East, the challenge to the primacy of the dollar and the pound in the world's money markets; all these partially successful or wholly unsuccessful *démarches* were said to be based upon an apparently sound economy and an autonomous national defence.

Dazzled by the virtuosity of the master tactician in the diplomatic field, the world often overlooked de Gaulle's dependence on the foundations laid by his much despised predecessors. Quite apart from a national nuclear policy, the Fourth Republic witnessed the establishment of an economic policy which could not come to full fruition until the national finances were put in order and the war in Algeria had come to an end. Nonetheless, the system of economic planning which had helped to make France competitive in many industrial sectors was worked out soon after the war. Similarly, some of the basic choices in foreign policy were made in the 1940s and the 1950s, notably the policies of accepting American economic aid, of European functional integration, which played a very large part in French economic recovery, and of Franco-German collaboration.

After ten years of Gaullist rule the events of the spring of 1968 revealed the fragility of the national base. They marked the true end of the Gaullist era for they cast doubt on the economic strength and social cohesion of the country and they undermined the effect of the General's international posturings. They also threw into relief the problems of an ambitious defence policy which informed observers had pointed out for a long time. The mandate given to the Gaullist movement in the legislative elections of June 1968 was for the restoration of order and the execution of social change. The General also construed it as support for his external policy. No doubt his assumption was partly correct but what the upheaval of 1968 proved was that the French, unlike their President, considered social and economic affairs far more important than foreign affairs. Gaullist foreign policy continued for as long as the President remained in office, but it operated under a triple handicap. It could no longer take precedence in the General's mind over domestic affairs, it had to take account of the economic and financial situation of France and it was less impressive in the eyes of other governments.

Within the ranks of the government's supporters there were some who would have been content with a symbolic nuclear force which would be efficient but limited. They favoured abandoning the second-generation nuclear weapons system of I.R.B.M.s in hardened sites and doubted the wisdom of developing I.C.B.M.s. Some ministers were known to share such thoughts. However, these reservations did not carry much weight as long as President de Gaulle dictated the basic orientation of French defence policy.

Foreign and defence policy did not play an important part in the programme and tactics of the opposition groups. M. Le-canuet's Democratic Centre Party with its emphatically European policy was the notable exception. Inheritor of the European Movement of Monnet and Schuman and of the waning political strength of the M.R.P., it campaigned vigorously against the Gaullist conception of Europe. Its relatively feeble electoral show-ing was proof of the absence of strong public feeling over the conduct of external relations.

Because of the nature of the regime, the opposition was forced to attack its very structure and give priority to constitutional and social reforms without which it had little hope of gaining power. The disturbances of May 1968 began with a student revolt against an educational system which was not elastic enough to meet a colossal expansion in numbers nor able to contain the wholly new social situation created by this expansion. The revolt spread to the industrial and agricultural sectors. In both the impetus came from economic conditions but for diametrically opposed reasons. The workers rebelled against a traditional wage and work structure which no longer corresponded to the technological changes of our time. The peasants and small shopkeepers reacted against changes – largely brought about through Common Market policies – in the same way that the Luddites reacted against new machinery. In the end, students, workers and peasants turned their anger against the social order and the institutions which clothed it. The opposition parties were therefore right in concentrating their attack on the social and economic system.

One other reason, besides the need to woo the public, accounts for the neglect of foreign and defence affairs. By 1968 President de Gaulle's personal popularity rested on two planks. At home he represented order and security for the mass of conservative-minded Frenchmen. Abroad he represented a revolutionary tradition in his encouragement of nationalism against super-power hegemony, thus appealing to the radical element in French politics. His policy of national independence and his occasional 'bull in the china shop' acts caused deep satisfaction to many French people, especially those old enough to remember a long string of national humiliations.

French national sentiment therefore affected opposition policy towards the national nuclear force. In the National Assembly the opposition groups, including the Centre Party, voted consistently against the successive 'loi-programmes', but there were marked differences in their official policies.

The party programmes for the legislative elections of March 1967[5] – those for 1968 showed no important differences and were completely overshadowed by preoccupations about the crisis in the spring of that year – revealed the lack of common purpose. Only the small P.S.U. stood for unilateral atomic disarmament. The communists and the Federation declared for the abandonment of the strategic nuclear force but did not suggest that this might be done unilaterally if general, simultaneous and controlled disarmament – which all the parties of the left advocated – was not achieved. The Federation proposed blocking military credits at the level reached in 1965 and implied a gradual running down of the nuclear force. It is possible that they were inspired by the actual if not declared policy of the British Labour Government. The Democratic Centre contented itself with a blanket condemnation of the government's military strategy as 'ruineuse, inefficace, dangereuse et rétrograde . . .'

214

The Centre insisted that the non-proliferation of nuclear weapons could only be settled through the United Nations but made no mention of its policy towards the Non-Proliferation Treaty nor other measures of arms control. The three parties of the left agreed on supporting the partial test ban treaty of August 1963, the Non-Proliferation Treaty and, in varying terms, called for participation in further arms control and disarmament measures.

The sharpest differences occurred over policy towards the Atlantic Alliance. The Centre and the Federation wanted France to continue in membership but called for a reorganization of the Alliance. The Centre saw this in terms of a European defence community, whereas the Federation envisaged a policy which would eventually make both the Atlantic and Warsaw Pacts unnecessary. The P.S.U. and communists made no bones about their intention to continue Gaullist policy and go further by advocating withdrawal from the Alliance in 1969. It is noteworthy that all the left parties thought it necessary to emphasize that Germany should not be allowed to have nuclear weapons. For the Centre this problem would presumably be taken care of within a united Europe.

When the Communist Party and the Federation published a joint text of their agreements and disagreements on the 24th February 1968, their differences over foreign policy were further underlined. The problem of national and international disarmament presented no serious difficulty. They agreed on 'la renonciation à la force de frappe et sa reconversion à des fins pacifiques', but the subsequent text suggested that they saw this in the context of an internationally negotiated reduction of nuclear weapons. Apart from support for existing arms control measures, they called for the creation of denuclearized zones in Europe.

Over NATO there was complete disagreement. Nothing illustrates better how de Gaulle had stolen the communists' clothes. Some of the language used by the party to oppose any continuation of membership after 1969 and by its Secretary-General, M. Waldeck Rochet, over the question of British admission to the Common Market could have been taken word for word out of a Gaullist declaration of policy. The Federation of the Left, on the other hand, considered it dangerous for France to leave the Atlantic Alliance before a new political situation had come into existence in Europe and the world. This disunity was demonstrated in April 1966 when the Communist Party supported the government in defeating a socialist motion censuring de Gaulle's policy towards NATO.

If one adds up the volume of electoral support given to the communists and Gaullists one must doubt whether there can be any return to NATO as it existed before 1966. Although the opposition was superficially united against Gaullist military policy, a clear alternative did not emerge from their vague and sometimes contradictory statements on the subject.

The Gaullist government created an instrument which it will be difficult to wish away. The extent of the vested interest and of political inertia will be such that after de Gaulle the French will have the same difficulty in deciding what to do with their strategic nuclear force that the British have had in the 1960s.

Making due allowance for the technical and military weakness of French nuclear policy, can we argue that the existence of an embryonic nuclear capability has, in fact, affected the position of France in the world? In only one sphere has the planned existence of a national nuclear force enabled the French government to take a particular stance. While accepting the need for a convincing deterrent against nuclear blackmail or attack, the government felt strong enough to disengage French forces from NATO. A cynic might suggest that for as long as the United States is willing to retain forces in Europe this withdrawal could have taken place without the existence of a national nuclear force. American forces would always provide a buffer against any onslaught from the east. Nevertheless, French policy aimed at weakening American influence in Europe, although it assumed that the United States would continue to deter any Russian move towards Europe. A strategic nuclear force, however small, would give France a claim to speak with the Soviet Union on a level to which no other European state–not even Britain–could aspire. Moreover, it would ensure Germany's partial dependence on France. Such were the arguments employed in support of Gaullist policy.

Against this we must consider two objections. In spite of her pretensions, France had not persuaded other European states to accept her title to leadership. In the Common Market she dictated terms over the British application for political reasons but had been successful not because of them, or her military strength, but because of the economic interests of the Community as a whole. In rapprochement with the East she may have opened doors but the Germans may eventually adopt an independent line and pursue a policy which owes little to co-ordination with France. The Federal Republic of Germany is in a particularly delicate position at this point in its history. Its external relations and domestic policies revolve around its 'Ostpolitik'. Caught between the need for military security from the United States and the need for political reassurance from France, German policy is hesitant and depends on initiatives and developments elsewhere, especially in the German Democratic Republic. However, this may not always be so and there are sufficient indications that German governments of the future might be prepared to strike out on their own if they consider time and circumstances to be favourable.

The Russians, though they might have welcomed the nuisance value of France as an embarrassment to the Atlantic Alliance, gave no indication that in serious negotiations over European security they would deal with any power other than the United States. When they have shown a concern over the future policy of a European state, it is the Federal Republic of Germany rather than France that held their attention.

A second objection is contained in the question whether nuclear weapons are necessary in order to have an independent foreign policy. Rumania and Yugoslavia were two members of an alliance system which have moved away from super-power domination. Neither is a nuclear power or likely to become one.

CONCLUSION

These countries may not have the same claims to status as France. Their interests are more narrowly confined to a particular geographical region. Yet whatever France might do in other parts of the world, French power is only relevant within Europe and in parts of Africa. If one therefore compares French influence in Western Europe and the influence exercised by Yugoslavia and Rumania in Eastern Europe one might be hard put to it to justify becoming a nuclear weapon state merely on the grounds that such weapons are an essential guarantee for the pursuit of an independent national policy.

Events in Czechoslovakia during 1968 could of course point to the opposite conclusion. The crisis in Czech-Russian relations underlines the essential differences between the Atlantic and Warsaw Pact Alliances. The former rests on a voluntary association of states, the latter is based on coercion by the super-power. For this reason alone, the success of the Rumanians in asserting their right to an independent foreign policy has been much more remarkable than that of France. Czechoslovakia, for a variety of reasons, is within the zone which the Russians regard as essential to their national security. Their intervention in that country may be likened to American concern over Cuba and San Domingo. Recent events may confirm de Gaulle's view of a world threatened by a directorate of super-powers, but it does not necessarily follow that an independent nuclear force is the most effective way in which to maintain national independence.

The existence of the French nuclear force has been used to justify French actions within the context of the Atlantic Alliance. It has yet to be shown that it is relevant to French policy outside that Alliance. In a negative sense it does, however, have a bearing on the problem of the spread of nuclear weapons around the world.

Quite naturally a number of potential nuclear weapon states have shown particular interest in the French experience. In Japan, for instance, many articles have appeared about the French nuclear programme. The interest focuses on the arguments used to justify French policy and the steps taken to implement it.

218

Nevertheless, it is clear that the decision to take up the nuclear weapons option will in the last resort depend on the peculiar position of each country. Thus, any Japanese initiatives will depend on a very delicate domestic political situation in relation to the issue, as well as on the triangular power relationship between the United States, the Soviet Union and China in the northern Pacific. India may have to balance the needs of security against a nuclear armed China with the impact on Pakistan of a decision to acquire nuclear weapons. Israel and the United Arab Republic will inevitably base their policies on the strict calculations of military balance. Switzerland and Sweden will decide theirs in relation to the long-standing traditions of armed neutrality.

Potential nuclear weapon states will, however, share one interest in the French programme. They will note what can be done largely through one's own efforts and they will try to evaluate the cost in economic and social terms, though the answer must remain partially unclear.

All states will be influenced to a greater or lesser extent by the international pressures to prevent the spread of nuclear weapons. They will assess the Non-Proliferation Treaty in terms of their security, in terms of their national atomic energy programme, in terms of its promise of more far-reaching arms control and disarmament measures, and in terms of an emerging pattern of world order in which the nuclear weapon states may seek to establish a permanent superiority over the rest.

If the French government had accepted the basic thesis propounded by General Gallois[6] then the proliferation of nuclear weapons might have been encouraged in the interests of stability and peace. Instead, it deserted the theoretical plane on which it justified the creation of a national deterrent force for the harsh realities of the world, arguing that the spread of nuclear weapons increases the danger of the outbreak of nuclear war because of irresponsibility or accident. French policy was identical to that of the other nuclear weapon states in its determination to do nothing which would increase the number of such states.[7] It may be objected that French assistance to Israel in building the nuclear reactor at Dimona was contrary to this policy. Undoubtedly General de Gaulle regretted the apparently free hand in its use left to the Israelis.

A brief glance at French disarmament policy since the war may further illustrate the basic objectives and continuity which have been characteristic of so much French policy in the post-war period.

In 1962 France formally dissociated herself from all negotiations concerned with disarmament and arms control. The paucity of any references to these problems in the French press and in official statements underlined the apparent disinterest. Yet a closer examination of French attitudes towards the negotiations and of the recent history of French policy in this field shows a remarkable consistency since the end of the Second World War. Historical experience and foreign policy objectives have shaped French attitudes to disarmament since 1945. Disarmament and collective security were indissolubly linked in the French mind between the two world wars. As we know, the failure to achieve both had disastrous results and has marked French policies ever since.[8]

Throughout the Fourth Republic M. Jules Moch was the key figure in the protracted international disarmament negotiations. His scientific background as a *Polytechnicien* and his political standing in the French Socialist Party undoubtedly gave him considerable weight in the counsels of successive governments. The exact extent of his influence over policy is difficult to determine. His views are well known and to be found in a number of books.[9] One may assume, however, that until 1957 French governments generally accepted his views. After that he officially represented a position which was increasingly at variance with his personal position.

We can distinguish three broad though overlapping phases in French disarmament policy since 1945. The first lasted until 1957 and was dominated by Moch. France sought to occupy an intermediary position between the United States and Russia. The objective was not so much to prevent an agreement between the two super-powers at the expense of the rest, something which was out of the question during this period, but to assert France's role as a major power. French weakness made the field of disarmament negotiations a particularly appropriate area of national initiatives. The attitude of Moch and a number of other political leaders at that time might be described as 'pacifistic patriotism'. This period was marked by the Franco-British Plan for disarmament which became mixed up with the whole issue of German rearmament; by Edgar Faure's proposals for a fund in aid of underdeveloped countries, to be provided by cuts in the military expenditures of the two super-powers, the United Kingdom and France; by Edgar Faure's and Guy Mollet's notably pacifistic policy statements about the French nuclear energy programme. Nevertheless, France consistently set two conditions as a *sine qua non* of her participation in any disarmament agreement. The agreement must not discriminate between one group of powers and another and it must mark a 'genuine' step forward in the direction of universal disarmament.

The emphasis on equal treatment in the sphere of disarmament and arms control became much more explicit during the second phase of post-war French disarmament policy which covers the years from 1957 until 1962 and marks the rise and consolidation of Gaullist power. The fear that the Anglo-Saxon powers and the Soviet Union might make a deal at the expense of France and other non-nuclear powers and thus reduce them to a permanent status of inferiority runs persistently through the declarations of French leaders during this phase. It was put most clearly by Christian Pineau in July 1957:

> ... We can agree to consider taking part in a disarmament agreement the result of which would be that all countries, without exception, would cease to manufacture fissile materials and that existing atomic weapons would be destroyed. This we could agree to. But what we could not agree to would be that a small number of countries—even if there were three of them—should have the exclusive right to manufacture fissile materials at a time when we had no disarmament agreement providing

for the cessation of this manufacture and the destruction of existing stocks. In other words, we accept a general disarmament, but we do not accept the creation of a club to which the manufacture of nuclear weapons would be limited.[10]

France opposed any arms control policies which threatened the military development of her atomic energy programme. The proposals advanced by Jules Moch tended to fit this requirement. He argued that stocks of nuclear explosives could no longer be controlled* but the means of delivery could still be checked. The official French position thus met a double objective. It concentrated on what seemed practicable and it left the door open to the French acquisition of nuclear explosives. In the spring of 1957 Moch warned the United Nations that an effective test ban must be linked to a cut-off in the production of fissile material for military purposes.

At this time there was much discussion of disengagement in Europe. France, like the Federal Republic of Germany, was reserved about such plans for military reasons. Apart from the dangers of an American withdrawal – in this respect the experience of the Rhineland crisis of 1936, more than six years after the last British troops had withdrawn from the Continent, had a profound effect on French psychology – the French argued that the limitation of effectives in Central Europe was useless in the atomic age while the limitation of nuclear weapons in this area was equally futile in view of the means of delivery and their range at the disposal of the super-powers. Nor would it be possible to verify stocks of nuclear weapons in a limited zone. Less openly voiced, but no less important in French eyes, was the suspicion that any agreement to disengage was another step towards Russo-American co-operation at Europe's expense.

The third phase in French policy began in 1962 when France refused to participate in the Eighteen-Nation Disarmament Conference at Geneva. The need to make sure of successful nuclear

* It is important to note a difference in the meaning of the word 'control' in French and in English. The French 'contrôle' is used in the sense of check or verification; the English 'control' assumes the meaning of restraint and direction.

test explosions (1960) and to bring the Algerian war to an end (1962) had dictated a certain caution. Now de Gaulle felt free to strike out on his own.

France voluntarily placed herself outside the main stream of contemporary disarmament and arms control negotiations, but this did not mean she had no policy in this respect. France opposed the dissemination of nuclear weapons by the existing nuclear powers. In the logic of her own position, she could not seriously object to any state acquiring such weapons through its own efforts.

The emphasis on non-dissemination led the French to insist that the existing nuclear powers should first proceed to negotiating an agreement over arms reduction. Hence the French not only criticized the composition of the eighteen-nation conference at Geneva because it included a number of non-nuclear powers but they also spurned the Chinese proposals for a world conference on disarmament. Since the discussions in Geneva shifted from the traditional Russo-American confrontation to a debate between the nuclear powers and the rest, the French position became even more ambiguous. As a nuclear power, France shared some of the preoccupations of other members of the 'club', yet her attitude to the question of the international control of atomic energy and her membership of EURATOM ranged her on the side of the other powers.

The history of French disarmament policies since 1945 is thus a faithful reflection of France's twin objectives: the restoration of her status among the powers of the world and the assurance of her national security. The former has led her to create a national nuclear armament, to resist any attempt by her nuclear predecessors to shut the door of the 'club' in her face and to insist that the effect of nuclear disarmament measures must be equally shared by all. The latter has led her to emphasize the importance of the non-dissemination of nuclear weapons with a special eye on Germany.[11] One of the first acts of a post-Gaullist government may be to rejoin the international disarmament negotiations but the basic policy is likely to remain the same.

CONCLUSION

The French case illustrates how a policy of national nuclear armament can be conceived and executed within a free society without substantial public discussion or control. The highly technical and complex nature of such an enterprise gives a small number of policy-makers at different levels and in various organs of government considerable power in pushing through basic decisions. Once a weapons programme is under way it gathers momentum through the sheer weight of resources which are necessary for its progress.

The motives which lie behind the decisions are varied. They are not confined to considerations of national security and foreign policy, though these play the most important part in any conscious formulation of the argument for a national nuclear armament. There are also economic motives and those which stem from industrial and technical vested interests. Personal factors are equally important, especially when the psychological make-up of the individual is rationalized in a *Weltanschauung*.

 The search for national security obviously steered French policy-makers towards the creation of a nuclear force. This was particularly true in the first decade or so after the war. An obsessional anxiety about security has marked French history in the past century and it will take some time before it is overcome. Paradoxically, this preoccupation was not translated into a concern about a particular enemy. Since 1945 the French have looked upon Germany as a potential threat in a distant and unspecified future. The transformation brought about by the Second World War in Europe has dwarfed Franco-German rivalry so that the debate in France today is about ways in which to co-operate with Germany rather than ways in which to fight her. The only other conceivable military threat has come from Russia. Yet from the beginning the French nuclear force was not thought of so much as a deterrent against Russia but as an instrument with which to control American reactions to Russia.

No amount of discussion about the why and wherefore of French nuclear strategy can hide the fact that the attempt to give French nuclear weapons a military justification has followed

224

rather than preceded their existence. Once the process of armament was under way, each new generation of nuclear weapons was heralded with attempts to define its military uses. Even so, the apologists of official policy freely admitted that if the deterrent value of the French nuclear force was undermined, if the bluff was called, then the whole policy behind the creation of such a force had failed. The cost of the deterrent led to a growing disparity between it and the means of conventional defence, so that French security rests increasingly on deterrence without defence.

We have seen how nuclear weapons serve the purpose of persuasion as well as of deterrence. As a support for diplomacy they have been used most in the realm of inter-allied relations. Under de Gaulle the F.N.S. was an instrument designed to give France the basic security which would enable her to pursue an independent foreign policy. After de Gaulle its principal use may revert to the function of supporting a policy of re-establishing the Western Alliance in which Europe will become the equal partner of the United States, and of furthering the cause of disarmament and détente within the framework of international co-operation.

For the time being national nuclear power, whatever its limitations, symbolizes security and independence for many Frenchmen. Eventually a new generation may arise which will no longer be obsessed by national security, which will have a humbler yet wider vision of the purpose of national policy and which may consider the contemporary conception of national interest as exaggerated and even trivial when compared with the colossal problems which are common to all men.

References

1. Scheinman, pp. 42 and 212.
2. *Le Monde*, 15th June 1968.
3. Jacques Isnard, 'La France disposera en 1975 d'une capacité nucléaire égale à celle d'un B-52 américain' (*Le Monde-Sélection Hebdomadaire*, 11th–17th July 1968); Georges Chaf-

fard, 'La Défense "Tous Azimuts" ' (*Le Monde Diplomatique*, January 1968).

4. Eric Rouleau, 'Au Moyen Orient, Diversification des Amitiés dans la Sauvegarde des intérêts nationaux' (*Le Monde Diplomatique*, January 1968).

5. The Centre Démocrate published its programme, 'Plateforme électorale', in the form of 29 mimeographed pages; the Fédération de la Gauche published its programme in a special number of *Cahiers de la Convention*, September 1966, supplement of *Combat Républicain*, official organ of La Convention des Institutions Républicaines; the programme of the Parti Socialiste Unifié was published in its weekly organ, *Tribune Socialiste*, 19th January 1967; the Communist Party's programme is to be found in *L'Humanité*, 17th June 1966.

6. See particularly General P.-M. Gallois, *Stratégie de l'Age Nucléaire* (Calmann-Lévy, Paris, 1960) and *Paradoxes de la Paix* (Presses du Temps Présent, Paris, 1967).

7. Goldschmidt, *Les Rivalités Atomiques*, p. 263.

8. Jean Klein, *L'Entreprise du Désarmement depuis 1945* (Paris, Editions Cujas, 1964), pp. 14–17.

9. Note particularly Jules Moch, *La Folie des Hommes* (Paris, Robert Laffont, 1955); *En Retard d'une Paix* (Paris, René Julliard, 1958); *Non à la Force de Frappe* (Paris, Robert Laffont, 1963).

10. *J.O.*, *Débats Parlementaires*, No. 46, C.R., 24 July 1957, session of 23rd July, pp. 1679–80.

11. Wolf Mendl, 'The Empty Chair–French Attitudes on Disarmament' (*Disarmament*, Information Bulletin published by the World Veterans Association, June 1967, pp. 13–17); reprinted in *Survival* (The Institute for Strategic Studies, December 1967, pp. 393–7).

Appendix

LIST OF THOSE RESPONSIBLE FOR
ATOMIC QUESTIONS UNDER THE FOURTH
AND FIFTH REPUBLICS

Général de Gaulle	October 1945	Président du Gouvernement Provisoire
Félix Gouin	January 1946	Président du Gouvernement Provisoire, Ministre de la Défense Nationale
Georges Bidault	June 1946	Président du Gouvernement Provisoire, Ministre des Affaires Etrangères
Léon Blum	December 1946	Président du Gouvernement Provisoire, Ministre des Affaires Etrangères
Paul Ramadier	January 1947	Président du Conseil
Pierre Abelin	November 1947	Secrétaire d'Etat à la Présidence du Conseil
Paul Devinat	September 1948	Secrétaire d'Etat à la Présidence du Conseil
Paul Bacon	October 1949	Secrétaire d'Etat à la Présidence du Conseil
Robert Prigent	February 1950	Secrétaire d'Etat à la Présidence du Conseil
Maurice Bourgès-Maunoury	July 1950	Secrétaire d'Etat à la Présidence du Conseil

APPENDIX

Félix Gaillard	August 1951	Secrétaire d'Etat à la Présidence du Conseil et aux Finances
Pierre July	June 1953	Secrétaire d'Etat à la Présidence du Conseil
Henri Longchambon	June 1954	Secrétaire d'Etat à la Recherche Scientifique et aux Progrès Techniques
Gaston Palewski	February 1955	Ministre Délégué à la Présidence du Conseil
Pierre July	October 1955	Ministre Délégué à la Présidence du Conseil
Georges Guille	February 1956	Secrétaire d'Etat à la Présidence du Conseil, chargé de la Recherche Scientifique et de l'Energie Atomique
François-Benard	June 1957	Sous-Secrétaire d'Etat à la Présidence du Conseil
Félix Gaillard	November 1957	Président du Conseil
Général de Gaulle	June 1958	Président du Conseil
Jacques Soustelle	January 1959	Ministre Délégué auprès du Premier Ministre
Pierre Guillaumat	March 1960	Ministre Délégué auprès du Premier Ministre
Gaston Palewski	April 1962	Ministre d'Etat de la Recherche Scientifique et des questions atomiques et spatiales
Yvon Bourges	February 1965	Secrétaire d'Etat chargé de la recherche scientifique et des questions atomiques et spatiales

Alain Peyrefitte	January 1966	Ministre délégué chargé de la recherche scientifique et des questions atomiques et spatiales
Maurice Schumann	April 1967	Ministre d'Etat de la Recherche Scientifique et des questions atomiques et spatiales
Christian de la Malène	June 1968	Ministre de la recherche scientifique et des questions atomiques et spatiales
Robert Galley	July 1968	Ministre délégué auprès du premier ministre, chargé de la recherche scientifique et des questions atomiques et spatiales

Bibliographical note

This is not an exhaustive bibliography nor a complete list of printed sources consulted in preparation of the book. I have thought it more useful to mention those books which may help to introduce the reader to various aspects of the subject. Many of them are in French, though details of translations are given where they are known to exist. French books, with very few exceptions, have limited indexes, where they deign to have any at all. Footnotes and references are rare, so that the student is deprived of those aids which abound profusely in American and English works of this kind.

Official publications, reference books and journals

For a study of official policy and of political argument, consult the decrees, laws and official records of parliamentary debates in the *Journal Officiel*. From time to time the Foreign Ministry issues documents giving background information about major events or policy innovations. These are often translated into English and may be obtained from the French Embassy.

At the time of the first French nuclear explosion, the Ministry of the Armed Forces published a White Paper, *La Première Explosion Atomique Française* (Notes et Etudes Documentaires, Documentation Française, Paris, No. 2648, 21st March 1960). The Foreign Ministry issued a less technical account with greater emphasis on the political and diplomatic background of French nuclear policy: *La France et la Puissance Atomique* (Situation de la France No. 2, 'Tendances', March 1960).

L'Année Politique (Paris, Presses Universitaires de France) is an indispensable work of reference for the political, economic and social events of the year.

A student of French defence policy should consult the monthly *Revue de Défense Nationale*. It is a semi-official organ of dreary and rather old-fashioned appearance which carries many articles by policy-makers, known and unknown. Occasionally an article will usher in a new orientation in government policy. Each issue includes very informative accounts of the latest developments in all aspects of national defence. The Ministry of the Armed Forces published a very glossy house organ, *Revue Militaire d'Information*, which ceased publication in 1964. In addition, there are the journals of the three services: *L'Armée, Forces Aériennes Françaises* and *La Revue Maritime*.

The *Revue Militaire Générale* appears monthly and has a strong bias towards NATO. It enjoys the patronage of the leading military figures in the Western Alliance except those of France since January 1963. It is trilingual (French, English and German). Each article is followed by abstracts in the other two languages. It is particularly useful as a forum for pro-NATO Frenchmen.

Politique Etrangère, published by Le Centre d'Etudes de Politique Etrangère, Paris, often contains interesting articles on French foreign and disarmament policies.

For handy reference, the annual *Military Balance* published by the Institute for Strategic Studies, London, and the recently added annual *Strategic Survey* provide excellent surveys of the state of French defences.

A surprising amount of useful information about the technical aspect of French nuclear armament may be culled from various technical journals, notably *Aviation Week and Space Technology*, published in New York.

The political and social scene

We are well served in this field by a number of excellent studies in English. Foremost among them are Philip Williams, *Politics in Post-War France* (London, Longmans, Green, 1954) and Dorothy Pickles, *French Politics: The First Years of the Fourth Republic* (London, the Royal Institute of International Affairs, 1953). David Thomson's *Democracy in France: The Third and Fourth Republics* (Oxford University Press, third edition, 1958) is not as detailed but puts things into a much broader historical perspective.

231

BIBLIOGRAPHICAL NOTE

Maurice Duverger has written an excellent introduction to the Fourth Republic, *The French Political System* (University of Chicago Press, 1958).

Among the books dealing with the Fifth Republic, one might start with Dorothy Pickles, *The Fifth French Republic* (London, Methuen & Co. Ltd., 1960) and Philip Williams and Martin Harrison, *De Gaulle's Republic* (London, Longmans, Green & Co., 1960).

For those who wish to go to French sources, Jacques Fauvet has written an entertaining and well-informed study, *La Quatrième République* (Paris, Arthème Fayard, 1959). A useful insight may also be gained from François Goguel, *Le Régime Politique Français* (Paris, Editions du Seuil, 1955) and René Massigli, *Sur Quelques Maladies de l'Etat* (Paris, Librairie Plon, 1958) which is an illuminating critique of the governmental machine under the Fourth Republic by someone who was very much involved in it.

For scholarly analyses of the role of the Secretaries of State in the Fourth Republic, see André Bertrand, 'La Présidence du Conseil et le Secrétariat Général du Gouvernement' (*Revue du Droit Public et de la Science Politique*, Vol. 64, No. 3, July–September 1948, pp. 435–51) and J. C. Groshens, 'Les Secrétaires d'Etat de la Quatrième République' in the same journal, Vol. 71, No. 2, April–June 1955, pp. 357–76. Roy Macridis also has a useful piece on 'The Cabinet Secretariat in France' (*The Journal of Politics*, Vol. 13, No. 4, November 1951, pp. 589–603). Jean-Louis Seurin has written an important study of 'Les Cabinets Ministériels' in the *Revue du Droit Public et de la Science Politique*, Vol. 72, No. 6, November–December 1956, pp. 1207–94. Peter Campbell has written a valuable analysis of 'The Cabinet and Constitution in France: 1956–1958' (*Parliamentary Affairs*, Winter 1958–9, pp. 27–36).

For a flavour of the political and social life of the Fourth Republic one should turn to David Schoenbrun, *As France Goes* (New York, Harper and Brothers, 1957) and Herbert Luethy, *France against Herself* (New York, Frederick A. Praeger, 1955).

BIBLIOGRAPHICAL NOTE

External policy
Easily the most outstanding treatment of the Fourth Republic's
foreign policy is in Alfred Grosser, *La Quatrième République et sa
Politique Extérieure* (Paris, Armand Colin, 1961). Quite apart from
its brilliant analysis, it has an excellent guide to further reading.
Grosser's *La Politique Extérieure de la Cinquième République* (Paris,
Editions du Seuil, 1965) is less satisfying for several reasons. It
lacks the depth and perspective of the earlier study and it is a
series of edited lectures with all the drawbacks of such an arrange-
ment. A translation has appeared under the title *French Foreign
Policy under de Gaulle* (Boston, Little, Brown & Co., 1967) but it
is no improvement, even though it has been brought up to date.

Among the studies of the Western Alliance which throw light
on French policy, one might single out Robert E. Osgood,
NATO – The Entangling Alliance (University of Chicago Press,
1962) as an outstanding analysis which succeeds in breaking out of
narrow American conceptions and interpretations. Mary M. Ball,
NATO and the European Union Movement (London, Stevens for
the London Institute of World Affairs, 1959) is rather ponderous
but full of hard facts.

The foreign policy of the Fifth Republic has been the source of a
number of books in French, most of which are polemic in tone
and make no pretence at scholarly detachment. The one notable
exception is Edmond Jouve's mammoth two-volume study *Le
Général de Gaulle et la Construction de l'Europe* (Paris, Librairie
Générale de Droit et de Jurisprudence, 1967) which is a compila-
tion of every conceivable document and piece of information
about de Gaulle's European policy since the end of the Second
World War. Roger Massip, *De Gaulle et l'Europe* (Paris, Flam-
marion, 1963) and Paul Reynaud, *La Politique Etrangère du
Gaullisme* (Paris, Julliard, 1964) are both critiques of the General's
foreign policy written by 'Europeans'. For a discussion of the
military implications of the French withdrawal from NATO see
Kenneth Hunt's excellent *NATO without France* (London, the
Institute for Strategic Studies, Adelphi Paper 32, December 1966).
Franco-British relations are the subject of a stimulating essay by

Dorothy Pickles, *The Uneasy Entente: French Foreign Policy and Franco-British Misunderstandings* (London, the Royal Institute of International Affairs, 1966).

Defence policy

The best historical introduction to the basic issues in French defence policy since the great Revolution is in Richard D. Challener, *The French Theory of the Nation in Arms: 1866–1939* (New York, Columbia University Press, 1955). This may be supplemented by Professor Raoul Girardet's brilliant essay on the French army in society, *La Société Militaire dans la France Contemporaine: 1815–1939* (Paris, Librairie Plon, 1953). There are a number of recently published histories of the modern French army of which Paul-Marie de la Gorce, *La République et son Armée* (Paris, Arthème Fayard, 1963) is one of the best. There is an English translation: *The French Army: A Military-Political History* (London, Weidenfeld & Nicolson, 1963). A two-volume political history of the French army since the First World War, J. Nobécourt, *Une Histoire Politique de l'Armée: Vol. I: 1919–1942, de Pétain à Pétain*; J. Planchais, *Une Histoire Politique de l'Armée: Vol. II: 1940–1967, de Gaulle à de Gaulle* (Paris, Editions du Seuil, 1967) gives us fascinating vignettes of French military leaders and their political ambitions but is too impressionistic to be of great value to students. The same criticism applies to Vincent Monteil's fascinating illustrated essay on the officer corps in the past century, *Les Officiers* (Paris, Editions du Seuil, 1958).

The most comprehensive and fully documented study of national defence since the war is Bernard Chantebout's *L'Organisation Générale de la Défense Nationale en France depuis la Fin de la Seconde Guerre Mondiale* (Paris, Librairie de Droit et de Jurisprudence, 1967). It is an essential work of reference.

A study of all the facets of national defence under the Fourth Republic should begin with *La Défense Nationale* (Paris, Presses Universitaires de France, 1958) which is a collection of lectures on the strategic and structural problems of national defence. Jean Planchais, *Le Malaise de l'Armée* (Paris, Plon, 1958) is a brilliant and prophetic essay about the mood of the army written before the events of May 1958. The same author's less well-known *L'Armée* (Paris, Buchet/Chastel, 1959) is an extremely useful little handbook about the armed forces and some of their leaders. Raoul Girardet and two collaborators have published a detailed sociological study of the French army since the war, *La Crise Militaire Française: 1945–1962* (Paris, Librairie Armand Colin, 1964). The best study in English on civil-military relations during this period is John Steward Ambler's scholarly *The French Army in Politics: 1945–1962* (Ohio State University Press, 1966).

A number of military men have written memoirs which throw some light on the period and on themselves. De Gaulle's *Mémoires de Guerre*, particularly *Vol. III: Le Salut: 1944–1946* (Paris, Librairie Plon, 1959) is an important source for the origins of the Fourth Republic and the General's *idées fixes*. Maréchal Juin, *Mémoires, Vol. II* (Paris, Librairie Arthème Fayard, 1960), is an interesting commentary on civil-military relations under the Fourth Republic. General Ely's *Mémoires: Vol. I: L'Indochine dans la Tourmente* (Paris, Librairie Plon, 1964), is disappointing. It confirms that he is a very cautious man. We are still waiting for the second volume.

Although many books have appeared on the war in Indochina, Donald Lancaster has written one of the most useful general histories in *The Emancipation of French Indochina* (London, the Royal Institute of International Affairs, 1961) and Bernard Fall, *Street without Joy* (Harrisburg, Pennsylvania, the Stackpole Company, 1961) brilliantly conveys the flavour of the war, its strategic and tactical problems and its effect on morale. The circumstances of the end of the conflict may be treated as a comparative study of three books written by men who were involved in the events surrounding Dien Bien Phu: the Prime Minister at the time, Josef Laniel, *Le Drame Indochinois: de Dien-Bien-Phu au Pari de Genève* (Paris, Librairie Plon, 1957); the Commander-in-Chief of the French forces in Indochina, General Navarre, *Agonie de l'Indochine: 1953–54* (Paris, Librairie Plon, 1956) and the head of the commission of inquiry into the disaster, General Catroux,

BIBLIOGRAPHICAL NOTE

Deux Actes du Drame Indochinois: Hanoi, Juin 1940; Dien Bien Phu, Mars–Mai 1954 (Paris, Librairie Plon, 1959).

The landmarks of the Algerian war and the problems of revolutionary warfare are the subjects of an abundant literature. Peter Paret's *French Revolutionary Warfare from Indochina to Algeria* (London, Pall Mall Press, 1964) is an excellent and comprehensive introduction to the subject. For lighter but instructive reading about the effect of the colonial wars on the soldiers, the student may turn to Jean Lartéguy's novels, *Les Centurions* (Paris, Presses de la Cité, 1960) and *Les Prétoriens* (Paris, Presses de la Cité, 1961), translated into English as *The Centurions* (London, Hutchinson, 1961) and *The Praetorians* (London, Hutchinson, 1963). The influence of the doctrine of revolutionary warfare on French military policy may be gauged in General Valluy, *Se Défendre? Contre Qui? Pour Quoi? et Comment?* (Paris, Plon, 1960) and General Paul Ely, *L'Armée dans la Nation* (Paris, Arthème Fayard, 1961). The revolt of the generals is treated by Jacques Fauvet and Jean Planchais in *La Fronde des Généraux* (Paris, B. Arthaud, 1961). For a more serious study of that event one should turn to the verbatim accounts of the trials of the insurgent generals.

Until the advent of nuclear weapons, little was written about general strategic problems as they affected France. General P. E. Jacquot wrote a revealing and interesting essay in the first decade after the war, *La Stratégie Périphérique devant la bombe atomique* (Paris, Gallimard, 1954). A study of Gaullist strategic concepts should start with General de Gaulle's *Vers l'Armée de Métier* (Paris, Editions Berger-Levrault, 1934), translated into English as *The Army of the Future* (London, Hutchinson & Co., 1940?), and *Le Fil de l'Epée* (Paris, Berger-Levrault, 1932). Edgar S. Furniss wrote an interesting but not altogether convincing interpretation of General de Gaulle's military policy in *De Gaulle and the French Army: A Crisis in Civil-Military Relations* (New York, the Twentieth Century Fund, 1964).

Nuclear policy

The best introduction to the history of the French atomic energy programme is to be found in Bertrand Goldschmidt, *L'Aventure Atomique* (Paris, Arthème Fayard, 1962) and *Les Rivalités Atomiques: 1939–1966* (Paris, Arthème Fayard, 1967). The latter is an expanded, more detailed and updated version of the earlier book. Although these studies deal with atomic energy throughout the world, they contain important sections on the French programme written by someone who participated in it at a high level. Lawrence Scheinman has produced a remarkably well-documented and detailed study of the programme under the Fourth Republic: *Atomic Energy Policy in France under the Fourth Republic* (Princeton University Press, 1965). Charles Ailleret's memoirs, *L'Aventure Atomique Française, Souvenirs et Réflexions* (Paris, Editions Bernard Grasset, 1968), contain an interesting account of the pressures for a nuclear weapons programme among military circles and of the preparations for the first atomic tests in 1960. It is, however, a very personal story and the reader should beware against an exaggerated impression of Ailleret's part in the enterprise.

Goldschmidt's account of the pre-war and wartime origins of the French programme should be supplemented with the relevant passages from Margaret Gowing, *Britain and Atomic Energy: 1939–1945* (London, Macmillan & Co. Ltd., 1964) and Richard G. Hewlett and Oscar E. Anderson, *The New World, 1939–1946: Vol. I: A History of the United States Atomic Energy Commission* (Pennsylvania State University Press, 1962).

Most French books dealing with the atomic energy programme are basically polemic and should be treated with considerable reserve as sources of information. Marc de Lacoste Lareymondie, *Mirages et Réalités: L'Arme Nucléaire Française* (Paris, Editions de la SERPE, 1964) offers interesting historical information in the first part of the book. Robert Gilpin has published an important work on scientific and technological policy-making since the war: *France in the Age of the Scientific State* (Princeton University Press, 1968). Chapter 9, 'Defence, Space and Atomic Power', is particularly germane to our study. The development of French missile technology is dealt with by Judith H. Young in *The French*

Strategic Missile Programme (London, the Institute for Strategic Studies, Adelphi Paper 38, July 1967).

Books which discuss French nuclear policy fall roughly into three groups. The first group includes those that offer a theoretical justification in its support. They are best represented by the works of General P.-M. Gallois: *Stratégie de l'Âge Nucléaire* (Paris, Calmann-Lévy, 1960), translated as *The Balance of Terror* (Boston, Houghton Mifflin, 1961), and *Paradoxes de la Paix* (Paris, Presses du Temps Présent, 1967). An anonymous group of officers and officials has also published an apologia of contemporary policy: Club de Grenelle, *Siècle de Damoclès: La Force Nucléaire Stratégique* (Paris, Les Editions Pierre Couderc, 1964). Alexandre Sanguinetti, *La France et l'Arme Atomique* (Paris, René Julliard, 1964) accepts Gaullist nuclear policy but has reservations about other aspects of defence policy.

The second group of books accepts the existence of a French nuclear force but criticizes its dimensions and the assumptions on which it is based. Most of them advocate a more modest policy. They include Maurice Bertrand, *Pour une Doctrine Militaire Française* (Paris, Gallimard, 1965) and the book by Lacoste Lareymondie which I have already mentioned.

The last category includes those which oppose the basic orientation of French policy for one reason or another. Not all of them, however, advocate the complete renunciation of nuclear weapons as do Jules Moch, *Non à la Force de Frappe* (Paris, Robert Laffont, 1963) and Dominique Halévy, *Contre la Bombe* (Paris, Editions de Minuit, 1960). Detailed technical and economic criticisms are made by Daniel Dollfus in *La Force de Frappe* (Paris, Julliard, 1960) and by some members of the Club Jean Moulin in *La Force de Frappe et le Citoyen* (Paris, Editions du Seuil, 1963). A recent biting criticism of French policy is contained in the second part of Alfred Fabre-Luce's *L'Or et la Bombe* (Paris, Calmann-Lévy, 1968). A more profound analysis has been written by a former Gaullist minister, Pierre Sudreau, *L'Enchaînement* (Paris, Librairie Plon, 1967).

Raymond Aron, *Le Grand Débat: Initiation à la Stratégie*

Atomique (Paris, Calmann-Lévy, 1963), translated in *The Great Debate* (New York, Doubleday, 1965), and *Paix et Guerre entre les Nations* (Paris, Calmann-Lévy, 1962), translated in *Peace and War: A Theory of International Relations* (London, Weidenfeld & Nicolson, 1966), deals with the whole problem of nuclear strategy in a wider context. So does Léo Hamon in *La Stratégie Contre la Guerre* (Paris, Bernard Grasset, 1966).

General André Beaufre's prolific output is in a class by itself and represents an interesting attempt to reinterpret the concept of strategy in the nuclear age. The trilogy has been admirably translated by Major-General Barry in *An Introduction to Strategy* (London, Faber & Faber, 1965); *Deterrence and Strategy* (London, Faber and Faber, 1965); *Strategy of Action* (London, Faber & Faber, 1967). In addition, his *L'OTAN et l'Europe* (Paris, Calmann-Lévy, 1966) throws an interesting light on NATO's past as seen through French eyes and makes suggestions about a possible future organization of the Atlantic Alliance.

Apart from scattered articles in various journals, French writers, with the notable exception of Jules Moch, have given little serious attention to disarmament. Moch's *La Folie des Hommes* (Paris, Robert Laffont, 1954) and *En Retard d'une Paix* (Paris, Julliard, 1958) outline the situation in the pre-Gaullist period. A little-known study by Jean Klein, *L'Entreprise du Désarmement: 1945–1964* (Paris, Editions Cujas, 1964) analyses the course of post-war disarmament and arms control negotiations but includes valuable information about French policy in this field and an excellent bibliography of French writing on the subject.

A study of the wider implications of French policy for the proliferation of nuclear weapons might begin with Leonard Beaton and John Maddox, *The Spread of Nuclear Weapons* (London, Chatto & Windus for the Institute for Strategic Studies, 1962) and then continue with the symposium edited by Alastair Buchan, *A World of Nuclear Powers?* (Englewood Cliffs, Prentice-Hall Inc., 1966).

For purposes of comparison with British nuclear policy, the student may wish to read Alfred Goldberg's most informative articles in *International Affairs* (London, the Royal Institute of International Affairs), 'The Atomic Origins of the British Nuclear Deterrent' (Vol. 40, No. 3, July 1964), and 'The Military Origins of the British Nuclear Deterrent' (Vol. 40, No. 4, October 1964). Useful books about the British experience include William P. Snyder, *The Politics of British Defense Policy: 1945–1962* (Ohio State University Press, 1964), a study of the policy-making process, and R. N. Rosecrance, *Defense of the Realm; British Strategy in the Nuclear Epoch* (New York, Columbia University Press, 1968) which is inclined to treat strategic questions without sufficient reference to their political context.

Index

INDEX

arms race, scientific, 50
  nuclear, 210
army, French, 22–3, 25–7, 39, 69–72,
  75, 77, 82–3, 86, 88–91, 96–7, 99,
  101, 107, 109–10, 113–15, 138,
  183, 193, 202–3
  anti-communist ideology, 23
  attachment to the cause of French
  Algeria, 203
  attitude to E.D.C., 25–7
  attitude to new weapons, 71
  challenges the government's authority, 110
  effect of its experience in Indochina, 96–7
  emotional effect of the Algerian
  war, 110
  exerts pressure in favour of de
  Gaulle (May 1958), 193
  favours tactical nuclear artillery, 83
  fear of loss of identity, 26
  half-way between 'armée de métier'
  and 'armée de conscription' (law
  of 1965), 114
  involvement in N. Africa, 77
  'mass armies or professional army'
  controversy, 69–71, 88–9
  officers selected to study nuclear
  physics, 72, cf 138
  real vocation restored, 110
  reduction of army estimates, 113–14
  regarded as a spendthrift by Ramadier, 86
  role in Germany after F. withdrawal from NATO, 39
  strategic controversy between army
  and air force, 82–3, 109
  theory and practice of counter-
  revolutionary activity, 91
  traditional preponderance in F. defence, 107, cf 115
Asia, 97

British influence in, 44
Atlantic Alliance, see NATO
Atlantic Council meeting (1960), 80
'Atlantism', policy of, 23
Atomic Energy Act, amendment of
  (July 1958), 57
Atomic Energy Committee, see Comité de l'Energie Atomique
atomic energy, harmful effects of, 132
Atomic Energy, Joint Congressional
  Committee on, 59
atomic energy, peaceful uses of, 53,
  129, 163, 177–8
atomic energy programme, French,
  122 sqq., 138, 157, 164, 166, 173,
  177, 182, 187, 192, 200–1, 221
  for industrial purposes, 27, 45,
  176–7, 184, 201–2
atomic engineers, training of, 72
atomic explosion, first French, 15,
  30, 57, 73, 144, 150, 184, 188, 203
atomic secrets, sharing of recommended by McNamara and Maxwell Taylor in 1962, 60
atom-powered aircraft engines, studies
  of, 76
Aubinière, General, 151
Augarde, M., 75
Auger, Pierre, 126, 129, 137, 151

balance of payments, French, 177
Barjot, Admiral, 72
Baruch Plan, 163
Beaufre, General, 16, 78, 123
Becquerel, M., 123
Belgium, 124, 158
Benelux, 156
Bergeron, General, 135
Berlin, 22, 27, 36, 38–9, 52
  crisis over, 22
  four-power conference of foreign
  ministers (1954), 52

INDEX

de Gaulle, Charles—*cont.*
declining authority of, 85
feelings of resentment over treatment by allies, 128
first visit to C.E.A. (Jan. 1956), 168
his concept of an 'armée de métier', 88
his concept of international relations, 61
his dependence on foundations laid by predecessors, 212
his European policy, 62
his secretariat the nerve-centre of government, 193
impatient with party squabbles, 30
objective of absolute national independence, 210
personal popularity of, 69, 214
personal rancour at end of 1962, 80
press conference of Feb. 4th, 1965, 38
pressure by scientists on, 129
proposes a directorate within NATO, 54
recognizes importance of Germany, 39
speech at Ecole Militaire, Nov. 1959, 57, 77, 122; Jan. 1967, 82
speech in Hamburg (1962), 37
visit to Ottawa, July 1944, 129
de Larminat, General, 25
de Lattre de Tassigny, General, 71–2
de Maupeou, M., 53, 184
Democratic Centre Party, 213–14
de Monsabert, General, 26
denuclearized zones in Europe, 215
dependence on others for security, 70, 92
deterrence, 78, 83, 97, 110, 112–13, 115, 202, 209, 225
credibility of, 115, 202
without defence, 225

Dien Bien Phu, 28, 96, 99–100, 103, 203
Dimona reactor, 220
Direction des Applications Millitaires (D.A.M.), 143
Direction des Poudres, 72
Direction des Etudes et Fabrications des Armements, 37, 72, 182
disarmament, 54, 220–3, 225
and collective security, 220
and détente, 225
Chinese proposals for world conference on, 223
Eighteen Nation Conference, 222–223
Franco-British Plan, 221
French post-war policy, 220–3
negotiations for, 220–1, 223
universal, 221–2
dispersal of industry, plans for, 72
'dissuasion, force de', nuclear weapons as, 18, 43, 104
Division Mécanique Rapide, 107
development of light motorized divisions, 74
D.M.R., *see* Division Mécanique Rapide
D.O.T., *see* Défense Opérationelle du Territoire
Douzane, Jacques, 34
Dulles, John Foster, 59, 82

Eastern Europe, 38, 211–12
East Germany (*see* German Democratic Republic)
East-West détente, possible effect of, 54
East-West relations, 42, 54
E.B.R. armoured reconnaissance vehicle, 74
Ecole Militaire de Spécialisation de l'Armée de Terre, 138

INDEX

Ecole Polytechnique, 134, 147, 150, 182, 189, 192, 200, 220
(see also Polytechnicien(s))
economic and social crisis of 1968, 114
economic planning, French, 19
E.D.C., see European Defence Community
EDF, see Electricité de France
E.E.C., see European Economic Community
Egypt, 30, 103
Einstein's warnings, 169
Eisenhower, President, 58, 60, 83, 103, 159
Elbe, frontier on the, 96, cf 210
Electricité de France, 140, 146, 178, 185
Ely, General, 102, 104
energy, search for new sources, 177
England, 158
(see also Britain and United Kingdom)
Erhard, Chancellor, 37
Erler, Fritz, 37
Etzel, M., 148
EURATOM, 31–5, 43–5, 52–3, 75, 147–9, 155, 157–61, 167–9, 176, 179, 184, 188, 205, 223
as a design to ensure American control, 31–2
as a means to become independent of U.S., 160
British aloofness towards, 43
conceived as a plot to avenge E.D.C., 31
conditions for acceptance, 168
debate on, 32–5, 45, 52–3, 149, 155, 159, 161, 167, 179, 184
decision to set up, 148
discussions on, 31–5
French policy a step towards a U.S. of Europe, 205

M.R.P. and socialists favour, 169
negotiations over, 147, 157–8, 188, 205
European army, 24, 94
European Coal and Steel Community, 24, 31–2, 44, 159, 168
European Community, 27, 40, 44, 46, 161, 205–6, 217
European co-operation in the field of armaments, 57
European Defence Community, 23–31, 34–5, 46, 100, 156, 159–60, 172, 204–5, 215
European defence system, French national force as kernel of, 80
European Economic Community, 159, 211
(see also Common Market)
European nuclear force, idea of, 79, 172
European security system, 38
European unity, 24, 100, 156, 167
Europe, 35, 58, 63, 93–5, 210, 213
British commitment to, 210
defence of, 93–5
Gaullist conception of, 213
I.R.B.M.s in, 58
of fatherlands, 35
settlement of, 63

Faure, Edgar, 25, 145, 156–7, 159, 189, 201, 204, 221
Faure, Maurice, 44–5, 81, 161
Federal Republic of Germany, 27, 31–3, 36, 147–8, 172, 202–3, 217, 222
Federation of the Left, 214–16
Fifth Republic, 19, 25, 57, 85, 106, 109, 144, 170, 180–1, 189, 190, 192, 199–200, 211
First World War, 22–3, 69, 84, 92, 172

247

INDEX

INDEX

INDEX